What some of the leading WEALTH-building authorities are saying about *Wealth Strategies*

"Todd Duncan has done an admirable job of explaining how to create a foundation for a balanced life in *Wealth Strategies: 9½ Steps to Achieving Physical, Financial, and Spiritual Abundance.* In this book, he deftly guides the reader through the questions of "why" and "how," allowing one to evaluate his or her own life as it relates to being, doing and having all that is available to them. Good, helpful information."

Zig Ziglar
Author

"This book is rich with life-living stuff. It will cause a transformation of your spirit, your health, your relationships, and your ultimate destiny. Todd's advice is practical, immediately useable, and life changing, all at once. I loved it and I know you will too. Read it now and experience life abundantly!"

Dr. John C. Maxwell
Founder, The INJOY Group

"This book will enrich every aspect of your life!"

Ken Blanchard
Co-author of *The One Minute Manager* and *Leadership By The Book*

"I have said often, 'If you have faith, nothing shall be impossible to you.' Todd Duncan's new book makes everything you have ever dreamed of having or becoming in your life possible. *Wealth Strategies* is the owner's manual for living a powerful, productive, and positive life. Read it and experience abundance!"

Dr. Robert Schuller
Author and Founder, The Crystal Cathedral

"WOW! This is a great book. Every chapter is potentially life changing – it is a handbook for lifelong success!"

Brian Tracy
Best-selling author and speaker

"Few men are more gifted or experienced in the arena of consulting regarding living life to the fullest than my friend, Todd Duncan. Without doubt, this book will prove tremendously valuable and helpful to those who seek to live the abundant life promised to us by our Savior."

Dr. Ted Engstrom
President Emeritus, World Vision

"Every once in awhile, you come across someone who actually lives what he teaches. Todd Duncan is one of those teachers and he has done it again. He's written Gold Medal wisdom in *Wealth Strategies: 9½ Steps for Achieving Physical, Financial, and Spiritual Abundance*. If you feel a desire for growth in any part of your life, read this book! You'll be glad you did."

Peter Vidmar
Olympic Gold Medalist, Former Member of the President's Council on Physical Fitness and Sports

"Todd Duncan knows how to get people to 'raise the bar' by showing them practical ways to take their life to new highs. *Wealth Strategies* is a great book."

Diane Deacon
President, Creative Thinking Association

"I have seen Todd Duncan build his *Wealth Strategies* over a number of years. His financial, physical, and spiritual growth offer a real life example for all of us to follow. Now his proven methods are revealed to you. Learn and use them now and don't miss this opportunity to grow wealthy."

Jim Cathcart
Author, *The Acorn Principle*

"Today's culture has caused incredible confusion for us. The pursuit of wealth and success has left many burned out, broke and broken hearted. In his book*, Wealth Strategies: 9½ Steps for Achieving Physical, Financial, and Spiritual Abundance*, Todd Duncan shows you how to clear up the confusion and put a plan in place for true success. He will show you how to build and enjoy wealth in the most important areas of your life. Follow his steps and enjoy the journey!"

Daniel Harkavy
CEO/Coach, Building Champions–The Coaching Company

"Todd Duncan is passionate about the topic, *Wealth Strategies*. In this compelling book, he redefines true and lasting success and gives you a step by step plan for living a rich and rewarding life! If you have kids, this will get them off to the right start."

Skip and Susan Ross
Founders, The Circle "A" Youth Ranch

"Todd Duncan consistently shows us in a very practical way, what can be ours physically, financially and spiritually. You can rise up . . . and Todd will walk with you in this powerful book of hope."

Dr. Gregg Jantz
Author, Speaker and Radio Talk Show Host

"Todd Duncan's *Wealth Strategies* is the first book I have come across that addresses ALL of the core aspects of our life, and gives concrete steps, thoughts, and perspectives that can help everyone live with peace, balance and power. Todd has put together the essentials for living a full rich life in the modern world, addressing real issues and difficulties. Incredible resource!"

Mark Allen
Six-Time Ironman Triathlon Champion

"Todd Duncan's new book has a wealth of great ideas and action plans to turn your dreams into realities. Learn from a man who practices what he preaches and has become a phenomenal success pursuing a life based on the principles he shares with you in his newest blockbuster, *Wealth Strategies*."

Tony Alessandra, Ph.D.
Author of *Charisma* and *The Platinum Rule*

"Read *Wealth Strategies* and achieve a new understanding of how to create abundance in your life in the lives of those around you."

Les Brown
Speaker and Author

Wealth Strategies

Wealth Strategies

9½ Steps to Achieving Physical, Financial, and Spiritual Abundance

Todd Duncan

WORD PUBLISHING

NASHVILLE

A Thomas Nelson Company

Published by Word Publishing, a unit of Thomas Nelson, Inc., P.O. Box 141000, Nashville, Tennessee 37214. No portion of this book may be reproduced, stored in a retrieval system, or transmitted in any form or by any means—electronic, mechanical, photocopy, recording, or other—except for brief quotations in printed reviews, without the prior permission of the publisher.

Unless otherwise indicated, Scripture quotations used in this book are from the New American Standard Bible (NASB), copyright © 1960, 1977 by the Lockman Foundation.

Other Scripture references are from the following sources:

The Holy Bible, New International Version, copyright © 1973, 1978, 1984, International Bible Society. Used by permission of Zondervan Bible Publishers.

The Good News Bible: The Bible in Today's English Version (TEV), copyright © 1976 by the American Bible Society.

The New King James Version (NKJV). Copyright © 1979, 1980, 1982, Thomas Nelson , Inc., Publishers.

The information in this book provides a general overview of health-related topics and may not apply to everyone. To find out if this information applies to you and to get more information about any health-related issue, talk to your family doctor. The health claims stated in this book are those of the author. Neither Word Publishing nor Thomas Nelson, Inc., expresses any opinion as to the validity of those health claims.

This book is intended to provide accurate and authoritative information in regard to the financial subject matter covered. Nonetheless, inadvertent errors can occur, and financial products, market conditions, rules and regulations, and laws or interpretations of laws are subject to change. Consequently, the publisher and the author specifically disclaim any liability or loss that may be incurred as a consequence of the use and applications, directly or indirectly, of any information presented in this book. Because every reader's financial situation and goals are unique, it is recommended that a financial, legal, or tax professional be consulted prior to implementing any of the suggestions herein.

Library of Congress Cataloging-in-Publication Data

Duncan, Todd, 1957–
    Wealth Strategies: 9½ steps to acheiving physical, financial, and spiritual abundance / Todd
    Duncan.
      p. cm.
    ISBN 0-8499-1653-4 (hc)
    1. Wealth—Religious aspects—Christianity. I. Title.
  BR115.W4 D86 2000
  332.024—dc21   00-036678

Printed in the United States of America

00 01 02 03 04 05 BVG 6 5 4 3 2 1

I would like to dedicate this book to you!
I hope and pray that as a result of your journey through these pages,
life will spring up within you and you will be positively and passionately
transformed at your very core.

Contents

Contents

Part Two: Financial Abundance

Step Four: Take Stock of Your Net Worth

Step Five: Learn from the Best

Step Six: Win with Wealth

Part Three: Spiritual Abundance

Step Seven: Breathe Life into Your Relationships

Contents

Foreword

Our INJOY Christmas party was coming to an end, and the evening was winding down. I started to feel a little sick to my stomach—something wasn't right. One of my associates was hugging me good-bye when she said, "John, your neck is cold, and you're breaking out in a sweat. Is everything all right?" My wife, Margaret, looked at me and immediately knew that something was wrong. She said to my associate, "Call 911."

I never thought it would happen to me, but it was. I was having a heart attack. As I lay on the floor in the 755 Club at Turner Field, the chest pains intensified, and I did not know what was going to happen. I was looking at death's door. After I was transferred to a hospital in Atlanta, the doctors were not able to stabilize my heart.

My definition of true success is having those who are closest to you love and respect you the most. That night I witnessed the power of these relationships in a mighty way. Six months earlier, I had met cardiologist Dr. John Bright Cage. I did not know why, but I would learn this night. My assistant, Linda Eggers, upon learning of my heart attack, had the foresight to stop at the office and grab our Rolodex, sensing she might need to make some phone calls that evening. Dr. Cage had told me months earlier that I was not in good health—I was overweight, working too hard, and traveling too much. He said I was a perfect candidate for a heart attack. He ended our conversation by saying, "John, call me anytime, night or day, if you ever need help."

Linda made that call at 1:00 in the morning, and within five minutes, Dr. Cage had called a team of Atlanta doctors from his home in Tennessee. Within several hours, these doctors suctioned a clot out of one of my main arteries and saved my life. If I had not met Dr. Cage, or if my assistant had not brought his number to the hospital, I might not be telling you this story today—that's the power of relationships.

This brings up another point: Why did it happen this way? God has a plan for your life, and it more than likely is better than the plan you have for your life. I firmly believe that what happened on that night was not coincidental, but part of the Creator's plan for my life. When I was on that table, not knowing whether I would live or die, the warmth of God overwhelmed me. The peace that He gave me and the assurance that He loved me removed my fear. And in the end, as is always the case, God knew what He was doing. Through this near-fatal experience, He taught me some powerful lessons.

First, be a good steward of your body. Second, get serious about your calling and pursue it with intensity and focus. Third, never take your relationships for granted. When I was on that table, I wanted so badly, just one more time, to tell my wife, Margaret, and my children, Elizabeth and Joel Porter, that I loved them. Wake up to God's plan for your life, and never, ever take life for granted.

These lessons are why I am so impressed with Todd Duncan's new book, *Wealth Strategies: 9½ Steps to Acheiving Physical, Financial, and Spiritual Abundance.* Life is fragile! You never know what's around the next corner. You have to live it with purpose, passion, and balance. Todd Duncan shares with you incredibly simple yet profound ways to live the life you have imagined. Step by step, he walks you through the process of making your dreams come true. This book will cause a transformation of your spirit, your health, your relationships, and your ultimate destiny. Todd's advice is practical, immediately usable, and life changing, all at once. I loved it, and I know you will too. Read it now, and experience life abundantly!

—Dr. John C. Maxwell
Founder, The INJOY Group

Acknowledgments

What began as a vision is now a reality! Whether writing a book or designing a life, you and I can make things happen, but it all starts with vision. When a vision springs forth you can't execute it alone. That was clearly the case with *Wealth Strategies: 9½ Steps to Acheiving Physical, Financial, and Spiritual Abundance.* I would like to thank the following people for the incredible impact they have made in my life and, as a direct or indirect result, this book.

Thank you, Sheryl, for being my life mate and for constantly shaping me so that I experience life with you and our two wonderful boys abundantly. You have given me true *wealth!*

In 1989, I met Zig Ziglar for the first time in a church service in Arizona. He had profound impact on me then as I first began to understand true *wealth.* Today, as a friend and mentor, his commitment to excellence in all areas of his life is the standard I strive to achieve. Thanks, Zig!

In 1995, Dr. John C. Maxwell, founder of INJOY, Inc., was placed in my path as I navigated some tough waters in my life. In that moment in time, a relationship was forged that will forever change how I look at *wealth* in the home, as a husband, and as a dad. I thank God for giving you life, John, so that you can give it to others.

This book would not be possible without the incredible belief and commitment in the end result of a host of people. Thank you, Bob Larson, for shaping this manuscript. I thank my entire team in San Diego—Amy, Julia, and Vicky—for all of the painstaking hours of research and proofing. You have given this book life. Thank you, Daniel Harkavy, for holding me accountable every Friday to the standard of a life of excellence. You have fine-tuned my "engine"; it's firing on all cylinders. Thank you, Dr. Greg Jantz, for assisting in the health section of this book. Thank you, Jeff Duncan. As a brother, you're one in a million—and as a top financial planner, I especially appreciate your contribution to the financial section of this book.

Introduction

When Socrates said, "If a rich man is proud of his wealth, he should not be praised until it is known how he employs it," it is not clear whether he was speaking of money alone. Since we do not know the full meaning of the great philosopher's statement, I will take the liberty to suggest that he is indeed right—in *all* areas of wealth: monetary fortune, good health, and the indomitable human spirit. In brief, that is what this book you are about to read is all about—developing an on-purpose life plan to help you create, sustain, and enjoy an abundance of wealth in each of these areas of your life. When these areas are pursued with equal passion, their synergy promises to create an unstoppable dynamic that will set the stage for you to have abundance in your life.

I know this to be true from personal experience. Using the information that fills these pages, I have quit severe addictive behaviors, lost weight and kept it off, built financial wealth, and developed high levels of intimacy with my family and with God. I follow the information in this book every day to be my best! My life is not any easier than yours—quite possibly, it is laced with the same challenges every day, in every area. However, one thing I have learned is that to be your best, there are certain daily disciplines that create a life of abundance. That is what this book is about.

On the path to a life of abundance will come the tough disciplines and decisions, the unexpected turns in the road, the people who may disappoint you, and the pesky self-doubts that cause you to ask yourself, *Is it worth the hard work necessary to become a fulfilled and happy person with great wealth?* If you have ever been there—or if that is where you are right now—you know what I am talking about.

So does my colleague and mentor Zig Ziglar, a human dynamo who has likely touched the lives of more people than any other speaker or writer today. But on his way to fame and fortune, Zig has been up, and he has been down. In the process, he has come to know the meaning of true wealth for himself, his family, and others whom he loves. I recall that he once quoted the great western writer Zane Grey on the subject of becoming a great person—a paragraph I think is apropos to the beginning of this book. I share that with you now.

> These are the tests of greatness—to bear up under loss, to fight the bitterness of defeat and the weakness of grief, to be a victor over anger, to smile when tears are close, to resist disease and evil men and base instincts, to hate hate and to love love, to go on when it would seem good to die, to seek ever the glory and the dream, to look up with unquenchable faith to something even more about to be. These things any [person] can do and so be great.

You will experience many tests along your way to wealth. However, as you live your life increasingly on-purpose, your challenges, rather than restricting you, will suddenly become the driving force to carry you to victory. God created you for abundance. He has filled you with His power and literally soaked you with His Spirit. Now, the ball is in your court. Will you pursue the *true* wealth that the Creator so generously offers you?

We live in an abundant universe—one that encourages us to ask, ask, and ask again. If we do not ask, or if we fail to take action, however, we have no one to blame but ourselves. If we lack money, health, and richness of spirit, we dare not blame the universe, our environment, our background, or our last run of bad luck. It is we who have chosen not to tap the bounty available to us all—*up until now.*

That's why I believe that today can be the day you turn your life around. Abundance can and will be yours. In each of these short chapters, there are time-tested clues to help you discover the true abundance you seek for your life. All you need is a commitment to living your days and years on-purpose and an uncompromising attitude that says, *I'm going for it!* As your coach and mentor, I promise you that I will be with you each step of your exciting, wealth-laden journey. You are on your way to a perfect "10," so let's get started.

Part One

Physical Abundance

Get Your Body's Attention

Chapter 1

Are You in Shape?

On a brisk December evening, he stood on the edge of death. Have you ever been there? Imagine being so close to death that you would do or give anything to have your life back. That is how my friend Dr. John C. Maxwell ended his year—on the brink of death.

John had it all—a successful business, a great marriage, two wonderful children, and several best-selling books. In the blink of an eye, he almost lost it all at the age of fifty-one. His heart attack got his attention. The three lessons he learned could also change your life. First, be a good steward of your body. Second, get serious about your calling and pursue it with intensity and focus. Third, never take your relationships for granted.

If John's story does not get your attention, the only one that will could be your own. So the question is, Are you physically fit? Are you doing the things that will minimize the risk of a life-ending or life-altering event? Are you being proactive about your health, or will you be forced to react one day like John did to your personal wake-up call? If you suffer any symptoms of poor health, such as fatigue, obesity, or low self-esteem, how much longer will you wait to reverse those challenges in your life? One way to help you move forward is to ask yourself, *Is this the way I want to live?* If the answer is no, then let's look at some practical ways to discover physical abundance by getting your body's attention.

Here Are the Facts

According to the Centers for Disease Control, more than 50 percent of American adults are overweight.[1] Other such studies report that as many as three in four Americans are too heavy. This problem leads to all sorts of other issues that affect our health.

According to the Centers for Disease Control, six of the top ten leading causes of death are directly or partially related to what we put into our bodies and whether we follow a regular and proper exercise program.[2] The risk for heart disease, cancer, stroke, chronic obstructive pulmonary disease, diabetes, and cirrhosis is often reduced by being in shape. In spite of an onslaught of helpful books, tapes, and infomercials that encourage us to get in shape, the research still suggests that more work remains to be done.

The Psychology of Health

At the "heart" of the health game is you. Have you ever made the connection that your lifestyle habits might have some relevance to how you think and feel about yourself? You and I have a choice each day about how we fuel the most important piece of equipment we own—our bodies.

When we exercise our right to choose a healthy, new path, we give ourselves permission to change. This change is always difficult because it requires undoing habits that have kept us in knots for years—even decades. The good news, however, is that it *is* possible to change. For change to happen, you must go from a "should" approach to a "must" approach. The only way you will ever have the urgency to develop a healthy lifestyle is by reinventing yourself and then locking onto a new vision that is powered by fulfillment, pleasure, and confidence. Hang on to your negative self-talk, self-esteem battering, and mediocrity, and you will stay exactly where you are.

The Fitness Checkup

Here are some questions that should help you get your body's attention:

1. Would you like to feel better about yourself?
2. What are the top three things you want to change about yourself?
3. Would you feel better about yourself one month from now if you made these changes?

4. Would you like to be able to exert yourself without fatiguing easily?
5. Do you feel you should be spending more time working out?
6. Would you like to have more energy after you eat?
7. Would you like to fall asleep easier and stay asleep longer?
8. Would you like to have less stress in your life?
9. Would you like to live as long as you can rather than die prematurely?
10. Did you answer any of these questions no?

Chances are you only answered no to the last question. Out of design, I want you to start thinking in terms of yes. *Yes* is a positive word, and it is the first indication that you desire to make the move to achieve optimum health. The more you pursue your goal, the more you begin to realize that health leads to wealth, which I broadly define as "enjoying the abundance of feeling great." Yes, you can achieve optimum health, if you truly think you can. Here is an anonymous poem entitled "The Winner's Creed" that embraces the attitude I want you to have as you move forward.

> If you think you are beaten, you are.
> If you think you dare not, you don't.
> If you like to win, but you think you can't,
> It is almost certain you won't.
>
> If you think you'll lose, you're lost.
> For out of the world we find,
> Success begins with a person's will—
> It's all in the state of mind.
>
> If you think you're outclassed, you are.
> You've got to think high to rise.
> You've got to be sure of yourself before
> You can ever win the prize.
>
> Life's battles don't always go
> To the stronger woman or man,
> But sooner or later the one who wins
> Is the one WHO THINKS HE CAN.

The Perfect You

With twenty more chapters to go in our discussion on achieving optimum health, it is important for you to begin to outline some of the changes you want to make. On the lines below, describe your perfect future health. Use descriptive words and great energy as you describe the new you. Have fun with this. Your better health begins with a clear vision of who you want to be.

My vision of my health future is:

_____

_____

_____

_____

_____

_____

_____

_____

_____

_____

_____

_____

_____

_____

_____

Chapter 2

How to Face Your Fears

Not long ago, I was with a client whose company was holding its annual president's club meeting in Negril, Jamaica. We had journeyed by bus to spend the afternoon at Rick's Café. Perched on the edge of the cliffs, the restaurant overlooked the Caribbean to the west. Just south of the restaurant was a cove where the waves ebbed and flowed and where timing was everything, especially if you were a cliff diver.

Hundreds of people lined the edge of the cliff that day and stared in amazement as local Jamaican men dived effortlessly from the cliffs into the ocean below. The spectators stood quietly by as each man took his dive. Then they breathlessly waited until each emerged from the blue waters. The cliffs, however, were not reserved for local talent alone; anyone who had a swimsuit could pick one of ten different areas from which to dive. However, none of the spectators was going for it. We were all paralyzed by fear.

Finally, confidence sprang forth from someone in our group. Michael had watched the other divers for almost twenty minutes. During that time, he had gained not only the knowledge of other divers' techniques, but also the certainty of their outcomes. Michael edged his way out onto the cliff, took a deep breath, and made the plunge. He hit the water, disappeared, and then resurfaced to the cheers of everyone. As you might imagine, his action said to everyone else, "Come on in; the water's fine." Within moments, a line of people from our group, including me, were diving off those Jamaican cliffs. We had all replaced fear with belief. And the more we dived into the water, the less fearful we became.

That is how it is with our bodies—and with the overall game of health. People usually put off their positive course of action toward optimum health because they are afraid. They do not know the outcome, nor do they have the certainty that once they start, they will be able to keep it up. They are putting off achieving a healthy life instead of observing others then *jumping into the water.*

Doubting Success at Thirty-Five Thousand Feet

While on a recent flight from New York to San Diego, a flight attendant learned that I was a motivational speaker. During our conversation, she asked me, "Is it possible to be afraid of success?" Her question lingered in my mind for several days. What about you? Are you not where you want to be because you are afraid? Does fear so fill your spirit that you are reduced to a state of paralysis? Did you once try a new course of action and fail so terribly that you are certain you would fail again?

Your focus is usually an indicator of your results. People tell me all the time what they do not want. They tell me they do not want to be fat, they do not want to be broke, and they do not want to feel separated from God and family. Yet these negatives invariably become their reality. What they focus on *not wanting* is exactly what they have attained. On the contrary, the people who tell me what they *do* want and who can articulate their vision for a better future have a goal to move toward. When they focus on positive results, their fears are usually overcome by momentum.

A Lesson from a King

King David was a man of God. In the Scriptures, his songs of praise articulate the fact that fear produces better performance. All successful athletes channel the fear of losing into their preparation for victory. They resist staying in the pain of losing and move mentally, psychologically, and physiologically to the immense pleasure of winning. This mind-set shapes their wisdom and, therefore, their actions. As King David wrote, "The fear of the LORD is the beginning of wisdom" (Ps. 111:10 NIV).

Failure is the key to success.

Let me help you reset your sails. Failure is part of the game. Failure is growth. Failure is learning how not to do it so you can learn how to do it. Failure is a launching pad for new discoveries about what and why you are doing things. Failure is going forward. Failure is the key to success.

A Near-Death Experience

To make positive changes, you must develop new beliefs. I found this out the hard way. Fourteen years ago, I was forty pounds overweight and addicted to cocaine and alcohol. Suffering from a low-self-esteem and an identity problem, I was burying my fear of facing life in these negative patterns. I wanted to change, but no matter how hard I tried to lose the weight or quit the addictions, I couldn't. I was riding a roller coaster of pleasure when I was high and one of pain when I wasn't. I was motivated to change my lifestyle, but I kept doing the same crazy things over and over, which led to more pain and more frustration. What began as recreational fun was chipping away at who I was and who I wanted to be.

The day I finally discovered how to stop the insanity is as vivid now as it was then. First, my fiancée postponed our wedding until we could both be free from our cocaine addictions. Sheryl, who is now my wife, set a deadline of eighteen months. She said that if we could stay away from cocaine for that long, we would schedule our wedding. This was the leverage I needed. I wanted to spend the rest of my life with Sheryl, and the pain of not being able to do that gave me the inner resolve to change my actions.

The key to lasting change is leverage, not will power.

Then the sports headlines reported that Maryland basketball great Len Bias died from a cocaine overdose. At that point, cocaine went from meaning fun to meaning death. I did not want to die, because then I could not spend my life with Sheryl. These two new beliefs changed my behavior, gave me confidence, shaped my resolve, and altered my life forever. I then used this new leverage to lose forty-two pounds and to eliminate my addiction to alcohol. I hope you will remember this: The key to lasting change is leverage, not will power.

Leveraging Your Fears

Here are three ideas to help you gain leverage and manage your fears.

Face your fears. Fear is instrumental for growth. Without fear, you are probably not growing. When it comes to facing your fear, however, your choices are relatively few: (1) You can avoid it and live a life of mediocrity and stress, (2) you can hope it will go away and be frustrated when it doesn't, or (3) you can deal with it. All great accomplishments involve people who deal with fear and failure. Look at a child learning to ride a bike, a pilot learning to fly a plane, or parents deciding to have children: All have fear components.

See fear as power. What would you attempt if you knew you could not fail? *You would do the thing you fear.* There is power in fear, and that power comes from your purpose, which is the bedrock of your motivation. When your purpose is clear, your decisions are easy. You now approach the things you once feared with confidence. Suddenly, you raise the bar for yourself and for those around you. When you align your fears with your purpose, then you are able to replace fear with faith and action.

Focus on your future. Be more concerned with your direction than your perfection. Focus on your growth, not your regression. When you focus on your future, you will begin to have one. If you stay stuck in your present, you will remain there. The choice is yours. Fear is always at the edge of excellence. Remember that, and you are on your way to a better future.

Chapter 3

Confessions of a Couch Potato

A ll movement toward optimum health begins with and ends with energy. Your energy level affects every aspect of your life. Energy is defined, among other things, as strength, power, and the capacity for vigorous action. Not only are we dependent on great supplies of energy, but these sources of energy are interdependent as well.

We are dependent on energy because it gives us strength, power, and the capacity to act. Each of these is interdependent on the other. As strength increases, so does our power; when power increases, so does our capacity to act. As Vince Lombardi once said, "Fatigue makes cowards of us all." Lack of energy makes us unhappy and inefficient human machines.

I admit that *knowing* the importance of energy in our lives is the easy part. Even *believing* it is relatively easy. The difficulty for most of us is *pursuing a course of action* toward increasing our energy that is positive and productive. So serious is this problem that the Office of the Surgeon General in 1997 issued its report on physical activity and health. It is to the '90s what the same office's report on smoking was to the '60s. The message: We are in trouble. Oh, did I forget to mention the problem? It is called exercise excusitis.

Your energy level affects every aspect of your life.

The president's council has said that more than 60 percent of adults are not active enough. The Department of Adolescent Health says that from the ninth to the twelfth grades, participation in physical education drops from 100 percent to 50 percent. Their research concluded that:

Only 22 percent of Americans meet at least the minimum exercise guidelines of thirty minutes of moderate activity most days of the week.

Fifty-four percent of Americans exercise sporadically.

Twenty-four percent of Americans are sedentary.[1]

Lack of activity is killing people, and it may be killing you. The U.S. government estimates that about three hundred thousand people die prematurely each year because of lack of physical activity and poor diet.[2]

According to the Campbell Survey on Well Being, conducted by the Canadian Fitness and Lifestyle Research Institute, the greatest perceived obstacles to physical activity are lack of time, lack of self-discipline, lack of a partner, and lack of ability.[3]

Activity Is a Lifestyle

Since these excuses can kill you, let's deal with each one so you can be on your way to optimum health.

Lack of time. The good news is that you have all the time there is. (If you can find hour number twenty-five, drop me a line and tell me how you found it.) What you must do is make different choices. If one large chunk of time for exercise does not work for you, spread it out and begin to look for exercise alternatives. Take the stairs instead of using the elevator. Park far away from the supermarket or mall instead of circling the parking lot for ten minutes looking for a parking place in front of the store. Take a walk during your lunch break. Read your mail on a treadmill instead of at your desk. Walk around the block at night instead of watching meaningless TV. Walk the golf course instead of using a cart.

Lack of self-discipline. The key to starting and maintaining a lifestyle of activity is picking the activities you enjoy that are beneficial to your health. If you hate jogging, don't do it. If you do not like swimming, give it up. If you are stuck in the same boring exercise routine, change it. Here's the key: When you look forward to the activities you do in your pursuit of health, you will do them more consistently and with greater commitment and joy. Your motives, and therefore your motivation, will become natural, and you will begin operating from a position of pleasure, not pain.

Lack of a partner. Accountability is one of the keys to staying on course with your workouts. As you finally settle into the things you enjoy when working out, find a partner who enjoys them as well. Then develop a mutual commitment to your schedules and to your exercise activities. Generally, when one is weak, the other will be strong. Once you have made the commitment to show up, you are more likely to keep your commitment because you don't want to disappoint your exercise partner.

Lack of ability. In any form of exercise, you have to be *your best*, not good enough to be *the best*. Too many people use "lack of ability" as their excuse for not being active. It's as if they want to fail with dignity. Let's face it. You probably will not play in the NBA, but shooting baskets for thirty minutes still has enormous health benefits for you, even if you do not make all the shots. If you need to get a few lessons, go ahead and do it. Your increase in talent will increase your excitement for and enjoyment of the activity.

You can either be a spectator and sit on the couch, or you can be an active participant and get into the game. Unless you choose to go in-line skating down a steep hill against traffic, getting—and staying—active will generally be a safe bet.

Chapter 4

Lessons from a Sumo Wrestler

To sumo wrestling fans in Japan, Hawaiian Chad Rowan-Akebono is one mean, but not lean, machine. Here's his take:

Eating isn't what I get paid for, but it's key to my success. The object of sumo is to push the other man out of the ring, so bigger is better. Right now I'm six-foot-eight and weigh 465 pounds. That's two hundred pounds more than when I played college basketball. If I didn't eat so much, I wouldn't be so successful. And if I didn't train three hours every day, I surely wouldn't be a yokozuna, or grand champion sumo wrestler—the only non-Japanese to hold the title.

Sumo wrestlers don't eat breakfast. I work out first thing in the morning, so by 11:30, I'm very hungry. The training table staple is a hearty potluck stew called chanko nabe. I often eat four bowls of it at a sitting and also chow down a couple dozen chicken nuggets, four or five eggs (both raw and fried), and lots of pickled vegetables, fried noodles, and grilled fish. I eat rice, of course (about three pounds a day), and I drink a gallon of ice tea with my meal. Then I take a three-hour nap. That's important to my training too. Dinner is the same as lunch, but sometimes I ask the kitchen to cook up a package or two of hot dogs— they're very good with rice. I really like the food here in Japan. I'd better—If my citizenship application is accepted, I'll be here for a while. But I do miss a few things about America: canned spaghetti, chili, Spam, poi and, most of all, my mom's meatloaf.

I don't know about you, but I don't think I'll pursue the fine art of sumo wrestling. However, Chad proves the point that if you eat enough, you will get fat. After all, he gained two hundred pounds! If you pig out, you will grow out. The key to not being fat is found in a simple, balanced approach to eating the right things in the right portions.

The Basics of Fat

More than ever, consumers are now aware of the effects of food on their health and overall performance. Unfortunately, so many messages are flying at us that we are left to decipher them on our own. The real danger today, then, is not whether we have *enough* information, but whether we have *accurate* information. The decisions we make based on this information can affect us for life.

My advice to people is not to be too regimented about their food-intake program, but instead to use the knowledge they have to make intelligent choices consistently. Balance this approach with a good exercise program, and you will be in great shape. One of the great misconceptions of this game called health, however, is the role that fat plays in our food-consumption habits.

Why We Crave Fat

You can be overweight and fat, or you can be underweight and fat. Weight is not the issue; fat is the real issue. If you expand the definition of fat to include the nonmuscular (what others can see) and muscular (what others cannot see), then it becomes easier to understand this concept. Therefore, reaching an ideal body weight would include not only losing weight, but also losing excess body fat. Too much fat is not good, because it can lead to obesity, diabetes, heart disease, and other illnesses. More than 50 percent of our world's population are considered overweight. These individuals exceed their ideal body weights by 20 percent, and a large percentage of them are also labeled "overfat." Men are considered overfat when their body fat is higher than 15 percent of their total weight; women are overfat when their body fat exceeds 22 percent of their total weight.

"But fat tastes good," you insist. You're right. Fats and fatty acids activate cells in the tongue, throat, and upper esophagus that send pleasurable messages to the brain. It feels good, so you do it, and you do more of it. Unfortunately, too much fat can kill you.

Low-Fat Does Not Guarantee Weight Loss

If you are trying to lose weight, you need to stay away from low-fat, reduced-fat, and nonfat cookies, potato chips, and other processed foods. Unfortunately, most people increase their portions when eating these types of food, a habit that creates excessive calories, not to mention the wrong dietary fat. If these excessive calories and fat are not burned through the body's natural metabolism, they are converted to and stored as body fat.

We actually need some fat, because the right kind of fat can aid in overall weight reduction and reduce the possibility of life-ending heart disease. The right kinds of fat are polyunsaturated and monounsaturated fats. The wrong kinds are saturated and transunsaturated fats. While most scientific research suggests that we should limit our fat intake to 20 to 30 percent of our total daily calorie consumption, you need to go one step further. Replace the bad fat with the good fat wherever and whenever possible. As a rule of thumb, your daily fat intake should come from at least one-third monounsaturated fats, one-third polyunsaturated fats, and no more than one-third saturated or transunsaturated fats. You do not have to look for the latter, since these "hidden" fats are already in the foods most people eat daily. With this strategy, you will reduce your risk of heart disease, stroke, and cancer. The *New England Journal of Medicine* reported that energy (calorie) replacement of bad fat with good fat had an exponential impact on heart disease, the number one killer in the world. Here are some sobering statistics:

Every increase of 5 percent in caloric intake from saturated fats, such as butter, was associated with a 17-percent increase in the risk of coronary disease. Olive oil, monounsaturated and corn oil, and polyunsaturated oil produced no reportable increases.

The replacement of 5 percent of calories from saturated fat with an equivalent amount of unsaturated fat reduced the risk of heart disease by 42 percent.

Replacing 2 percent of caloric intake from transunsaturated

(hydrogenated) fats with unhydrogenated, unsaturated fats re-duced heart-disease risk by 53 percent.[1]

It's a Good Bet

The bad fats are destructive because they are the hard fats. They are made hard through the hydrogenation process, which returns hydrogen atoms back to unsaturated fat. A good visual would be butter versus olive oil. Butter is hard (hydrogenated); olive oil is soft (unhydrogenated). How it is *before you eat it* is how it can end up *after you eat it*.

I remember a graphic example of the good fat/bad fat para-digm as demonstrated in one of my college science classes. One vial was filled with the blood from an athlete with 6-percent body fat; the other was filled with the blood from a student with 32-percent body fat. By the end of the class, the blood in the athlete's vial was crimson red, while the blood in the overfat person's vial had separated, with the bottom two-thirds a dull-ish red and the top one-third a milky brownish white—the fat.

Clearing Up Cholesterol Concerns

Cholesterol is sort of a "cousin" to fat. Both fat and cholesterol are part of a larger family of chemical compounds referred to as *lipids*. A lipid is a chemical compound characterized by the fact that it is not soluble in water. Cholesterol is a chemical com-pound manufactured by the body that is used to build cell mem-branes and brain and nerve tissue. It also helps the body produce steroid hormones for processing food and bile acids needed for digestion.

You do not need to consume dietary cholesterol, since the body is able to make enough for its needs. However, most diets contain substantial amounts of this killer in foods such as egg yolks, meat, some shellfish, and whole-milk products.

Cholesterol is carried through the bloodstream in large fat and protein molecules called *lipoproteins*. Low-density lipoproteins are called LDL, and high-density lipoproteins are called HDL. LDL, or "bad" cholesterol, in your blood increases the risk that fatty deposits will form in the arteries, thus increasing the risk of heart attack. HDL, or "good" cholesterol, seems to have a protective effect against heart disease. Your cholesterol number refers to the total amount of cholesterol in the blood. Most physicians, and the National Institute of Health, recommend that your total cholesterol be less than 200 milligrams per deciliter [100 ccs], with your HDL level above 35 mg/dl and your LDL less than 130 mg/dl to minimize the risk of heart disease.

There is little question that fat and cholesterol are killers if consumed the wrong way for an extended period. As you read on, you will:

- Learn how to group foods correctly to help reduce fat and cholesterol and to maximize your metabolism
- Learn how to read labels to discover and avoid the hidden fats
- Learn how a regular exercise routine helps you burn more of your calories, thereby bringing you to your ideal weight without depriving your body of the nutrients it needs to operate at peak performance

Optimum health is just around the corner!

Chapter 5

Sugar and Spice and Everything Bad

My friend Hyrum Smith, CEO of the Franklin Covey Company, defines *addictive behavior* as "compulsive behavior with short-term benefits and long-term destruction."[1] Addictions are a reflection of our lack of worth, our need for inner health, or, in some cases, our bad habits. In other instances, we simply refuse to question decisions that may be bad for us because of a lack of knowledge of how to care for our bodies. Lasting, healthy self-esteem, and thus the power to conquer an entire range of addictions, comes only when we measure our worth by God's unconditional love for us, not by our misguided attempts to try to get it right by ourselves. As King David observed, "I will give thanks to Thee, for I am . . . wonderfully made" (Ps. 139:14).

I am amazed at the things we do to our bodies that have been so "wonderfully made." In my own life, and in observing the lives of others, I have found the following to be the five most frequent "addictions" in the area of consumption:

- alcohol
- nicotine
- overeating
- caffeine
- adding sugar and salt to food before tasting

Limit Your Alcohol

In my book *Closing the Gap,* I illustrated this concept in the following way. One of the richest men of all time, King Solomon, has great advice for you if you drink too much. About three thousand years ago, wise Solomon said, "Who has redness of eyes? Those who linger long over wine, those who go to taste mixed wine" (Prov. 23:29–30). King Solomon goes on to create a remarkably clear word picture about the attraction and havoc of alcohol. He says, "Do not look on the wine when it is red, when it sparkles in the cup, when it goes down smoothly; at the last it bites like a serpent, and stings like a viper. Your eyes will see strange things, and your mouth will utter perverse things" (vv. 31–33).

I can still remember the moment I decided to change my drinking behavior. I was confronted with some sobering statistics and considered, for the first time, their validity in the overall game of my health. Medically, alcohol consumption in moderation—one to two glasses of wine per day—has been linked to lowering the risk of heart disease. However, since moderation leads many to excess, why increase the risk of stroke, high blood pressure, heart disease, cancer, and cirrhosis of the liver? These can all lead to premature death.

The average alcoholic drink is six fluid ounces. If you combine beer, wine, and 100-proof vodka, the average calories per ounce are thirty-eight. Add the mixers, and the average drink packs 278 calories (fifty calories per drink for mixers). Consider this: If you have only two drinks per day, in moderation, *you are adding a whopping fifty-eight pounds of calories to your body each year.* Further, since these are sugar calories, they turn to fat more quickly and easily. The additional side effects of alcohol consumption—reduced mental clarity and energy—can wreak havoc on the other positive elements of your life. You cannot be on top of the game of life if alcohol or any other abusive substances are taking you down.

> If you have only two drinks per day, in moderation, you are adding a whopping fifty-eight pounds of calories to your body each year.

Starting today, think of your body as God's temple, a masterpiece that He does not want you to ruin. Each day, God offers you new opportunities to live well. Begin to take advantage of them, and watch your life turn around.

Going Up in Smoke

It's estimated that in the United States 25.2 million men (26.7 percent) and 23.2 million women (22.8 percent) are smokers, all of whom are putting themselves at increased risk of heart attack, lung cancer, osteoporosis, hearing loss, and stroke. They also look and feel older—something never mentioned by the ad wizards of Madison Avenue. Further, 4.1 million young people ages twelve through seventeen are smokers. More than six thousand kids under eighteen years of age try one cigarette each day, and more than three thousand kids under eighteen join the smoking ranks every twenty-four hours. If these trends continue, some five million children and teenagers will eventually die from a smoking-related disease. If you are putting yourself at risk, do these statistics convince you that it is time to stop?

Let me tell you a story. My dad was a radiologist. I remember from an early age how my dad introduced us to the impact of smoking. (He and my mother had smoked an average of eighty cigarettes per day for many years.) Somewhere en route to becoming a medical professional, my dad decided he could not do to his body what he was seeing others do to theirs. This picture was magnified for him through x-ray technology.

For years, as patients would die from diseases associated with smoking, he would bring home their x-rays to show us their lungs. Once clear, vibrant, life-sustaining mechanisms were now cloudy, opaque, and congested with the adversity of tar, nicotine, and cancer. After looking at those disgusting lungs, I decided that I was not going to be a smoker.

If tobacco isn't safe to walk on, why would anyone inhale it?

The National Institute of Occupational Health in Ahmedabad, India, found that tobacco harvesters often complained of headaches and other symptoms of nicotine poisoning. Wearing rubber gloves relieved the symptoms in 20 percent of the harvesters. The others did not get relief until they added rubber boots and socks. The question is, If tobacco isn't safe to walk on, why would anyone inhale it?

Overcome Your Addiction

If you want to quit drinking or smoking, I encourage you to do the following three things:

Set a target date for when you will be a nonsmoker or a nondrinker. Link a major reward to that day. Examples might include departure for a vacation, a shopping spree, a new car, or new clothes. It does not matter what you choose to do. Just make it a reward you would truly enjoy.

Commit to a daily plan that coincides with your target date. If you want to go from twenty cigarettes a day to none, lower your intake by just one per day (twenty-day plan) or every other day (forty-two-day plan). If you want to go from ten drinks a week to none, lower it by two drinks per week (five-week plan) or one drink per week (ten-week plan). When you begin to think about lighting up or having a drink, replace that activity immediately with something else you love to do. Make sure the activity is not associated with creating the crave (such as eating, drinking, etc.). Use medically approved tools for assistance if appropriate, or if you feel you need them. Always check with your doctor first.

Ask a friend to hold you accountable for each day you are on your new plan. This friend must be a nonsmoker or nondrinker. My brother, Jeff, and his wife, Gabriella, followed these three steps and have not smoked a cigarette in more than five years.

Stop Pigging Out

"I never eat more than I can lift," boasts Miss Piggy with a twinkle in her eye. However, her humor fast loses its edge when we take it as our formula for our own life. Overeating, second helpings, eating the wrong foods—and too much of them too often—will make you feel sluggish, shorten your life span, and reduce your capacity to be the person God designed you to be. Diets are guilt driven, producing one result: failure. We lose every time. A well-executed *eating plan* is one of the most productive strategies for thinness available to you.

Here are three action steps to help you control how much you eat.

Decide if you are really hungry. Are you a victim of biological hunger? Does a gurgling stomach, lightheadedness, or difficulty concentrating send you to food? Or when scheduled mealtimes arrive, do you eat out of habit? My rule when hunger strikes is to drink a glass of water and then see if the hunger leaves within the next ten to twenty minutes. I then ask myself, *What else can I do to replace my urge for food?*

Eat slowly. When I was a kid, my dad always told me to eat slowly and to chew my food until it was no longer in my mouth. He said it would satisfy my taste buds and ease the digestion process. Dad was right! Another good rule is to stop eating as soon as you are starting to feel full. What you have consumed will catch up with your hunger as your food is absorbed into the bloodstream.

Control your portions. To avoid overeating, limit all portions to the size of your palm (without the fingers), and eat only one of those portions at a single sitting. This is a powerful weight-loss and weight-management strategy.

Reduce Your Sugar and Salt Intake

We can all get by with less sugar and salt than we think. I am always amazed to see people who, out of habit, pour excess salt or sugar onto their soon-to-be-consumed food products *before they taste their food.* You should be aware of some of the research on each of these substances.

Here are the facts on sugar. Avoiding sugars alone will not correct your being overweight. For active people with high calorie needs, sugars can be an additional source of energy. However, because maintaining a nutritious diet and a healthy weight is so important, sugars should be used in moderation by most healthy people and sparingly by people with low calorie needs.

Sugar-free foods can be as misleading as fat-free foods. Sugar substitutes such as sorbitol, saccharin, and aspartame are ingredients found in many of our foods. Most sugar substitutes do not provide significant calories and therefore may be useful in the diets of people concerned about caloric intake. However, the foods that contain these substitutes may be higher in calories than the same foods containing real sugar. Therefore, sugar substitutes alone will not help you lose weight.

Here are the facts on salt. In the body, sodium plays an essential role in regulation of fluids and blood pressure. However, many studies in diverse populations have shown that a high sodium intake is associated with higher blood pressure. Most evidence suggests that people at risk of high blood pressure reduce their chances of developing this condition by consuming less salt or sodium. Adding salt to food is a learned behavior, not a dietary requirement.

Most people consume more sodium than necessary. In household measures, one level teaspoon of salt provides nearly 98 percent of the daily requirement. With a balanced eating program that has no added salt, you will generally get what your body needs. In the end, consuming less salt or sodium is not harmful and is recommended for the healthy normal adult.

Limit Your Caffeine

According to fitness expert Dr. Kenneth Cooper, use caffeine in moderation. As with any substance, it is up to you to weigh the pros and cons. Dr. Cooper recommends that as long as you do not have a medical reason to the contrary, you can have up to two cups of coffee or tea per day. However, be aware of some of the findings reported in his book *Regaining the Power of Youth:*

- You should be safe with no more than 240 mg of caffeine per day (two cups of coffee).
- More than five to six cups of coffee per day may trigger a higher incidence of heartbeat irregularities, increased blood pressure, shortness of breath, headaches, and other health problems.
- Studies have shown that boiled or nonfiltered coffee may raise cholesterol levels.
- Coffee drinking has been linked to a loss of the body's calcium through urination, a process that can decrease bone density and increase the risk of osteoporosis (thinning of the bone mass).
- More than three cups of coffee per day can reduce a woman's ability to conceive by as much as 26 percent.[2]

It is obviously your privilege to make your own choices. However, like any habit, you must evaluate any negative impact of caffeine against the possible rewards. In the case of caffeine, less is best.

Optimum health comes when you become clear on what you are putting into your body, all the time making the decision whether it is good for you. Overall health comes from balancing your intake of the things that are good for you and limiting or eliminating the things that are bad for you. When we journey into Step Three, "Develop Habits for Health," we will introduce you to some key factors to help you stay motivated as you are trying to rid yourself of some or all of these addictive behaviors.

Overall health comes from balancing your intake of the things that are good for you and limiting or eliminating the things that are bad for you.

Chapter 6

Let's Don't Do Lunch

It had become a routine. Forty-two pounds later, I realized it had to stop. I am talking about eating lousy lunches. Early in my career, I was often invited to lunch with other employees in our company. We regularly went to a restaurant in town where for the next hour or more we enjoyed our conversation and ate, and ate, and ate—and ate. Without the proper knowledge, most of what I consumed was rich with fat. Slowly but surely, the cheeseburgers, greasy fries, gobs of mayonnaise, and deep-fried (and oh-so-good) calamari took their toll on my waistline and my energy. I was stuck in the habit of "doing lunch."

On a recent trip to Australia, I was again impacted by the "lunch" culture. Not only were the lunches there generally longer than an hour, but they also were rich with high-fat foods and in many cases, a bottle of wine or a few beers. (And Foster's beer comes in very large cans!)

In both illustrations above, I was in a comfort zone—a zone that caused my personal and professional productivity to plunge, taking its toll on my self-esteem, which ultimately led to habits that became more life restricting than life enhancing.

Everyone has comfort zones—ways of life to which we have grown accustomed. Habits, good or bad, become an integral part of our lives, and we feel great resistance from the "habitized self" when we try to make corrections or change course to new habits.

Although lunch is the theme here, the lesson applies from sunup to sundown. It has as much to do with breakfast and dinner as it does with every snack in between. We are a world of eaters: We eat when we shouldn't, what we shouldn't, and more than we should. Add it up, and our eating habits are a surefire recipe for poor health.

The three keys to a balanced approach to food consumption

are (1) refusing to skip meals, (2) spreading out your consumption, and (3) consciously choosing the foods you will and will not eat. Let's look at each one of these keys.

Don't Skip Meals

Many people try to lose weight by skipping meals, especially breakfast and lunch. That is what I was doing for years. I was actually starving myself. And did I ever make up for my starvation when the next meal came around! When we are famished, we make up for lost calories by eating larger meals, consuming most of our calories when we are least active.

Skipping meals, especially breakfast, can drop your metabolic rate 4 to 5 percent. Eating raises your metabolism. Shunning the calories by skipping meals, then, has an adverse effect. When you skip meals, thereby reducing your calories, your body reacts with a built-in defense mechanism. Your body assumes that you are starving and, in a noble attempt to *save your life,* raises all sorts of barriers to protect against dramatic and unhealthy weight loss. Your body simply does what it thinks is best: It slows the metabolism and stores energy. If skipping meals is part of your weight-loss program, *your body is actually doing all it can to keep the weight on.* If you skip too many meals during the day, you will invariably eat more food—and the wrong kinds of food—when your will power finally caves in.

> **If skipping meals is part of your weight-loss program, your body is actually doing all it can to keep the weight on.**

Spread Out Your Consumption

My friend Dave Agena's body fat is below 10 percent. He eats five to seven times per day, but he eats smaller portions of the right foods, spread throughout the day. He calls this "grazing," and it works.

A good rule of thumb is to eat three meals and two snacks a day, with at least 60 percent of your total calories consumed by midafternoon. Another good rule is to eat the majority of your calories during those times of the day when you are most active, thus maximizing the conversion of calories to expended energy versus stored fat.

Choose the Food You Eat

A balanced approach to food consumption requires that you carefully choose the right foods to eat. Let's take a closer look at carbohydrates and proteins.

Carbohydrates. Too many carbohydrates (different forms of simple sugars linked together in polymers) consumed in any one day can make you fat. Here's why. The body needs carbohydrates to convert into glucose, which feeds the brain. If the body has more carbohydrates than it can use, the excess carbohydrates are stored as glycogen. Glycogen is then stored in the liver and muscles. The brain can only use the glycogen stored in the liver, which is further broken down and rechanneled to the bloodstream to help maintain adequate blood-sugar levels for proper brain function. The liver can hold a supply of carbohydrates, stored in the form of glycogen, that can be depleted in approximately twelve hours. Therefore, we need enough carbohydrates to maintain this essential function. The question is, How much is enough?

About 350 to 450 grams of glycogen are all that can be stored in the liver and muscles at any one time. Once the glycogen levels are full in these body parts, carbohydrates have one destiny: They are converted to fat and stored in the fatty tissue of the body. Here is where it starts to get confusing. Carbohydrates are fat-free, but if there are too many of them in your body, they are converted to fat. Hang on, because it gets worse.

Barry Sears, author of *The Zone,* explains another danger of excess carbohydrates in the body:

> Any meal or snack high in carbohydrates will generate a rapid rise in blood glucose. To adjust for this, the pancreas secretes the hormone insulin into the bloodstream. Insulin then lowers the levels of blood glucose. . . . The problem is that insulin is essentially a storage hormone, evolved to put aside excess carbohydrate calories in the form of fat in case of future famine. . . . Insulin stimulated

by excess carbohydrates aggressively promotes the accumulation of body fat. . . . Increased insulin levels also tell
the body not to release any stored fat.[1]

If you are trying to lose weight, too many carbohydrates,
especially those in the high-sugar category, can have the reverse
effect.

Proteins. Proteins are the building blocks of life. We need them
for our survival. In fact, they represent the largest substance in
the human body, second only to water. Protein makes up our
cells, our immune systems, and the enzymes that keep the
whole thing going. Amino acids, the underlying structure of proteins, are key to our survival. However, nine of the twenty
amino acids cannot be created by the body and therefore must
be consumed from food products.

Therefore, it would make sense to eat a high-protein, low-
carbohydrate diet, right? Wrong. Although there are undoubtedly
tens of thousands of people throughout the world who have lost
thousands of pounds by following the host of high-protein, low-
carbohydrate diets, most of them gain back their weight simply
because they have short-circuited the process of converting fat
into energy. Their weight loss is typically water, not fat. These
types of diets create abnormal metabolism called *ketosis*—not
enough stored carbohydrates to fulfill the body and brain requirements—and force the body to make its own carbohydrates. The
outcome is that nitrogen is converted to ammonia, which is toxic
and is quickly converted into urea, which is also toxic and
diluted into urine. Since the body has no need for urine, it jetti-
sons the fluid through urination, thus putting a great strain on
the kidneys.

Too much protein also causes insulin levels themselves to
increase, as they feebly attempt to get rid of the excess amino
acids. Then what happens? You guessed it. The excess insulin is
converted to fat. Too much protein can "reinvent" your fat cells,
making them harder to get rid of than before this type of diet
was initiated. In addition, God forbid that you ever go off the
diet with this permanent change in your fat cells because you
will now accumulate fat faster than ever.

The final danger in this whole scheme of protein conversion

is the loss of muscle and the degeneration of muscle tone and efficiency. Since most of the high-protein, low-carbohydrate diets are low in total calories, there typically is not enough protein to give the liver the resources it needs to produce blood sugar for the brain. Therefore, if there is not enough glucose in the liver, the muscles must supply the glucose needed to keep the brain going. Over time, the muscles break down and are not repaired or rebuilt.

Finally, high-protein, low-carbohydrate diets can produce a pound of muscle loss for every pound of fat loss. It is simply not the smart way to lose weight. A well-balanced approach to eating should include enough carbohydrates for glucose production, leaving the protein available for muscle repair.

High-protein, low-carbohydrate diets can produce a pound of muscle loss for every pound of fat loss.

In chapters 10 and 11, I will discuss the power of combining carbohydrates, proteins, and fat, and I will give you some ideas on the best types of each of these to eat on a regular basis. Since this book is about lifestyle management, we will not discuss specific diet plans; instead, we will continue to think about a *way of life* that can move you closer to your ideal weight.

Chapter 7

On a Scale of One to Four Hundred Pounds

L et me tell you about Joe (not his real name), who had been heavy all his life. At the tender age of two, he weighed seventy-five pounds, and by the time he was thirteen, he weighed in at 225. Joe soon reached a weight of 385 pounds, after which he fell into bouts of severe depression. Still, his weight kept climbing, topping out at a whopping 528 pounds.

This may not be your story. In fact, chances are good it is not. However, whenever you stand on your scale, if you discover you do not like what it reads, you probably experience some of the same emotional and physical problems that Joe faced. You may be depressed, unhappy, and lacking in energy. You simply do not feel good about yourself. In that state, it will always be difficult to get up and get going. By continuing to focus on what you do not like, however, you have little choice but to continue your downward spiral. The key to change is the power of your vision—to set your sights on the new you and to harness the power of momentum toward becoming the person, physically, you want to be.

Here is the rest of Joe's story.

Thirty days after starting a modified health-management program, Joe had lost forty pounds. Two months later, he had lost a total of sixty-two pounds. After only four months in the program, he had lost one hundred pounds. After two years, he had dropped an incredible 275 pounds. Today, Joe weighs 253 pounds less, and his waist has gone from eighty-eight to forty-two inches. As he says, "I have newfound energy and a zest for living." Good for you, Joe.

There are three basic pillars to the optimum health game—diet, exercise, and stress management, both on and off the job. Diet and exercise will be covered in future chapters. Here we will deal with poorly managed stress, the one thing that generally causes us to make wrong choices with diet and exercise, all of which lead to a state of weak self-image, depression, unhappiness, and low energy.

What Is Stress?

Stress is the reaction of our bodies and minds to something that upsets their normal balance. Things like interpersonal conflicts, financial worries, time constraints, fatigue, illness, and job insecurity can be stressful to the point of physical and psychological dysfunction. Some people are especially vulnerable to these stressful situations and respond in extreme ways to everyday decisions. In many cases, their inability to manage the stress leads to overeating, excessive drinking, smoking, drug use, and, in some cases, suicide.

The most important thing to realize about stress is that it can be either good or bad. Stress in its bad form is *dis*tress and in its good form is *eu*stress. The prefixes here are the key. *Dis-* is the opposite of *eu-,* which means good. Invariably, the center of our distress is worry, and Scripture tells us what we should do about it: "Do not worry about tomorrow, for tomorrow will worry about itself. Each day has enough trouble of its own" (Matt. 6:34 NIV).

Bad stress is a negative response to outer or inner pressures that can lead to poor health choices. By contrast, good stress involves healthy internal responses to outward circumstances. Good stress enhances our health choices and increases our energy levels, thus allowing us to go beyond our usual limits of stamina and strength.

Besides eating well and developing a workout program, the removal of bad stress and the pursuit of good stress complete this three-part approach to optimum health. You will usually experience bad stress because you are in a situation you either do not want to be in or from which you cannot extricate yourself. Dr. Kenneth Cooper counsels that the best response to the first situation is to avoid it.[1] The most effective response to the second situation is to determine immediately how to control it.

The Negative Health Impact of Stress

There are three areas that bad stress generally affects—physical, psychological, and behavioral. Here are several symptoms for each area:

- **Physical.** Headaches, chest pain, shortness of breath, pounding heart, high blood pressure, muscle aches, indigestion, constipation or diarrhea, increased perspiration, fatigue, insomnia, and frequent illness.

- **Psychological.** Anxiety, irritability, sadness, defensiveness, anger, hostility, hypersensitivity, apathy, depression, slowed thinking, and feelings of helplessness, hopelessness, worthlessness, lack of direction, and insecurity.

- **Behavorial.** Overeating or loss of appetite, impatience, quickness to argue, procrastination, increased use of alcohol or drugs, increased smoking, neglect of responsibility, poor job performance, withdrawal or isolation, change in religious practices, and change in close family relationships.

Stress Cures for Better Health

Research shows that long periods of bad stress can contribute to physical or emotional illness that manifests itself generally in what we end up doing to our bodies. Here are three ways to eliminate the bad stress in your life.

Take care of yourself. The best way to relieve bad stress is to live a healthy lifestyle. That includes good exercise, adequate sleep, and a balanced eating program. Why do these three things work? Aerobic exercise helps burn off excess energy that can create stress. Sleep helps us manage problems with a clearer mental capacity. And a balanced food program, including fruits, vegetables, and lots of water, keeps our bodies fine-tuned and strong.

Manage your time events. Being overscheduled, committing to too many projects, and setting unrealistic goals and deadlines can all lead to more bad stress in our lives. Simplify your life. Give yourself more time than necessary to complete your goals. Align scheduled tasks with your most important values. If the task does not feed a value, drop it or delay it to a block of time that is not as important. Do your more challenging tasks during a peak energy state, and do your easier, less demanding work when your energy levels are not as high.

Rest. Our model for rest is found in the Creator Himself. After all God did to create our world and its abundance, on the seventh day, He rested. Get into the habit of slowing down. The best way not to go too fast is to move more slowly. Burnout and blowout are wicked realities for those who refuse to slow their pace.

High-performance machines need regular care and maintenance. Without these two critical components, they will sputter and fail to perform. You and I are also high-performance machines, designed to last a lifetime, but only if we subject ourselves to regular maintenance and proper care. *Resting our machine* is one of the best ways to prolong its life. Nurturing it and letting it stop for a while—sharpening the proverbial saw—are necessary for a lifetime of usefulness. Rest is an intentional act, not something you simply hope will happen. You must make time for it. Not to do so is a prelude to disaster.

As you become more skilled at removing bad stress from your day, you will begin to live a fuller, healthier life. That is my hope for you today and always.

Pay Attention to Your Body

Chapter 8

Mirror, Mirror on the Wall

Lhe Scriptures remind us to "prove [ourselves] doers of the word, and not merely hearers who delude themselves. For if anyone is a hearer of the word and not a doer, he is like a man who looks at his natural face in the mirror; for once he has looked at himself and gone away, he has immediately forgotten what kind of person he was" (James 1:22–24).

What do you see when you look in the mirror? Do you like the image? Does your comparison with "perfect" fall short? Does the image of the reflected you hurt so much that you ignore the truth and remain in slavery to your bad habits and poor choices?

It Can Be Different

I was once so disgusted with what I saw in the mirror that I made myself throw up. I was masking my unhealthy self-image by drowning myself in food, drugs, and alcohol. In many ways, I "had it all," but every time I looked in the mirror, I felt bankrupt. I remember the day I got some pictures back from a trip I had taken with my fiancée, Sheryl. One photo showed me wearing only my walking shorts as I stood next to my Porsche with its top down. All I could see was fat. God had created me in His image, and I thought that I was either fouling it up royally or He had not done such a great job in the first place. Since I believe God is perfect, it was clear to me who was ruining His masterpiece.

All I could see was fat.

In my book *The Power to Be Your Best,* I introduced readers to three important laws that will always affect who we are and what we do. These laws ultimately govern our choices and consequently play a major role in how we see ourselves, for they shape our self-image. These are the laws of responsibility, cause and effect, and repetition. Let me briefly explain each one.

The law of responsibility. The gap between where you are and where you want to be can only close when you accept full responsibility that *you are where you are because of the lifetime of choices you have made.* All movement toward the life you want comes from how you manage your response to past and present situations. Those who get what they want in life do not blame their circumstances. They take control.

The law of cause and effect. The gap that has been created in an area of your life because of wrong choices can close only when you create new actions or causes. For example, when you eat too much, you get fat. When you drink too much, you get a hangover. When you smoke too much, you set yourself up for cancer. To change your results, you need to make different— and better—choices.

The law of repetition. To continue to close a gap in some area of your life, you must repeat your new and better choices until this behavior becomes a habit. Only then will you begin to experience consistent results. To do otherwise produces little more than the "yo-yo" effect—a phenomenon that extends well beyond dieting. Without repeating your good choices often, you continue to "yo-yo" your way through life.

How to Get a New You

If you do not like what you see in the mirror, only you have the power to change it. Take a good look inside. Tell yourself what you see. Be honest. No one will ever know what's really going on but you, so there is no reason to hide the truth. See yourself as you are, and then go to work on creating the new you.

When I lost forty-two pounds, lowered my cholesterol to 160, and changed my body-fat percentage from 28 percent to a lean body mass of 13 percent—and as I observed many of my students who accomplished similar results—I discovered three things that happened before we began to make the transformations: (1) we developed a new mind-set, (2) we established a vision for our better selves, and (3) we modeled a program. Let's look at each one of these in more detail.

Develop a New Mind-Set

You become what you focus on. People who become thin and healthy stop thinking about being fat and unhealthy. For the next thirty days, instead of sending messages to your brain that say, "I'm fat," say, "I'm thin." Then immediately ask yourself, *What can I do this instant to give myself pleasure—something that is good for me and that does not consist of food?* This shift in self-talk will help you begin to make different decisions and, in the moment, will give you the power to change. Strength is not about what others tell you to do or say you should do. Strength is leverage. It is the capacity to reach deep inside and to grab on to what matters—that "something" that anchors you when nothing else will. Strength is what brings you back to your center. A healthier self-esteem also begins to emerge when you tap into the strength that God has given you, especially as you see the changing picture of the person you are becoming. People always act consistently with their view of who they are, whether it is positive or negative. That's why your mind-set is crucial to your success.

Establish a New Vision

All movement toward a healthier you begins with having a new vision. Vision drives everything—the choices you make and the purpose for which you live your life. The person in the mirror with a changed mind-set can no longer act in the ways he or she once lived. In the area of health, those who succeed know the power they receive when they continually pursue a new vision. They may not have all the details worked out, and their new course remains a work in progress, but they resolve to continue taking the kind of action that is in sync with their purpose.

The Scriptures speak at length of the importance of vision. They tell us that without a vision, we will surely perish (see Prov. 29:18). God gave the men and women of the Bible visions regularly, and through these visions, He provided guidance, direction, encouragement, warnings, judgment, and ultimately action for His glory.

Your assignment is to develop a clear vision of the new you, that person who will someday be looking at you in the mirror—a person you can be proud of because you have done the hard work to become the person God designed you to be.

Model Successful People and Programs

You can learn to eliminate the risk of failure and simultaneously increase the certainty of positive outcome. That is the advice I heard when I was overweight and down on myself. Successful models exist everywhere for us to copy. In the area of health, I would recommend these three courses of action.

Hire a coach or trainer. Not only will you have a fitness model because of your coach or trainer's own experience and credentials, but you also will be encouraged by the students who have come before you.

Read health magazines. *Men's Fitness* and *Women's Fitness,* along with other health-focused magazines, can be a great resource for staying in shape and maintaining your motivation to make physical change. For example, a year's subscription to *Men's Fitness* or *Women's Fitness* for only fifteen dollars can help you lose weight, build muscle, increase stamina, work out more effectively, spot tone or reduce, and, overall, feel better about yourself.

Join a gym. One of the best ways to stay motivated in the health game is to surround yourself with people who are also motivated to make changes in their bodies. Not long ago, I increased my commitment to working out because someone who saw me in the gym each morning asked me, "Hey, Todd, where have you been?" after I missed only two workouts. There is something compelling about surrounding yourself regularly with ten or twenty others who are committed to getting—and staying—fit.

> **Comparison—at any level—is a fast track to misery.**

Above all, be true to yourself. There is no need to compare yourself to others. Here's a phrase to remember—and perhaps tack on the fridge: *Comparison—at any level—is a fast track to misery.* Make the decision to stop comparing yourself to others. Simply determine to be your best.

Being true to yourself allows you to lay the groundwork for a clear conscience that will help you reduce your negative self-talk and give you peace that goes beyond all understanding. Welcome the highs and lows of life as your teachers. Learn the lessons of passion, faith, focus, and commitment, all of which have the power to sustain you as you pursue your vision. When you learn to respect yourself, you have begun to acquire one of life's most precious possessions.

Remember that you will always be a work in progress. Honor the masterpiece that God is creating through you.

Chapter 9

The Seven Laws of a King

Recent statistics suggest that a majority of people in the world believe in a universal God. Although many world religions have different slants on His existence, the fact remains that most people believe that there is a God. What does this have to do with paying attention to your body? Actually, quite a lot. Particularly when you read about a man by the name of King Solomon, the author of the Book of Proverbs in the Old Testament. I mentioned him in chapter 5 when we discussed the downsides of alcohol. I want to bring him back to the core of our conversation on health because of his profound commentary on life and proper conduct. The fact that he was a wise king does not alone make his advice worth heeding. His advice simply makes too much sense not to follow it.

The positive and negative standards in the Book of Proverbs provide a valuable test of personal conduct—the most basic key to obtaining optimum health.

In Proverbs, wisdom begins with God—His centrality is assumed. The wise, upright, righteous, and godly people are described as those who trust and know their God and mirror their beliefs by how they order their lives. Good and bad behaviors are linked to rewards and penalties. The positive and negative standards in the Book of Proverbs provide a valuable test of personal conduct—the most basic key to obtaining optimum health.

The Law of Possessing Wisdom: Excellence Develops over Time

King Solomon said, "Fools despise wisdom and instruction . . . The wisdom of the prudent is to understand his way . . . The naive believes everything, but the prudent man considers his steps . . .

How much better it is to get wisdom than gold! And to get understanding is to be chosen above silver" (Prov. 1:7, 14:8, 15; 16:16).

If you are going to pay attention to your body and live the life you want, you must seek wisdom. Wisdom is knowledge in action. Wisdom allows you to make better choices and follow the soundest course of action. Wisdom is based on knowledge, experience, and understanding.

At the heart of wisdom is a long-term commitment to excellence. The wisest people I know have made the commitment not to make the same poor choice more than once. This commitment is the essence of building a life on God-honoring standards and the standards of those whom you admire. With this lifelong commitment to excellence, you will find yourself operating at new levels each day.

With wisdom, you can lose weight and keep it off, you can give up addictive behaviors that are holding you back from being the person God designed you to be, you can develop a high self-image, and you can enjoy the life that God has given to you.

The Law of Gaining Knowledge: Progress Is the Result of Sound Choices

The key to possessing wisdom is rooted in the habit of gaining knowledge. King Solomon said, "Also it is not good for a person to be without knowledge" (Prov. 19:2). I am sure you are already committed to this law. However, let me expand on it a bit. Knowledge is having an acquaintance with the facts, a range of information, awareness, and understanding. The more knowledge you have, the more likely you can take advantage of the law of possessing wisdom. And the more knowledge you enjoy, generally the more automatic your responses will be to good health patterns.

> **The key to possessing wisdom is rooted in the habit of gaining knowledge.**

My dad practiced medicine for twenty-five years. Each year, he had to gain more knowledge about his profession for him to be effective on the job. Imagine if the doctor performing heart surgery on you today had stopped gaining knowledge ten years ago. That would be life threatening. So the question is, Do you have a commitment, beyond finishing this book, to gain the knowledge you need to make your good choices automatic and your results predictable?

The Law of Having Discretion: Sound Decisions Determine Your Destiny

How do you treat your body? Discretion and discernment are wisdom in action. You have the freedom and authority to manage your health any way you see fit. However, good judgment is the key. Every day, you have thousands of choices flying at you, many of which affect your health. At any given second, some of those decisions could determine your physical destiny.

Research has shown that poor health generally does not result from one bad decision. Extended periods where the same bad decision is made time and time again contribute to poor health. The smoker says, "Just one more cigarette." The alcoholic says, "I'll quit drinking next week." The overweight person says, "I'll start my diet on Monday." The only way you will achieve optimum health is to decide now that you refuse to live this way any longer. Another central figure in the Scriptures is a man named Paul, who said, "No temptation has overtaken you but such as is common to man; and God is faithful, who will not allow you to be tempted beyond what you are able, but with the temptation will provide the way of escape also, that you may be able to endure it" (1 Cor. 10:13). When you accept this truth, your life will not end up as a moment of misery, but rather a moment of momentum and forward progress.

The Law of Maintaining Integrity: Honesty Is the Foundation for Growth

King Solomon said, "He who walks in integrity walks securely, but he who perverts his ways will be found out" (Prov. 10:9). There is no more important law to help get you on your way to the new you than arriving at the point where you can be brutally honest with yourself. Living a life of lies is a direct route to self-destruction and to becoming more of the person *you don't want to be.*

Let me tell you a story to help illustrate this point. One day after a three-day party, I placed a call to the man from whom

Sheryl and I were buying our cocaine. I ordered more, and within several hours he was at our door with the delivery. As I forked over the cash, he looked into my eyes and said, "I think you guys are getting out of control with this stuff, and it concerns me." Imagine it. The guy who was profiting from our poor choice of buying a steady flow of cocaine was concerned more for our well-being than we were. In that moment, we knew we had to become honest with ourselves. Although it was months before Sheryl and I got serious about quitting, that was a transformational moment in time. So here's the question: Is it going to take someone else to help you get honest with you, or could you save yourself some time and come clean in this moment?

The Law of Living Humbly: Imperfection Leads to Exponential Growth

King Solomon said that the rewards of humility are "riches, honor and life" (Prov. 22:4). In the effort to obtain optimum health, humility is the "breaking of the dam." To arrive at a place where you are aware of your shortcomings, where you can rid yourself of the false pride, and where you can finally understand that you can no longer live the lie . . . that is when you know you are on your path to exponential growth.

This is a lifestyle choice. Humility leads to the discovery and admission of your shortcomings—those gaps that indicate you are not what you pretend to be. Only with awareness plus action will you begin to close those gaps. Only when you make the commitment to get right with yourself, your loved ones, and God will your life make its about-face. It is important that you know and believe that this path is a lifelong path. Your new you is not a moment in time but a time of moments strung end to end like fine pearls, so that when your life is over, you can look back on it and say with confidence that your life was worth living.

The Law of Self-Discipline: No One Will Do It for You

This is a law of action. King Solomon said, "He who neglects discipline despises himself" (Prov. 15:32). What does it mean to despise yourself? It means to live below your dignity, to look down on yourself with contempt. In fact, living a life without self-discipline is the very thing that creates a low self-image.

Many people go only so far and then give up. However, the small percentage of people who *do* master this law always deter-

Your new you is not a moment in time but a time of moments.

mine to go a few steps further, and their forward progress makes all the difference in the world. Which person will you be? Will you go the extra steps and do the tough work? Or will you continue to wallow in a destructive zone of complacency? King Solomon addressed this issue when he said, "The complacency of fools will destroy them" (Prov. 1:32 NIV).

The key is to get momentum on your side, and the best way to develop this is by harnessing and then unleashing the power to act based on your purpose and your values. In chapters 15 and 16, I will give you this road map.

The Law of Moderation: Limits Create Liftoff

In every area of life, and especially in the search for optimum health, limits are necessary to create liftoff. The people at NASA have limits, standards, and procedures. If there is ever a doubt whether any one of their predetermined procedures is followed, they postpone liftoff. What good advice for the rest of us. However, many people postpone liftoff accidentally. They do not have their limits or standards set; therefore, they end up living their lives on the "platform," never really ascending to the heights of their potential.

King Solomon said, "Do not be with heavy drinkers of wine, or with gluttonous eaters of meat; for the heavy drinker and the glutton will come to poverty, and drowsiness will clothe a man with rags" (Prov. 23:20–21). In this context, the king is saying essentially this: Be careful whom you associate with, and keep your standards high.

I am sure that many of us have succumbed to the influence of others when, in certain situations, we have consumed alcohol to the extreme. My advice? It is best not to go into those situations in the first place. If you do, you need to determine your limits beforehand. As you use the power of these other *kingly* laws, you should be able to maintain your focus and soar to new heights.

Your Future Will Happen

"Trust in the LORD with all your heart, and lean not on your own understanding; in all your ways acknowledge Him, and He shall direct your paths" (Prov. 3:5–6 NKJV).

Faith is being assured of things that you hope for while experiencing the conviction that although you have not seen these things come to fruition, you believe that they will (see Heb. 11:1). The Seven Laws of a King can set you up for victory in any area of your life. When all seven laws line up, and when you realize that God loves you and that He wants you to have the power to be your best, it is almost impossible not to have faith in your future.

Take these words and apply them to how you pay attention to your body. Do it now. Don't wait for a wake-up call. You can have the body, the health, and the life you want. However, it will take these seven laws, practiced daily, for you to succeed.

Chapter 10

A Funny Thing Happened on the Way to the Fridge

You are what you eat, and perhaps the best way to find out what you are eating is to look inside your refrigerator. Besides the year-old jar of pickles, the pizza with fuzz on top, and the ice cream coated with "protective ice," what other kinds of foods do you see? Take a look, and ask yourself, *Do I have a "heart-healthy" fridge?*

Open the Door to a Healthy Heart

Whether it is your refrigerator or your pantry, what is on the other side of that door presents you with your major challenge: Should you put what's inside into your body? If the answer is no, then why are those foods there at all? Being healthy begins with your state of mind, a consciousness that must influence your every thought. A new way of thinking must be part of your daily routine. Let's start with what kinds of foods you are buying. From now on, I hope that stocking your refrigerator and pantry will become an exercise in health. If that is to be, it is important to have some guidelines to help you with your purchase decisions.

Read the Labels; Save a Life

Under the guidelines that have been established by the Food and Drug Administration, the Department of Health and Human Services, and the Department of Agriculture, foods must contain an official nutrition label. In the past, these labels have often been misleading and full of loopholes. Today, food products must have nutrition labels that provide pertinent, accurate information. Fortunately, these new label requirements are in your favor. With only a few exemptions, such as food malls, food for immediate consumption, wild game, and food corporations that sell to less than certain FDA established numbers of consumers, all other food products must have a label. Here are some highlights regarding food labels that are critical for you to know:

- Easy-to-read formats enable you to find the information you need to make healthful choices. The most important things to look for are serving size, calories, fat, cholesterol, sodium, dietary fiber, vitamins, and minerals.
- Nutrient reference values, expressed as percentages of daily values, help you see how a food fits into an overall diet of two thousand calories per day.
- Claims about the relationship between a nutrient or food and a disease or health-related condition are helpful for people who are concerned about eating foods that may help keep them healthier longer.[1]

Armed with this information, you can now determine—in advance—how stocking these foods on your shelves at home will affect your body, your health, and your life.

Read the Lines . . . and between the Lines

There is an abundance of information on a nutrition label, and understanding only what is important is the key to your better health. The three things I see people consistently overlook are total calories, total fat, and hidden fat. Although the guidelines are clear, people still tend to eat larger servings than the label statistics apply to, thereby consuming more calories than necessary. For example, you can look at the label on a Snickers bar, see 170 calories, and think that's okay. You eat the bar, take one more look, and notice that the serving size was one-third of a bar. Oops. You got it—*you just consumed 510 calories*, more than 25 percent of the daily calorie guideline in one consumed product. You also just ate an abundance of simple carbohydrates, and you know the negative impact they will have on your body!

In the fat category, the FDA says there is mandatory disclosure of total fat and saturated fat. To keep it simple, instead of trying to calculate your total fat intake for the day as a percentage of total calories, focus on the total fat grams consumed. Ladies, stay under sixty grams for the day; guys, keep it under eighty. Make sure that most of the fat is neither saturated nor transunsaturated fats. The FDA does not force companies to disclose the amounts of transunsaturated fats—at least not yet—but a little math will help you uncover this killer. For example, if a stick of margarine discloses that one serving has ten grams of fat and that two grams are saturated, two grams are polyunsaturated, and two and one-half grams are monounsaturated, that totals only six and one-half grams. While only one-fifth of the fat is saturated, a full three and one-half grams of fat are unaccounted for. This is the transunsaturated fat—hydrogenated—and, in our example, it is a whopping 35 percent of the total fat. Add that to the saturated fat, and you can see that more than 50 percent is bad, artery-clogging fat. This example is particularly helpful when looking at "light" and "low-calorie" products.

> **Once each month, take everything out of your refrigerator and pantry, and see what is in there.**

Great Tips for a Heart-Healthy Refrigerator

By now you're probably getting it down: Calories and fat are two of the three essential components for healthy living. Now, the key is for you to take this knowledge to the place where your food is stored—the refrigerator. Here are some ideas on how to make your fridge friendly to your heart.

Take inventory. Once each month, take everything out of your refrigerator and pantry, and see what is in there. You may be surprised. Make sure you have plenty of low-fat, high-fiber, and low-sugar foods.

Eat more fruit and produce, fewer desserts. On average, each week Americans throw away ten dollars' worth of spoiled fruit and produce. "Out of sight, out of mind" is generally the thinking—or lack of it. Here is an idea. Put these products on a shelf where you can see them, and put the other stuff in the drawers where you can't. When you do this, you will probably eat more of the good food and less of the bad. Also, make sure the good food is easily seen. Shove the bad stuff to the back—or, better yet, trash it.

Replace high-fat products with low-fat ones. Go from whole milk to 2 percent, or from 2 percent to skim. Go from stick butter to margarine and from margarine to soft margarine. You can make great strides in cutting the saturated and transunsaturated fats from your system by doing this.

Make healthy snacks ready to eat. When you return from the store, prepare your fruits and vegetables so they are ready to go. It's a good idea to store them in their own containers. People often avoid eating healthy snacks because their food is not ready to eat. You will be pleased with yourself when you take the time to do it right.

Make the healthy food fun to eat. Eat nonfat frozen yogurt with low-fat chocolate topping or a few mixed nuts.

This process can be fun—and habit forming. While I was losing weight, I did two things that helped me most: I learned to understand the food labels, and I acted on my new awareness every day. You can do the same. When you do, the new you will begin to emerge. Proceed with passion.

Chapter 11

Eat, Drink, and Be Merry for Tomorrow We Die(t)

You cannot lose weight by dieting and expect to keep it off. You have no choice but to reinvent your lifestyle if you want to have a healthy outside and a healthy inside. Eating and drinking too much and then trying to lose it the wrong way will not create pleasant results for you. If anything, it will only keep you on the treadmill of inconsistency. If, over your lifetime, you have lost and then gained back 50 percent of your present body weight, no matter how many cycles you have been through, you have a dieting challenge. For example, if you weigh two hundred pounds and in the last ten years you have lost and gained ten pounds on several different occasions, dieting is obviously not your answer to responsible weight management.

It is no secret. People who feel good about themselves tend to keep their weight consistent. In this section, we will focus on why diets do not work and never will. We will then arm you with the information you need to put an effective food-management program into place. As you begin to lose weight, you will start to feel good, and the momentum you create will carry you into your new way of living.

Diets Are Shortcuts That Lead to Disaster

Have you ever tried to hurry somewhere only to find out that your shortcut had added hours to your trip? This is the way most people approach dieting—with irresponsible shortcuts. They follow every diet that comes along because they have never addressed the need for underlying psychological reinvention of the person who is trying to lose the weight. I think we all know that most weight eventually returns when our "dieting will power" runs out of gas. For most people on the weight-loss "treadmill," dieting is an up-and-down battle of the fiercest kind. It is both exhilarating and debilitating, depending on the results.

Have you heard of negative energy balance? That is what most diets produce when they lower the caloric intake below the basal metabolic rate. You lose weight, but this loss of weight turns out to be muscle, not fat. We mentioned this earlier, but let's do a quick review. Food gives you energy, and when you have less energy than is required, your body thinks it is starving and goes into high gear to burn muscle to fuel its energy requirements. During the process, your metabolism (the rate at which you burn off calories—your internal "fire") actually slows down. When the body thinks it is starving, it will store whatever it can as body fat to protect itself. This is simply the way nature works. The body will also respond to a threat of starvation by increasing the number of fat-depositing enzymes, which in turn store more fat. Bottom line: It is almost impossible to lose weight simply by restricting calories.

> **For most people on the weight-loss "treadmill," dieting is an up-and-down battle of the fiercest kind.**

Why Do I Gain Weight after I've Lost It?

When you lower your metabolism, your body requires fewer calories. When you stop dieting, your body starts to crave what it has been deprived of. Generally, when this happens, you will increase your caloric intake and gain back more fat than lean muscle. This is the infamous "yo-yo" effect that plagues millions of people worldwide every year.

There is also a negative side effect to the low-calorie approach to losing weight. When you diet, it is doubtful that your overall protein, carbohydrate, vitamin, and mineral needs are being met. When you are deficient in your daily nutrients, this deficiency will also affect your metabolism.

Dieting Can Be Hazardous to Your Health

Diets that eliminate certain food groups can zap you of the vitamins and nutrients you need. They can also become quickly boring because of their lack of variety.

Diets also create a negative psychological impact, especially when you eat the bad food. I believe in "fudge days"—a fudge day gives me the opportunity to eat the bad food and still feel okay about it since I know I have eaten the good food for six previous days.

Dieting itself implies a start and a stop, setting you up for the perfect "yo-yo" syndrome. You must make eating healthy a habit, as I will show you in the chapters to come.

Want to Lose Twenty Pounds the Easy Way?

I recently spoke with one of the great motivational speakers of our time, Zig Ziglar. He said that he was sick and tired of being sick and tired, so he decided to start changing that feeling by losing some weight. He said that in twenty-four years of dieting he had lost well over two thousand pounds and had gained it all back. He suddenly realized he had not gained his excess thirty-seven pounds in thirty days, and therefore he should not try to lose it in thirty days. So Zig set a realistic goal of ten months, and then he committed to losing an average of 1.9 ounces per day. For twenty-seven years, he has not gained the weight back. The lesson? It is easy to lose weight when your goals are big and your steps are small.

> **It is easy to lose weight when your goals are big and your steps are small.**

What Should I Eat?

Eating foods with the right amount of calories and that are low in total fat, saturated fat, and cholesterol can be like juggling fresh eggs while standing on the edge of a hammock on one foot. However, with the following information and your commitment to an eating plan every day, before long, your weight will fall off and stay off. Remember, this is not a diet; it is a way of life.

Meat, Poultry, Fish, and Shellfish

- **Choose more often**—Lean cuts of meat with fat trimmed, poultry without skin, fish and shellfish, lean luncheon meat

- **Choose less often**—Fatty cuts of meat, bacon and sausage, organ meats, fried chicken, fried fish, fried shellfish, high-fat luncheon meat (bologna)

Eggs and Dairy Products

- **Choose more often**—Egg whites, egg substitutes, skim milk, low-fat and nonfat cheeses, and yogurt
- **Choose less often**—Egg yolks, whole milk or 2-percent milk, whole milk products

Fats and Oils

- **Choose more often**—Unsaturated fat products in the reduced and nonfat categories, including margarine, salad dressings, mayonnaise, liquid cooking oils, seeds, and nuts
- **Choose less often**—Tropical oils, lard, bacon fat, full-fat butter and salad dressings

Breads, Cereals, Pasta, Rice, Dry Peas, Beans, and Soy Products

- **Choose more often**—Whole-grain bread, cereal, pasta, and rice; beans; baked goods made with unsaturated oil or margarine
- **Choose less often**—Egg breads; granola-type cereals; pasta, rice, dry peas, or beans made with cream, butter, or cheese sauce

Vegetables

- **Choose more often**—Fresh (including at least one helping of "cruciferous") vegetables every day. These include broccoli, Brussels sprouts, cauliflower, and cabbage. These have been proved to reduce risks of cancer and heart disease. Frozen, canned, prepared plain or with lemon, stir-fried with unsaturated oils or margarine
- **Choose less often**—Vegetables prepared with butter, cheese, or cream sauces

Fruits

- **Choose more often**—Fresh, frozen, canned, or dried; real fruit juices
- **Choose less often**—Fried fruit or fruit served with butter or cream sauce

Sweets and Snacks (WARNING: While low in fat, these still contain calories.)

- **Choose more often**—low-fat or fat-free frozen desserts, low-fat cookies, flavored Jell-O, pretzels, baked chips, air-popped popcorn
- **Choose less often**—Candy and baked goods made with butter, cream, or tropical oils; full-fat ice cream; frozen desserts; doughnuts; regular snack chips[1]

With this healthy eating program, you will be on your way to a more physically fit you. Pay attention to your body. Focus on what goes into it. Over time, you will be surprised at the results.

There is also another element of the diet game of which most people lack knowledge—fast food. Read on to see how fast-food consumption is becoming a national—and international—tragedy.

Chapter 12

Feasting on Fast Food

A government report says people are eating out more often, and they are eating more meals that are high in fat and low in nutrients. This comes after researchers found that the number of people eating out has doubled in the past two decades. Most people surveyed know they should not be eating as much fast food as they are, but they continue to eat it anyway.

Here's the problem. Foods eaten away from home are higher in saturated fat and lower in fiber, calcium, and iron. In fact, the report says, fat makes up only 31 percent of the calories in foods cooked at home, while fat comprises 37.6 percent of the calories served outside of the home.

The Pace of Life

It is not news that our entire world is moving faster than ever—with e-mail, voice mail, hand-held computers, and cell phones that seem to do everything, all designed to give us "more time." Well, we may be moving through life faster, but are we really being blessed with the gift of more time?

A Senate subcommittee in 1967 predicted that within twenty years, the average person would work twenty-seven hours per week, thirty-six weeks per year, and retire by the time they were forty. They said the main challenge facing people at the turn of the century would be what to do with all their free time.[1] Hmm. Is that your challenge as we enter a new millennium?

In 1937, Dick and Maurice McDonald started a small restaurant in Pasadena, California. The sign on the building read "McDonald's Hamburgers," and fast food was born. Shortly after, they felt that fast food wasn't fast enough, so the industry invented drive-though eating. The real issue here is not whether it is fast, but whether it is good for you. The short answer? No, it is not.

It's Not the Fat; It's the Frequency

Sticking to a healthy diet can be tough, especially for those of us who give in easily to temptation. However, you do not need

You do not need to give up burgers and fries altogether to stay on a cholesterol- and fat-lowering diet.

to give up burgers and fries altogether to stay on a cholesterol- and fat-lowering diet. In fact, according to a recent study, half of the eighty-nine volunteers ate the National Coalition Education Program Step One diet to lower their cholesterol, while the others ate a version of the same diet, modified to include five meals per week at McDonald's. The participants trimmed fat from other meals on the days they indulged in fast food.

After two months, the group on the nonmodified plan lowered their total cholesterol by 8 percent, and their LDL, or "bad" cholesterol, by 10 percent. The McDonald's group lowered their total cholesterol by 3 percent and their LDL cholesterol by 4 percent.[2] If you cannot live without fast food, the good news is that you can still lower your cholesterol. However, it is even better if you do not eat it, because cutting out the fat and the grease will help you reduce your cholesterol and decrease your risk of heart disease.

Chapter 13

Let's Go Swimming

Yʎou're surrounded by it, you're mostly made of it, and you can't live without it. It is the key ingredient your body requires to maintain all other vital systems and processes. What is this miracle substance? Water.

Why Do We Need Water?

The human body is composed of approximately 70 percent water. Without water, the body can survive for only five days. The body's water supply is responsible for or involved in nearly every bodily process, including digestion, absorption, circulation, and excretion. Water is the primary transporter of nutrients throughout the body, and it is necessary for all building functions in the body. Therefore, we must commit to replacing the water that leaves our bodies with an equal or greater amount of water. If we exercise, we must drink even more.

How Much Do We Need?

Dehydration is one of our greatest energy zappers. When it is dehydrated, the body's available water supply is rationed and distributed to those systems that need it most. The body does not have a water reserve, like an automobile's gas tank, and no red warning light comes on when we are low on water. Water is supplied to the body only through the fluids and foods we drink and eat.

Caffeine and alcohol increase dehydration, not improve it.

We are talking pure water here. The recommendations from most of the research indicate that the average person should be consuming the equivalent of two and one-half liters of water, or ten and one-half glasses per day. Since we get some of this water from foods, it nets out to around six to eight actual glasses of water. If you are counting your coffee, lattes, and wine in this number, don't. Caffeine and alcohol increase dehydration, not improve it. If you drink these regularly, add one eight-ounce glass of water for every cup of coffee or glass of alcohol you drink.

Water Flushes before You Do

Here are some things water does to help flush your system and provide health for your body:

- Water suppresses the appetite.
- Water assists the body in metabolizing stored fat.
- Water reduces fat deposits in the body.
- Water reduces sodium buildup.
- Water helps maintain muscle tone.
- Water rids the body of waste and toxins.
- Water relieves constipation.

The Wet Workout

If you exercise regularly, drink plenty of water during your workout. "It is absolutely critical to keep hydrated when you are exercising. Without the right amount of fluids during a workout, your performance deteriorates," says Nancy Clark, M.S., R.D., director of nutrition services at Sports Medicine Brookline, a Boston area clinic.[1]

A lack of adequate fluids stresses the heart, raises core body temperature, and compromises performance.

A lack of adequate fluids stresses the heart, raises core body temperature, and compromises performance. For every liter of sweat you lose, your heart rate increases about eight beats per minute. Depending on conditions, you can lose one liter of sweat in thirty minutes.

The American College of Sports Medicine recommends that you consume two glasses of water two hours before every workout. During the workout, drink an additional five to ten ounces of water every twenty minutes and then again during the first hour after the activity.

You seldom need to be concerned about drinking too much water. Your body is a miracle machine, and it will excrete what it does not need. Here are some more great tips on drinking water:

- Water is the best source of rehydration for workouts that last less than one hour.
- Sports drinks containing carbohydrates are a better bet for restoring blood glucose during longer sessions. However, fluids containing more than 10-percent carbohydrates slow gastric emptying and should be avoided.
- Water needs are dependent on activity levels, temperature, humidity, and whether you are carrying extra weight like a backpack or a football uniform. Depending on these factors, you can become dehydrated in less than thirty minutes.
- A high volume of fluid intake can increase the rate at which fluid is absorbed from the stomach if you exercise above 80 percent of maximum capacity.

Keep your water cool, between 60 and 70 degrees. Cool water promotes the increased intake of fluids during exercise.

Are You Drinking Enough?

There are tests that let you know if you are drinking enough water during the day. Water deprivation leaves telltale signs. How do you check out on these?

- Dark circles under your eyes that are not caused by lack of sleep or usual stress
- Dark yellow or discolored urine instead of pale, whitish yellow
- Infrequent urination instead of passing water several times a day
- A urinary output of less than two quarts per day, the amount required to clear the kidneys adequately and flush the system

Have you ever been really hot on a summer day and jumped into a cool pool? Remember how it felt? That's what your body says every time you give it a drink . . . *Ah!*

Chapter 14

How to Fail in Twelve Easy Steps

We are now coming to the end of Step Two, "Pay Attention to Your Body," and we have presented an enormous amount of information on how to gain and maintain the body you deserve. In Step Three, I will focus on systems and strategies for maintaining your maximum weight, along with a psychology of success to help you stay motivated. However, before we move on, I want to give you twelve surefire things to do if you do not want to succeed. Many people find the "pain" side of the equation to be a great motivation. So, with tongue in cheek, here we go.

Step One: Don't Bother to Exercise

You'll get nice and fat, feel lethargic, and have a nonproactive lifestyle. What a wonderful way to live. Besides, who wants to get all sweaty, anyway?

Step Two: Don't Drink Your Water

Let fat accumulate in your body like scum on a stagnant lake. Let toxins build up in your body and choke your cells into life-less oblivion. Drink something that tastes good, for heaven's sake—like a few bottles of sugar-laden Coke or a couple of beers.

Step Three: Don't Take the Stairs

You could fall down and hurt yourself. Besides, it might be too hard on your heart, your knees, your legs, and your feet. You will even wear out your shoes eventually. Take your paunch for a ride on the elevator. It's the easy way to die.

Step Four: Don't Eat Fresh Vegetables

Lay off those green, red, and yellow foods that are "hidden" on the perimeter of your supermarket. Head for the chips. Remember, McDonald's is always the better dining choice. Vegetables aren't messy like burgers. They don't make you smell like mustard or grease. They're boring.

Step Five: Don't Read the Labels

Labels are for wimps. After all, the Surgeon General says smoking can kill you, and people still smoke. The FDA also tells you what the food you eat will do to you—good or bad. Are you going to ignore the FDA's warnings? Sure, why not? It's just a big, impersonal bureaucracy, anyway!

Step Six: Have Some More Chips

What's a night of TV without a big bag of chips or some popcorn with rich butter and salt poured all over it? Why, it's un-American! That tasty salt, fat, and girth-expanding cholesterol are what make life worthwhile. And make sure it's a routine. Do it every night, like clockwork. You will achieve some amazing results.

Step Seven: Double Your Fat-Free Portions

Eat more food if it's fat-free. Hey, it says "fat-free" on the label, so it must be true. Come on, would a marketing firm lie to you? Be sure to believe everything you read. "Eat it today; wear it tomorrow" can be your hallmark for the rest of your life. Double your portions; double your girth. Die early.

Step Eight: Don't Walk When You Can Drive

Park as close to the mall as possible; even if you have to burn five dollars' worth of gas circling the place. Hey, you've bought a nice car. Use it to go everywhere. Bikes are for kids. You can burn up quite a lot of energy just adjusting your car seat, tuning to your favorite radio station, and shouting at the person who just took your spot while you were fiddling around.

Step Nine: Don't Run When You Can Walk

If you decide to walk, do it slowly. Running is for runners, and you're no runner. Running could hurt your back and mess up your knees. And you don't want to get your heart rate too high. Just sort of meander through life. Besides, you might lose weight—even feel better. Better stay in your comfort zone—the couch.

Step Ten: Set a New Year's Resolution to Lose Weight

You know how well you have always done with resolutions. You never set yourself up for failure, do you? So try it just one more time. And be sure to wait until January 1—even if you are giving serious thought to losing weight in June. There's no rush. You don't want to get too enthusiastic about this decision. Take your time. You've got a lifetime of fat to live with.

Step Eleven: Add Sugar and Salt before You Taste Your Food

Pour on the sugar and salt. Really intelligent people can tell the taste by just looking at their food. So heap it on. Besides, you never know when you'll have to sweat a lot. So you better have plenty of salt stored up. And refined sugar? Nothing will give you a bigger high. Eat a lot of the white stuff, especially just before you go to bed. You've had quite enough sleep lately any-way, so let sugar keep you awake all night. Besides, the sugar high is fantastic. Who cares that your "letdown" will feel like you've been hit with a ton of bricks?

Step Twelve: Drink a Lot of Alcohol

Drink like a fish. You've done well. Celebrate. And make sure your children see you drink. You're their model, and you want them to do what you do. And there's more sugar here too—an added bonus. So, fatten yourself up however you can . . . and what is easier than sugar in a bottle? There are so many benefits to drinking alcohol: sickness, liver damage, bad modeling, drunken driving, prison . . . and death. Cheers!

Okay . . . I hope I have made my point with good humor. Get your body's attention, then start paying attention to your body. What remains after that is to turn these new practices into habits for health. So as the Italians say, *Andiamo* . . . let's go!

Develop Habits for Health

Chapter 15

Putting the Act in Action

People who lose weight and keep it off typically exercise for at least one hour per day, far more than the federal guidelines that recommend exercising a minimum of thirty minutes each day to improve overall health. The key to taking action, especially in the areas of health and fitness, is to harness the power you have within to overcome inertia, to begin an exercise routine, and to turn that commitment into a lifelong habit. You have the power to change, and that power can be found in discovering your purpose.

The Power of Purpose

The bridge between success and mastery in life management is purpose. A purpose is more ongoing and gives meaning to our lives. When people have a purpose in life, they enjoy everything they do more, including following an exercise routine. People go on chasing goals, trying to prove something that does not need to be proved: *that they are already worthwhile.* The fastest way to achieve goals, physically, financially, spiritually, and vocationally is to stay on-purpose.

So the question is, What's your purpose? Do you know?

If you have ever started and then stopped an exercise program, somehow not able to stay with the discipline to make it happen, there is a good chance that you were not clear on your purpose or that you did not successfully link exercising to that purpose.

> **Mastery is the result of living your life on-purpose in those areas that are important to you.**

The discovery of your purpose is the first requirement for your success in life mastery. Mastery is the result of living your life on-purpose in those areas that are important to you. The alternative to living your life on-purpose is to live it off-purpose, or without purpose, which is how most people spend their days—and their lives. If this is where you are, you may never be able to maintain the self-discipline to make your commitment to exercise stick.

The Power of Observation

I have been observing people for the last twenty years, trying to understand what contributes to their success in the important areas of their lives. I have learned that people fall into three categories. People in the first group are those who seem to get what they want in life and who are happy. People in the second group seem to get what they want in life but are unhappy once they achieve their goals. People in the third group want something different in life and are unhappy, but they do not know how to move toward what they want. All three groups have one thing in common: purpose. They either know their purposes or they do not, and that awareness or unawareness makes all the difference.

Your purpose is the foundation of your existence and the platform on which to build your life. To know your purpose and to align your life with it is to live purposefully. It begins through introspection as you look at tough answers to tough questions. Chances are you may not have asked yourself these questions in a way that has provided clarity of purpose. As you answer them now, think about how you could become more congruent with the person you are becoming, not who you now are. I suggest that you do this exercise when you will not be interrupted. Journal your answers, and let your purpose take over.

The Purpose-Discovery Question

What is important about success to me? We start with the word *success* because that is what most people identify with. Success has different meanings to different people. That is why it is important to know what success means to you. Ultimately, your answer to the question will yield stronger distinctions, stronger motives, and stronger reasons for wanting to be successful. The deeper this dialogue goes, the more profound the impact of each answer becomes. Here are two examples from my research of how the same question delivers different, but equally power-ful, platforms on which to build one's life.

Person A: Money→Freedom→Time→Making a Difference
Person B: Accomplishment→Happiness→Fulfillment→
Peace of Mind

How Does This Apply to an Exercise Routine?

Person A awakens every day knowing that her purpose is to align the actions in every important area of her life so that at the end of the day she will have *made a difference.* Let's look at exercise. If your purpose is making a difference, would you be able to make that difference more consistently and more effec-tively if you were in good physical shape? Of course! You can now use your purpose of "making a difference" to act as a cata-lyst to making a commitment to a workout regimen. Watch how the motivation works.

Most people know they should exercise more, but they don't do it. Now you can overcome that lack of commitment—not with will power, but with purpose. For the person in this exam-ple, not working out means she will not be in good shape. This reality then affects her energy level and her weight, which com-bine to prevent her from making a difference in her life and in the lives of others. Her motivation to act comes either by avoid-ing the pain of not living her purpose or by harnessing the power that comes from living it.

Person B awakens each morning knowing that his purpose is to align the actions in every important area of his life so that at the end of the day he will have *peace of mind.* This person's motivation to exercise each day will be fueled by his purpose of "peace of mind." I do not know of a better way to have seren-ity of spirit than to know you are doing everything within your power to live a healthy life and to work at getting—and stay-ing—in good physical condition.

This kind of purpose-driven thinking provides focus, makes decision making easier, and provides the motivation to help you work toward your objectives with passion. Your purpose is your life. Discover it. Live it. Benefit from it.

Chapter 16

Hooked on a Feeling

People who are dissatisfied with their bodies and tired of weight that goes up and down like a yo-yo have the most difficulty losing their girth, say researchers from the Stanford University School of Medicine. Researchers found that people who are unhappy with their bodies have the least success losing weight. So what is the first key to permanent weight loss? Become happy with your body. One of the best ways to do that is to start combining exercise with the food-intake knowledge you have gained so far in your reading.

In the study detailed in the September 1998 issue of *Annals of Behavioral Medicine,* 177 men and women who were mildly overweight were sent to one of two weight-loss programs: (1) diet and exercise or (2) diet only. Study results showed 49 percent of the diet-and-exercise group successfully lost weight compared with only 26 percent of the diet-only group.

The University of Pittsburgh School of Medicine and the University of Colorado Health Sciences Center have compiled a National Weight Control Registry of people who have lost weight and kept it off. Experts have analyzed the data from detailed questionnaires of twenty-eight hundred individuals (80 percent women) who have lost an average of sixty-five pounds and kept at least thirty pounds off for five and one-half years. Among the findings so far:

- People who have lost weight and kept it off burn an average of twenty-eight hundred calories per week with exercise—about four hundred calories daily.
- On average, participants burn about one thousand calories per week by walking.
- On average, participants burn eighteen hundred calories with a combination of activities, including aerobics, strength training, and cycling.

A key point to this study is that "members of the registry increased their exercise gradually over time until exercise had become an important part of their lives," says Rina Wing, cofounder of the registry and professor of psychiatry at the University of Pittsburgh School of Medicine.

A separate study of 140 exercisers, mostly walkers, showed that those who maintained weight loss averaged 280 minutes per week, or fifty-six minutes five days per week. Some exercised at one time, while others broke this time into ten- to fifteen-minute sections and spread them throughout the day. The key is they exercised.[1]

Ultimately, everyone who gets "hooked on the feeling" of working out enjoys the physical, mental, and emotional success that an exercise program produces.

The Science of Exercise

Exercise makes you healthier. It strengthens your heart and blood vessels, and it improves your circulation. The heart is a muscle that needs regular conditioning, and a well-conditioned heart can more effectively pump a large supply of blood with fewer beats than a weak heart. Exercise will make your heart more resistant to stress, heart attacks, and other health problems.

> **Exercise will make your heart more resistant to stress, heart attacks, and other health problems.**

Lack of exercise threatens the heart by producing unwanted changes in the body. For example, if you combine lack of exercise with overeating, your weight and cholesterol increase. This can cause heart disease and blood-circulation problems. As you exercise, your body and heart become fit, your blood pressure goes down, your HDL ("good") cholesterol goes up, and you begin to lose fat.

Exercise simply makes you feel better. It gives you more energy, helps you cope with stress, improves your self-image, increases your resistance to fatigue, helps counter anxiety and depression, helps you to relax and feel less tense, and enables you to fall asleep more quickly and sleep more soundly. A regular physical exercise routine also helps you become more productive on the job, increases your capacity for physical work, aids in muscle strength, and helps your body's organs work more efficiently. Exercise tones your muscles, helps you control your appetite, and increases the efficiency with which you burn calories.

The Furnace

Exercise helps you maintain weight loss by increasing the intensity of your internal fire, which burns the energy you put into the body. If you are not exercising, your internal fire is not hot enough to burn the stuff you are putting into it. Combine that with putting the wrong kinds of food in your stomach, and your body has a difficult time trying to process food. As you exercise consistently, you not only raise the temperature of this fire, but, because it is now hotter, you also burn the food you eat faster and more efficiently.

> **You need to burn off thirty-five hundred calories more than you take in to lose one pound.**

The Simple Truth

Here is the scoop: You need to burn off thirty-five hundred calories more than you take in to lose one pound. The key to efficient weight loss is to combine your increased metabolism, generated through regular exercise, with the right diet. Remember, you are now "burning" your energy intake through the smallest activities of your daily life, even when you are sleeping, when the body is repairing itself for the next day. The average calories burned per hour for a 150-pound person are listed below.

Activity	Calories Burned per Hour
Walking briskly at 3.5 mph	360
Walking briskly at 3.5 mph uphill	480–900
Bicycling at 5 mph	240
Bicycling at 13 mph	660
Running at 10 mph	1280

Activity	Calories Burned per Hour
Running at 8 mph	900
Running in place	650
Swimming 50 yards per minute	500
Tennis—singles	400
Sitting, watching TV	100
Gardening	400

As you can see, there are many ways to stay active and increase the intensity with which your internal fire burns. Ask yourself these questions: *How can I best burn the fat I do not want while not reducing my lean body mass? What program should I begin to help me do this consistently?* Read on, and get healthy.

Chapter 17

Jump in Heart-First

In 1998 I got to know Mark Allen. Mark Allen is a world-class triathlete who has won the grueling Hawaii Ironman six times. The Ironman combines a 1.2 mile ocean swim, a 112 mile bike ride, and a 26.2 mile marathon run. This intense competition plays out every October in the rugged volcanic terrain of Hawaii's Big Island. The Hawaii Ironman is considered to be the toughest single day athletic event in the world. Mark won the race five years in a row from 1989 to 1993. He took 1994 off. When he returned in 1995 he was thirty-seven years old and competing against the best triathletes in the world who were younger and stronger. And Mark beat them all, but not easily. Trailing by over 13 minutes when he started the run, Mark's victory in 1995 was the greatest comeback in Ironman history and capped a brilliant triathlon career.

Aerobic exercise is the best way to burn excess body fat for energy, because the exercise itself builds fat-burning enzymes.

I met Mark because my friend Bill Bachrach was training for the 1998 Ironman and Mark was his coach. When Bill began training for the Ironman in December of 1997 he naturally focused on what he was comfortable with, biking and running. Mark had him add a weight training regimen to improve his strength and reduce chances of injuries. For several months Bill procrastinated his swim training because he was uncomfortable in the water. "Besides," Bill rationalized, "the swim is only ten percent of the race. Biking and running are what really count." By March of 1998 Bill still wasn't in the pool! He had just six months before the big race and he hadn't started to swim. Not good. Of course Bill knew this, but sometimes what we know we should do and what we actually do are two different things. One afternoon Bill and Mark were discussing Bill's training progress. Bill was telling

Mark all about his running, biking, and weight lifting hoping Mark wouldn't notice there was no conversation about swimming. Mark finally asked the inevitable question, "So how's the swimming going?" Bill replied weakly, "Uh, I haven't really started yet." Mark then uttered the great coaching wisdom, "You know, Bill, you really are going to have to get in the pool."

So Bill finally got off the dime and jumped in the pool. With the right swim coaching and the right amount of inspiration from Mark, Bill went on to have a successful swim and achieve his Ironman goal. Sometimes all we need is the right push at the right time.

That is how it might be for you. There is a time when you, too, will simply have to "jump in" to the exercise commitment. My advice is to jump in with your heart, not just your head. In these next two chapters, I want to talk about the right way to exercise for maximum fat burning and minimum muscle loss. I will also share with you some of the lessons I have learned about the power of having a program. At the heart of the exercise game, there are two ways to burn fat and energy: aerobically and anaerobically.

What Is Aerobic Exercise?

Aerobic exercise means exercising in the presence of oxygen. Aerobic exercise is the best way to burn excess body fat for energy, because the exercise itself builds fat-burning enzymes. In this training zone, the heart and lungs are able to supply enough oxygen to the muscles so that the glucose is broken down, disassembled, and completely burned.

How Do You Know If You Are Exercising Aerobically?

The usual prescription for aerobic exercise is to do some kind of physical activity that raises your heart rate to between 65 and 80 percent of its maximum. You determine your maximum heart rate by subtracting your age from 220. Some people have slower hearts and others have faster hearts, but the above range is generally acceptable. Exercising at this level is important because it allows you to burn more fat than carbohydrates. If you exercise above these limits, the demand for moving the fat from the tissue in which it is stored to the muscles that convert it into energy is limited. If the muscles cannot get enough fat, they switch over to stored carbohydrates, thus defeating their purpose. The key to aerobic exercise is high-intensity exercise for an extended period of time. This reduces insulin levels, thereby allowing the release of more stored body fat.

Aerobic Exercise: The Good, the Bad, and the Ugly

The old rule of exercising at these levels for thirty minutes for at least three days of the week was good, but not good enough. Research now says that you should be exercising almost every day of the week. The key is selecting the right exercises, mixing them up for fun, listening to your Walkman while you do them, and, whenever possible, doing them with a friend. In his book *The New Fit or Fat,* fitness expert Covert Bailey shares the following findings on the best kinds of aerobic exercises and their impact on fat burning.[1]

Jogging/running. This exercise has high fat-burning potential. The risk of injury is relatively low if you jog or run fewer than thirty-five miles per week. This type of aerobic exercise is great for young, relatively fit people and older folks who have prior conditioning from a walking program.

Walking. This exercise has moderately low fat-burning potential unless your pace is less than fifteen minutes per mile for longer than thirty minutes. If you speed walk, the fat-burning potential is high. This is an excellent program for beginning exercisers, obese people, older people, pregnant women, and for anyone who is recovering from an injury or illness. Jogging and running achieve the same results as walking in half the time.

Cycling. This exercise has moderate fat-burning potential. You must double the time on a bike to get the same results you would get from a run.

Stationary bicycle. This exercise has moderate fat-burning potential and is good for older people, people with joint problems, overweight people, pregnant women, and beginning exercisers.

Rowing, stair stepping, chair stepping, bench stepping, and jumping rope. These exercises all have high fat-burning potential and are good for beginners, older people, and overweight people. Jumping rope, however, should be reserved for moderately fit people as a second exercise.

A rule of thumb when exercising is to make sure you stay in the 65 to 80 percent range of your maximum heart rate. Stop periodically, check your pulse, count it for ten seconds, and then multiply that number by six. There is an even simpler way of determining if you are in your target range: If you cannot catch your breath or talk while doing this exercise, you are close to exceeding the 80-percent level. When this happens, you go anaerobic.

What Is Anaerobic Exercise?

During anaerobic exercise, your heart rate exceeds 80 percent of your maximum. In this range, oxygen transfer is limited; therefore, the muscle can no longer make energy from fat and goes to the stored carbohydrates. Although on the surface it may seem that this type of exercise does not burn fat, this is not entirely true.

Examples of anaerobic exercise include stadium loops, circuit training, heavy weightlifting, wind sprints, short races, and any other exercise that requires frequent bursts of energy.

Benefits of Anaerobic Exercise

According to Barry Sears, author of *The Zone,* anaerobic exercise is about 95 percent less efficient in energy generation than aerobic. However, there does appear to be a benefit, says Sears:

> If the intensity of the anaerobic exercise is high enough, it causes the body to release human growth hormone. This exceptionally potent hormone repairs microdamage done to the muscle tissue during the exercise. It takes a lot of energy to do the repair job, and that energy comes from your stored body fat. . . . This hormonal change gives you two crucial sweat benefits: It burns fat, and it allows you to build new muscle at the same time.[2]

My counsel is to read the next chapter, discover how to create the right fitness program for you, and then go for it! There are few feelings in the world better than the ones that come from getting—and staying—fit.

Chapter 18

Exercise Is Bite-Size

A body that is in motion will tend to stay in motion—that's momentum. Now that you perhaps have a better understanding of the basics of fitness, it is time to put a program together that you can get excited about and help you create the eagerness to do it again and again. Small, consistent steps will generally give you better results than inconsistent, large steps.

Getting Started

Developing a fitness routine does not require an advanced degree in chemistry or biology. It is a good idea, however, to check with your doctor before you begin so you will have some base lines on which to measure your improvement over time. For example, it would be helpful to know your body fat and lean body mass percentages, weight, cholesterol, and basic body measurements before you begin an exercise program.

The most basic fitness routine that addresses the areas we have discussed so far would look something like this:

- **Cardiovascular exercise.** Three days per week of aerobic training with a twenty- to thirty-minute target, getting your heart rate to between 65 and 80 percent of its maximum.
- **Resistance training.** Two days per week, working the major muscle groups of the upper and lower body with between eight and twelve exercises.
- **Flex training.** Four days per week, stretch major muscle groups, holding each stretch for twenty to thirty seconds.

The Nine Indispensable Laws of Working Out

If you want to have a successful workout regimen, keep these steps in mind.

Start slow. One of the greatest mistakes people make is they overcommit to a time frame and to a routine when they begin a workout regimen. Somehow, they think they can transform their bodies in a month and assume they can exercise for a full hour. What makes them think this is beyond all logic. The psychology of working out must focus more on direction than perfection; otherwise, your attitude may take a turn for the worse. Think in terms of six months or more as you get started. You did not get out of shape in a day, and you cannot get back in shape in a hard-fought twenty-four hours. Also, if your first workouts are too intense, you may sustain an injury and slow down the entire process. Work your way up, gradually increasing your workout time every two weeks until you begin to reach your workout goals.

> **You did not get out of shape in a day, and you cannot get back in shape in a hard-fought twenty-four hours.**

Choose the right equipment. I have been an avid skier since the age of ten. One year I decided that if I really built up my endurance, I wouldn't tire midafternoon on the slopes. So I picked a piece of equipment at the gym that resembled skiing—a Nordic Track. I had only one problem with the machine. I could not make it work like the TV commercials said it should. I felt clumsy and was in a constant state of feeling as if I were going to fall off. That kind of experience makes people want to quit. One of the most important laws of working out is to have fun. I know of no better way than to pick two or three machines that you like, are good on, and that you look forward to using to provide the benefits you are seeking.

Exercise as often as possible. I enjoy the good fortune of having a gym in my office building. There is nothing that should prevent me from working out every day. But I don't always go to the gym. I know a guy at the club whose name is Reed. Recently I was in my office early one morning and saw Reed's car parked in front of the gym. I worked late that day, and when I left, I saw his car again—in a different spot but still there! Later, I asked Reed, "How often do you work out, anyway?" He said, "Twice a day, seven days a week." Wow! He's the Energizer Bunny. Reed's body fat is 6 percent, and he looks fantastic. Here is the point: The more you work out, the better off you will be. Most do not need to follow Reed's schedule, but doing even half of what he does would work miracles for about 95 percent of us.

Come rain, sleet, or shine—just do it! There is no reason a scheduled workout should be canceled. If it is cold, raining, snowing, blowing, or anything else, work out indoors. If your routine is generally indoors, and it is a nice day, exercise outdoors. There must be no excuse for not working out. Our family has a home gym, a membership to the YMCA, and a membership to the club next to my office. Next time you see me, keep me accountable: Ask me if I have worked out that day. Chances are I have . . . or you will embarrass me into promising I will!

Exercise with a friend. More on this in chapter 20, but for now let me just say that having a friend who is as committed as you are to a healthy lifestyle and with whom you have common interests and values is a great strategy to help you keep your exercise commitments. Any exercise you can do with one, two, or three other individuals will greatly increase the likelihood that you will honor your fitness commitment to them and to yourself.

Burn and learn. My friend Brian Tracy is one of the top motivational speakers in the world. In his program, *The Twenty–One Habits of Self-Made Millionaires,* he places great emphasis on the importance of gaining knowledge and never stopping the learning process. In fact, he says that if you were to study any topic for one hour a day, in three years you would be an expert in that area. In our Business Line Seminars, we teach a program called "Time Mastery." The program's message is that, essentially, the people who get full reward out of life are the ones who maximize their time. I want to emphasize that there is nothing wrong with using a Walkman to listen to music. But what if you watched or listened each day to an hour of helpful hints, while working out, on financial, spiritual, relationship, or parenting issues? Do you think that might be more important for your overall well-being than knowing what's on the Top 40?

Out of breath? You're moving too fast. One of the keys to the fat-burning game is moderating your heart rate. This law is important to know if you are to maintain the maximum fat burn during a workout. Don't let your heart rate exceed the maximum target, or you will go anaerobic. If you are struggling with your breathing or have difficulty carrying on a conversation, chances are you are exercising at too fast a pace. *Do not stop!* Just slow down, because you are going too fast.

Don't get bored—change your routine or hire a trainer. Recently, the International Health, Racquet, and Sports Association, an industry association for health and fitness clubs, surveyed ten thousand former health-club members to find out why they stopped going to the gym. The survey discovered that many of the members were either bored or felt they did not receive enough personal attention. If you have ever felt this way, here is some advice. Don't quit; change your routine. If that doesn't work, hire a trainer. This will bring the vitality back to your workouts and will help you stay motivated.

> **Progress is always the result of increased excitement and commitment.**

Set goals and monitor your progress. I mentioned the importance of momentum earlier, but I want to go a little deeper. Progress is always the result of increased excitement and commitment. People who see the inches fall off, watch the size of their biceps increase, or run a mile for the first time in their lives get excited about doing it again and again. However, a successful workout program must be built on goals. Once a week—no less, no more—measure your results, and you will be hooked. When you follow these laws and begin to see positive results, take time to celebrate the new you. Have some fun with your new commitment as you start down the road of becoming fit for life.

Chapter 19

Do It a Few Hundred Times, and You Have It Made . . . Almost

M astering the workout game takes a special kind of attitude. It requires a commitment that few are willing to make due to a lack of patience and a lack of the awareness that success in fitness, as in anything, takes time—a great deal of time. I would like to share some thoughts with you that form the foundation of a workout attitude. In that context, the one word that comes quickly to mind is *perseverance*.

The Power of Perseverance

It is a rare individual who never loses his patience . . . whether it's waiting in a checkout line; living with a spouse, children, or roommate; or trying to stay focused on an exercise program. However, there is one formula that will win the day for you: *Perserverance requires patience.*

In a manufacturing town in Scotland, a young woman began teaching a Sunday-school class of poverty-stricken boys. The most unpromising youngster was a boy named Bob. After the first two or three Sundays, he did not return. So the teacher went to look for him. Although the superintendent had given **Perserverance requires patience.** Bob some new clothes, they were already worn and dirty when the teacher found him. He was given another new suit, and he came back to Sunday school. But soon he quit again, and the teacher went out once more to find him. When she did, she discovered that the second set of clothes had gone the way of the first.

"I am completely discouraged about Bob," she told the superintendent. "I guess we must give up on him."

"Please don't do that," he pleaded. "I believe there is still hope. Try him one more time."

They gave Bob a third suit of clothes, and this time he began to attend faithfully. It was not long until he became a Christian and eventually even taught in that same Sunday school. Who was that obstinate, ragged boy who for a time seemed so unreachable? None other than Robert Morrison, who later became the first Protestant missionary to China. He translated the Scripture into Chinese and brought the Word of God to teeming millions.[1] Patience, patience, patience. Sunflowers bloom and die within days; oaks take forever to grow but endure the test of time. It will be the same with you and your fitness program. No, it will not be easy. But as long as you stay on-purpose, continually review your objectives, and remember the commitment you made to yourself that day in the mirror, the pressure you place on yourself will pay off in ways unimaginable.

Don't Despise the Small Numbers

In 1853, a denominational mission society discussed closing a station in Ongole, India, because only ten converts had been won to Christ in fifteen years. Two men of God pleaded for the continued support of this field, however, arguing that these few believers must not be abandoned. They made up the single church, which someone called the "Lone Star" of India. Samuel Smith, author of "My Country 'Tis of Thee," was a member of the mission board. As he contemplated this matter, he was moved to write the following verse: "Shine on, Lone Star, in grief and tears, and sad reverses oft baptized; shine on amid thy founders' fears; lone stars in Heaven are not despised." The next day he read this poem to his colleagues, and they unanimously voted to continue the work. Because of this decision, God moved in such mighty power that hundreds in India were converted. Thirty years later, the Ongole church had grown to fifteen thousand members.[2]

With your workout program, your numbers will be small initially. You will not lose thirty pounds in thirty days. If you do, something is wrong. Your small numbers, over time, will add up to be large numbers, as long as you never, ever give up.

Working with Diligence

On October 18, 1879, a young inventor by the name of Thomas Edison sat in his laboratory. He was weary from thirteen months of repeated failure in his search for a filament that would stand the stress of electric current. To add to his problems, the men who had backed him financially were now refusing to put up any additional funds. Having tried every known metal in his experiment, Edison was admittedly baffled. Casually picking up a bit of lampblack, he mixed it with tar and rolled it into a thin thread.

Suddenly the thought struck him: Why not try a carbonized cotton fiber? For five hours, he worked on the first filament, but it broke before he could remove the mold. Two spools of thread were used in similar fruitless efforts. At last, a perfect strand emerged—only to be ruined when he tried to place it inside a glass tube. Still Edison refused to admit defeat. He continued to work without sleep for two more days and nights.

> **His persistance in the face of the most discouraging odds gave the world one of its greatest inventions—the electric light.**

Eventually he managed to insert one of the crude carbonized threads into a vacuum-sealed bulb. "When we turned on the current," he said, "the sight we had so long desired to see finally met our eyes." His persistence in the face of the most discouraging odds gave the world one of its greatest inventions—the electric light.[3]

The key to health is the "Edison Attitude." You must keep your eyes on your goal and pursue your goal with passion, never allowing yourself to be beaten down by little or no movement toward your objectives. Even when you gain a pound or two, do not be discouraged. Stay diligent, and you will succeed.

A Good Finisher

The name Mickey Thompson used to be one of the most recognized names in auto racing. His team built the fastest cars on the track. However, not one of those cars ever brought Thompson a checkered flag. That's right. Although his cars took the lead in the first twenty-nine races they entered, they never won a race. Why? Because they did not finish.

One of the things I learned from Ironman Hall of Famer Mark Allen is to "take it to completion" and to "finish the race." God built you to go all the way. Keep your eyes on the finish line, and run the race well.

The Law of Repetition

Change is tough. In my seminars, I demonstrate this challenge by having participants do the following three exercises. Try them now before you go any further:

- Take a ring, watch, or bracelet from one finger or arm and move it to the opposite one. Leave it there for a moment. How does that feel? Weird, I bet. But how would it feel if you left it there for as long as you have been wearing it on the other finger or wrist? Over time, it would become natural.
- Clap your hands ten times right now and then stop. Now turn your hands in the other direction, still letting your palms face each other, and clap ten times. Feels different, doesn't it? And it's not quite as loud.
- Cross your arms across your chest as you normally do. Now move your arms and cross them the other way across your chest. How does that feel?

Developing any habit takes time. Any one of the three exercises above, if done long enough, would feel natural. That is how it is with exercise. Do it a few hundred times, and working out will become a way of life.

This infallible law of repetition is the missing link to developing and maintaining your commitment to exercise. In closing, let me share with you three proven benefits when you put this law into effect.

A stronger self-image. Anything important to you that is done well enough and long enough will have a positive impact on your self-esteem. When this happens, commitment to any process soars.

A desire to expand your results. When your hopes become reality, you raise your own standards. You do new and more challenging things, which then feed the cycle of your personal growth.

A positive synergy. In all areas of health, you suddenly begin to see positive results. You discover you have more energy, stamina, less stress, more focus, and more discipline. You create higher levels of balance and fulfillment.

Now that you are on your way to achieving optimum health, the only other thing I recommend is a safety net, and that net is found through the power of accountability.

Chapter 20

My Wake-up Call

L et me tell you a story. To quote my friend Zig Ziglar, "I was sick and tired of being sick and tired. I had tried everything. I tried the thirty-day diet and lost a month. My idea of exercise was to fill the tub, take a bath, pull the plug, and fight the current. You see my problem was, I never accidentally ate anything."[1] Zig changed his ways, lost thirty-seven pounds, and has kept it off for more than twenty-seven years. His newfound energy has dramatically impacted his life. He is seventy-three and recently commented, "I'm not retired—I'm refired. I'm not gonna ease up, let up, shut up, or give up until

> **"My idea of exercise was to fill the tub, take a bath, pull the plug, and fight the current."**

I'm taken up. As a matter of fact, I'm just getting warmed up!" What is so remarkable about this? For Zig, it is a way of life. And it needs to become a way of life for you too.

Have you ever been sleeping soundly and then suddenly shaken into consciousness by the shrill ring of the telephone? That kind of wake-up call is not what most of us look forward to, especially when it is a good friend reminding you that your Saturday morning workout begins in one hour. That is how it was with Craig and me. We knew that with the pressures of relationships and the host of other responsibilities we had, the easiest thing to do was to blow off a workout. We also knew, through experience, that losing our "fitness" habit would be the first danger sign of losing our edge. In fact, it was the wake-up calls that created the habit in the first place.

Wild Oscar Wilde

What happens when, in the important areas of your life, you do not bother to ask for accountability? Here is a brief account from the pen of the famed writer Oscar Wilde that answers that question.

> The gods had given me almost everything. But I let myself be lured into long spells of senseless and sensual ease. . . . Tired of being on the heights, I deliberately went to the depths in search of new sensation. What the paradox was to me in the sphere of thought, perversity became to me in the sphere of passion. I grew careless of the lives of others. I took pleasure where it pleased me and passed on. I forgot that every little action of the common day makes or unmakes character, and therefore what one has done in the secret chamber, one has some day to cry aloud from the housetop. I ceased to be Lord over myself. I was no longer the captain of my soul, and did not know it. I allowed pleasure to dominate me. I ended in horrible disgrace.[2]

Five Benefits of Accountability

Having someone hold you accountable helps to produce a kind of personal excellence that you will find nowhere else. Here are just five of the major benefits.

Character. When you have someone to whom you are accountable, you have made the decision to work on building your *character*—defined broadly as "the person you are becoming every day." In the area of health, it is the framework for making automatic choices that are beneficial to you. You know that each time you follow through on an action, you are building yourself up for excellence.

Commitment. When someone holds you accountable, your commitment to take positive action increases. When commitment goes up, consistency goes up. When consistency is increased, so are the results, and so is the momentum. Accountability partners who have an interest in you will not let you fail.

Choices. An accountability partner helps you shape your choices. In fact, if you and your accountability partner go beyond the "wake-up" call to a deeper level of fitness commitment, for example, you will invariably make a different set of decisions during the week. If I know that on Friday I have to report on my health goals—weight, fat intake, and number of workouts—I will be more likely to stay the course throughout the week. If you have the right exercise partner, you cannot lie, and therefore you will make different decisions.

Clarity. Accountability partners help you clarify many of the decisions you will be forced to make about your fitness program. They can help you establish your goals, shape your routines, partner with you while working out, create a diet for you, and even give you your wake-up calls. This kind of accountability can be even further accelerated with a fitness trainer or coach—although this is not a prerequisite for personal growth. If you have neither a partner nor a coach, look around for someone who has the body and healthy lifestyle you want and talk with that person. Any positive relationship will increase your clarity.

Communication. Share your need for accountability. In your moments of challenge, when your discipline may be slipping, you can reach out to that person and communicate your weak, undisciplined state of mind. One brief conversation may help you change your course. Start appreciating the "little" moments. If you have ever been involved in or studied the work of Alcoholics Anonymous, you know this to be one of their key strategies. Honest communication—whether it is a quick telephone call or a long conversation over lunch—will win the day for you.

Hold My Feet to the Fire

Who is holding your feet to the fire of health? Do you have an accountability partner, someone you can count on? If not, here is a story that may motivate you to act now.

Pastor Bill Hybels of Willow Creek Church in South Barrington, Illinois, tells about being the chaplain for the Chicago Bears several years ago. He led a Bible study for the players at Halas Hall in Lake Forest, where they practiced. One day he arrived early and observed that some of the players and coaches were watching a film of the previous day's game.

Hybels joined them and was surprised by what he saw. Time after time, a player would request that the projector be stopped.

He would then ask his teammates and coaches, "Now what did I do wrong on that play?" Here were world-class athletes, highly paid champions, laying aside all pride and asking their teammates to tell them the truth. They realized they needed objective observers to point out how they could improve. They chose to be accountable.[3]

Do you have the same attitude toward your personal improvement? Are you able to be transparent and authentic enough to reach out for help? If not, you will be in for a rough ride in the health game for the rest of your life.

To Whom Are You Accountable?

Charles Colson, a prominent figure in the Watergate cover-up when Richard Nixon was president, wrote an article entitled, "The Problem of Power." In it he wrote, "Christians need to hold one another accountable. Though I know intellectually how vulnerable I am to pride and power, I am the last one to know when I succumb to their seduction. That's why spiritual Lone Rangers are so dangerous—and why we must depend on trusted brothers and sisters who love us enough to tell us the truth."[4]

Regardless of what you believe spiritually, Colson's words should have great impact on you in the area of your health. You and I are vulnerable to shortcuts and excuses. We can easily manufacture our own wrong reasons for not taking our eating plans or workouts to completion. In the end, however, we must depend on others to help motivate us to be our best.

Chapter 21

Smell the Roses
and Other Nice Scents

A strategy for optimum health and a habit we must all pursue is *rest!* In his bestseller *All I Ever Really Needed to Know I Learned in Kindergarten*, Robert Fulghum said one of the great secrets of life and a major lesson was . . . take a nap.

Have you ever gone on a long trip in your car? Chances are you have. Along the way, did you notice the many rest stops? Did you take advantage of them? Did you stop and take a rest, go for a brisk walk, or enjoy a catnap? Or were you in such a hurry to arrive at your destination that you simply sailed by, missing that special moment of fresh air, a brush with history, the enjoyment of nature, or the rare chance to experience life away from your regular routine?

Rest Is for the Health Conscious

Over the years, I have watched many of my friends and colleagues go through life in the fast lane—hurry, hurry, hurry up and get there. As writer Gordon MacDonald says, "We are on one fast, continuous trip; the destination, although elusive, is all-important. Rest stops along the way are not. And these places along the **Are you running on empty?** side of the road are only noticed when we are desperate; out of gas, in need of a bathroom, fighting an overheated engine."[1]

Are you running on empty? Are you in need of release? Do you need to cool your engine? The Bible gives us a glimpse into the life of a man, King David, who understood the importance of rest: "The LORD is my shepherd, I shall not be in want. He makes me lie down in green pastures, he leads me beside quiet waters, he restores my soul" (Ps. 23:1–3 NIV).

This is true rest—that special moment when you relinquish your needs, wants, and earthly desires for the peace and tranquillity of "safe" waters. This is where your mind, body, and soul are reordered and rejuvenated. As I mentioned in chapter 7, our model for rest is God Himself, who created this world in six days and rested on the seventh day.

Optimum Health Includes Slowing Down

As I've said before, the best way not to go too fast is to move more slowly. Burnout and blowout are wicked realitites for those who refuse to slow their pace.

Listen to the wise words from an anonymous author:

> Have you ever watched kids on a merry-go-round? Or listened to the rain slapping on the ground? Ever followed a butterfly's erratic flight? Or gazed at the sun into the fading night?
>
> You better slow down. Don't dance so fast. Time is short. The music won't last.
>
> Do you run through each day on the fly? When you ask, "How are you?" do you hear the reply? When the day is done, do you lie in your bed with the next hundred chores running through your head?
>
> You better slow down. Don't dance so fast. Time is short. The music won't last.
>
> Ever told your child, we'll do it tomorrow, and in your haste, not see his sorrow? Ever lost touch, let a good friendship die, 'cause you never had time to call and say hi?
>
> You better slow down. Don't dance so fast. Time is short. The music won't last.
>
> Life is not a race. Do take it slower. Hear the music before the song is over.

Congratulations. You are on your way to obtaining true wealth through health. You now, hopefully, are even more aware of the importance of the careful maintenance of your body. With this expanded awareness, you will now be able to maximize the next six steps of wealth. Here's what I want you to do. Skim through this first section again and set some healthy goals that will help you edge ever closer to your optimum health. When you are finished, join me as together we explore the world of financial abundance and gain valuable insights to help you put your financial house in order.

Part Two

Financial Abundance

Take Stock of Your Net Worth

Chapter 22

Ladieees and Gentlemen

I want to establish two things before we explore the very important topic of money. First, too many people do not know how to use their money intelligently to secure their future and their dreams. And if having money is how you validate your position in life—if you love it and worship it as if it were some kind of idol—you will never ever feel truly fulfilled. It has been said that he who buys what he does not need ends up needing what he cannot buy. There must be a plan for your life in the area of money. The sooner you develop such a plan, the better off you will be.

Avoid Going *Splat!*

My wife and I recently took our two sons to the circus. I remember how fascinated they were, especially when the performers started climbing the ladder on their way to the highest point under the tent. Have you ever been to the circus? If you have, you probably have some of those same memories. This act is generally reserved for the end of the show because it contains so much thrill, challenge, and danger. The brave trapeze artists practice long hours perfecting their routines, so when it is showtime, they can perform without a net. However, most of the other trapeze artists around the world operate *with* the safety of the net. If, by chance, they miss the trusted hands of their partner or the bar they must miraculously grab hold of, they have the confidence that on their way to the ground below, the net will catch them before they go *splat!*

That's how it should be in our lives financially. Unless we are among the smallest percentage of the truly brave, most of us would benefit greatly if we had a financial "safety net." Few of us who read these pages are excited about the prospect of not making it financially. Most of us realize that while money is not going to buy us happiness, it will certainly make the journey through life easier. You can seize this moment so you will never again need to worry about finances. You can do this for you and your family today, giving everyone you love the security of knowing their financial future is safe. Personal financial freedom is an option for everyone, and I hope you grab it as one for you now.

The Net-Worth Net

Contrary to the most commonly accepted definition of financial wealth, real wealth is not measured by the abundance of things acquired. Real wealth is measured by the total amount of acquired assets that will appreciate in value and create real abundance. A modern-day nice car may be nice, but it is not likely to appreciate in value. Cartier and Rolex watches are nice, but they are not likely to appreciate. They may hold their value, but appreciation is unlikely.

Building a safety net for the future requires that you begin where you are today. Net worth, positive or negative, must be your starting place for building true wealth. Your net worth is an accurate reflection of your financial affairs, and it marks those areas in which goal setting and planning begin. There is a danger here for the young reader. The longer you wait to begin to build real wealth, the more difficult it will be. The younger you are, the better. If you are older, take comfort that it is never too late to start. After all, having more later than you have now is still a very good thing.

> **Real wealth is measured by the total amount of acquired assets that will appreciate in value and create real abundance.**

Once your net-worth number is established, you should review the number every six to twelve months, measuring your progress in specific goal areas, always being aware of where you might be slacking off or losing your discipline. Do yourself a big favor: Respect the power of your net-worth number. It will drive everything you do financially.

Here are the specifics for creating a net-worth statement. Grab a pad of paper and complete the information below. When you have finished, I will tell you what your net-worth number means.

Part One: Your Personal Assets (total these amounts)

- cash (checking, savings, on-hand)
- certificates of deposit
- money-market accounts
- investments such as stocks, bonds, mutual funds, etc.
- vested dollar amounts of retirement accounts such as 401(k), 403(b), IRAs, Keoghs, annuities, etc.
- life insurance cash value
- estimated market value of your home
- other real estate owned
- all personal property
- trust funds
- valuation of your business

Part Two: Your Personal Liabilities (total these amounts)

- department store charge-card balances
- credit-card balances
- unpaid mortgage balance (include first trust deed and any equity line or seconds)
- unpaid auto loan balances
- medical loans
- student loans
- other loans, including personal property loans
- medical and dental loans
- other long-term obligations

Take your total assets and subtract them from your total liabilities: This is your true net worth. What does this number mean? To understand it, you should know, based on your age and your income, where you should be by now. I like what Thomas Stanley and William Danko say in their bestseller, *The Millionaire Next Door*. According to their research of wealthy people, they offer this formula for net worth: "Multiply your age times your realized pretax annual household income from all sources except inheritance. Divide by ten. This, less any inherited wealth, is what your net worth should be."[1]

Where are you? If your actual number is behind where it should be, then the chapters and steps that follow will do more to shore up your performance financially than anything you can get your hands on.

Chapter 23

The Top Ten Mistakes of Money Management

It is imperative for you to understand why you may not be where you want to be in your overall goal of financial abundance and freedom. While the opportunities are greater than ever for people to become well off financially, there are still many alarming realities that affect people today. Some of the most common include: people having too few liquid assets when they retire, more families needing two incomes or jobs to survive, only 30 percent of households having stocks or mutual funds, and only 20 percent of households having savings in a money-market account. Why is this so? There are many reasons, but you will find that these important few will do more to change your course than the hundreds of others combined. Here are the top ten mistakes people tend to make before and during their wealth-building and asset-management years.

Not Starting Early Enough

People who start late seem to think that they have all the time in the world, and *someday* they will start saving. *Someday* gets put off, day after day, week after week, and finally year after year. The person who truly wants to build wealth realizes that the best time to start is now. Such a person understands early that the lifestyle choices that consume cash need to be monitored, and in some cases delayed, so his or her wealth-building plan can take root.

No Vision or Written Plan

Any successful business leader will tell you that one of the absolute keys to business success is to have a clear vision of where you want the business to go. This vision is usually long-range, with goals and objectives comprising the short-term benchmarks that must be accomplished. Without this vision, setting short-term goals has little if any impact. The same is true with most people and their finances. True wealth building starts with a long-range vision, usually ten to thirty years, depending on when you start. If you want to be on your way to wealth, you must create this vision. The elements that shape it will be discussed in chapter 29. For now, recognize that the primary goal is not getting or having money, but rather experiencing more of the things that money will get you. The more you link the accumulation of money, and thus wealth, to those important values you have for your life, the more likely you will stay motivated for the long run, which is paramount to being truly wealthy.

Not Utilizing Asset Allocation

Another mistake people make in the area of money management is not allocating their cash and investment resources appropriately. In chapters 29 and 37, I will go much deeper into this issue. A definition now, however, will be helpful as you journey toward those chapters. The premise of asset allocation is that, over time, you will allocate your dollars to different investment mixes with varying risk sensitivity. Some investments will be low risk, others in between, some high risk. The amount of your portfolio that is allocated to any one class or risk category changes based on your goals, age, and your current realities. Generally, your risk factors are higher when you are building wealth and then decrease as you begin to rely on your portfolio for income, security, and retirement.

High-Interest-Rate Debt

The number one killer of building wealth is high-interest-rate debt. The amount of outstanding credit in this category continues to soar each year. This kind of debt occurs most often when the holder of a credit card that carries a high interest rate makes purchases that he or she cannot pay off within thirty days. The credit-card habit is born, driven by instant gratification, and soon, millions of people find themselves struggling every month simply to pay the minimums. When they are finally at their wits' end, in comes another offer from another credit-card company offering instant approval, and the cycle begins again. One of the happiest days in my life was when I made the commitment not to have credit-card debt. In chapter 30, I will give you several strategies to help rid yourself of this highly emotional addiction.

> **The number one killer of building wealth is high-interest-rate debt.**

Timing the Market, Following the Masses, and Chasing Hot Stocks and Funds

There is a difference between being a risktaker and a gambler in building wealth. Most of us who are trying to build wealth are not experts at it; therefore, we rely on the advice of friends, family, or perhaps a financial advisor. (But be especially careful of taking the counsel of good ol' Uncle Charlie who probably does not have a clue.) The most seasoned investors will tell you that a good alternative to the high-stress life of timing trades, buying and selling, and following runaway stocks and funds is to buy smart, hold long, and watch carefully. Here is the short course on wise investing:

- Never invest in anything simply because everyone is buying it.
- Never buy a stock or fund when the emotion and "heat" surrounding that stock are high. Slow down when you make investments. Just because a stock is selling off doesn't mean it is going to come back. And just because the stock is skyrocketing doesn't mean it will not return to the earth in flames.
- Never buy a stock or fund or make an investment without doing adequate research. Uncover the hype, get a sense for the long-term performance opportunity, and then make a decision. Go to the company's Web site and poke around. Read the annual report. Ask questions such as, Does this fund have a load? What do analysts think about the company right now? What are the tax consequences of those bonds? In the end, doing your homework will pay dividends.

Not Building Cash Reserves

One of the first goals anyone should have in the pursuit of wealth is to build your reserves. You should have at least six months of reserves that will cover 100 percent of your living expenses. If you have any unexpected items that surface, such as car repairs, a layoff, medical emergencies, home repairs, or the like, these funds can be liquidated and used to cover your expenses without having to use credit cards, credit-card cash advances, or investments. This money should be kept in a savings account, money-market fund, or bank certificate of deposit so it is easily accessible.

Improper Estate Planning

Another big mistake people make in the area of wealth building is improper or nonexistent estate planning. Some of the greatest errors in judgment can be found in not having a durable power of attorney for healthcare that gives a member of the family the right to make healthcare decisions if you cannot. Here are a few more:

- Not having a revocable living trust, which states who controls your assets while you are alive and what happens to them when you die
- Not having a will, a document that states where you want your assets to go after your death
- Not having a "bypass" provision in your living trust, which, if you are married, will let you and your spouse leave up to $1.35 million (year 2000) estate tax–free
- Not having the right insurance for health, life, and disability

All of these need to be taken care of in your pursuit of building and protecting wealth. The library, the Internet, a qualified estate-planning attorney, and a financial advisor are resources from which you draw the information to put these plans in place.

Short-Term Thinking

Many people fail in their pursuit of building wealth because they do not think long-term. They are chasing the highest yields and looking for quick returns, never fully understanding that the higher the yield, the riskier the investment. They have fallen into the habit of "churning" their portfolio—buying and selling often and, in the end, experiencing an overall lower-yield performance. It certainly is nice to enjoy the high returns we often see today. However, the best advice would be to balance those returns with an asset-allocation model and let the stock or fund work for you over the long haul. Consistent returns of 8 to 12 percent will amaze you when their earnings are compounded. One thousand dollars invested in small stocks in 1975 would be worth more than one hundred thousand dollars today.

Lack of Knowledge

Too many people lack even the most basic knowledge of financial planning. They simply do not realize the impact of their money decisions on their lives. We have all learned financial lessons the hard way, and it hurts. There are few things worse in life than financial stress, particularly if the pain could have been avoided. I think those prudent students, even if they haven't begun the financial wealth-building process, would benefit by doing two things besides finishing this book. The first would be to read *The Richest Man in Babylon,* by George Clason (more on this book in the next chapter). The second would be to subscribe to *Money* magazine. Both will be of tremendous benefit because they both keep the financial strategies simple. Most of us would benefit greatly if, in our pursuit of gaining knowledge, we were to keep it simple.

Improper Lifestyle Management

Lack of respect for money and for one's self leads to seeking gratification through the accumulation of things. Generally, these material possessions will not be income-producing assets, or assets that will appreciate in value. The temporary fulfillment lasts only days or weeks, and yet the long-term financial impact can be awesome. For example, if in 1950, Joe decided, as a twenty-five-year-old man, to invest one thousand dollars in small stocks instead of buying a new car, his investment would be worth more than seven hundred thousand dollars today. I'll bet you Joe is no longer driving the car he bought fifty years ago.

One of the keys to building wealth is to get healthy with your view of money. Nothing acquired to fill a void of self-worth will ever bring the happiness and peace of mind that come with building long-term financial security.

In the chapters to come, all of these issues will be dealt with comprehensively. Start thinking about where you need to be more responsible with your money.

Chapter 24

Start Acting Your Wage

Y ou cannot be successful in the years ahead unless you lock on to the key principles you must apply today. One of the most important is *the law of delayed gratification.*

If you desire greater financial rewards in the future, and if you want something of greater value in your later years, you are simply not allowed to have something else in its place today. I agree with my friend John Maxwell when he says, "Only if you pay now, will you be able to play later."

> "Only if you pay now, will you be able to play later."

There is no viable alternative to this formula. If you reverse this equation, chances are you are already in trouble, whether you know it or not.

On what do you place more value: things or money? Of the following two options, which makes more sense to you?

> Option A: Pay now and play later.
> Option B: Play now and pay later.

You need to make a choice. Put another way, are you comfortable trading your future freedom for current short-term pleasures that may lead only to temporary contentment? If you are going to gain personal financial freedom, you must adopt the following financial habits.

Know Where Your Cash Is Going

Becoming wealthy requires discipline. The world's wealthiest people know that the first key to building wealth is proper cashflow management. Until we start tracking where our money comes from and where it goes, we cannot appreciate how much we are spending that we do not need to spend. To build wealth, we must have more money coming in than we do going out. Appreciate the power of money and ask yourself, *In the midst of making expenditures, do I really need to part with this money for this thing?* In most cases, the answer will be no. Each time we arrive at this affirmation, we become more committed to making similar future decisions.

Don't Wait; Start Now

In the wealth-building classic mentioned earlier, *The Richest Man in Babylon*, author George Clason tells the story of Arkad, the richest and wisest money manager in all Babylon, and his son, Nomasir. The story told by Kalabab focuses on "The Five Laws of Gold." The first law is this: "Gold cometh gladly and in increasing quantity to any man who will put by not less than one-tenth of his earnings to create an estate for his future and that of his family."[1]

This habit must be formed, and the earlier, the better. Consider these facts as quoted from *Money* magazine's "100 Steps to Wealth":[2]

Age When Lifetime Savings Begins	Yearly Contribution	Lifetime Contribution	Lifetime Interest Earned at 6 Percent	Total Savings
21	$5,000	$220,000	$832,029	$1,052,029
31	$5,000	$170,000	$365,918	$540,918
41	$5,000	$120,000	$140,397	$260,397

Spend Less; Save More

The secret of wealth building is found in the basics of cash management. There are only two ways to have more money with which to build wealth: Earn more or spend less. For most people, this means they must spend less than they make. Wealth is not predicated by income, but by the amount of money accumulated and saved. This is so simple that most people miss it. No business could survive if it constantly spent more than it took in; likewise, no person or family

> **Wealth is not predicated by income, but by the amount of money accumulated and saved.**

can survive financially unless it develops the daily discipline of monitoring cash flow. The other way to have more money to invest is to earn more vocationally.

In most surveys available, we learn that people are spending disposable income on things they do not need. They are not channeling their money into active savings or accumulation accounts, such as money markets, stocks, and mutual funds, which are designed to give them the money that they will need for their future.

According to a number of financial resources, we are not a nation of savers. Americans save an average of 5 percent of their disposable income. Japanese households are socking away 12.2 percent. The Germans are saving 11.5 percent, and thrifty Belgians are putting aside 17 percent. The United States holds 14 percent of the world's total savings, yet we borrow 27 percent of the capital available in the world market. That's the big picture. What about you and your personal savings plan?

> **There are only two ways to have more money with which to build wealth: Earn more or spend less.**

There are three ways you can begin your savings plan today.

Make different lifestyle decisions. This is a powerful component. Researchers Thomas Stanley and William Danko have determined that the nation's wealthiest first-generation millionaires had seven things in common when it came to creating and building wealth. Number one was *that they lived well below their means.*[3] They could enjoy nicer and newer cars, homes, clothes, and other nice things, but they did not. Their lifestyle reflected their goals. They looked at every expenditure with a different eye. How do you answer the following questions?

- What is the real difference between a $5,000 watch and one that costs $500? They both tell time don't they? Invested, what would the $4,500 difference earn during the life span of these watches?
- What is the difference between enjoying a cup of coffee at home for three cents and one at Starbucks for $1.55? The answer is $46.00 per month, or $547.00 per year.
- What is the difference between a new car and a five-year-old

model? Don't they both get you from point A to point B?

- What is the difference between a deli sandwich, for which you pay $4.50, and one you make at home for thirty-five cents? Well, if you eat the $4.50 sandwich five days per week, it comes to a whopping $1,037.00 a year.

Look at every expense you have, track it, and decide where you can save. Is your money working for you, or are you working for your money?

Reduce debt. One of the killers of financial freedom—and one of the major things that zaps our ability to save—is high-interest-rate debt. Credit-card debt, the most common of high-interest-rate debt, will not only destroy your net worth, but it can also have a devastating impact on your self-worth. The first step is to make this sort of debt manageable; the second is to pay it off

> **Is your money working for you, or are you working for your money?**

gradually as you work on your other financial goals simultaneously. Again, as I mentioned earlier, we will talk more about this in chapter 30. However, for now, understand this: If you do not respect money, it will not respect you.

Develop automatic cash allocation. Make your money work for you. Every dollar freed up and saved is equivalent to earning two new dollars. Remember that your "net" dollar has all taxes and insurance taken out, so when you save, you are actually accumulating the purchase or investment power of two dollars.

Once the above two steps are in motion or moving toward completion, you should contact your personnel or payroll department or your bank and arrange for automatic deductions to be made from your paycheck or deposits for investment purposes. As you modify your lifestyle, your credit-card debt and other debts decrease, your available investment dollars increase, and you are on your way to having something of significance for your future. When that happy day arrives, it is time to build real wealth.

Chapter 25

Money Is Like a Brick

The Scriptures say, "Behold, I am laying in Zion a stone, a tested stone, a costly cornerstone for the foundation, firmly placed" (Isa. 28:16). Mortar and stone. A brick is hard, solid, and abrasive. It can be beautiful, or it can be ugly. What are the uses of a brick? You can build a wall—the Berlin Wall, the Great Wall of China, or a wall to keep your kids safe. It can be used to build a fence, a fountain, a church, a house, a prison, or a bridge. The brick is essentially morally neutral.

What we do with the brick is critical. It is the same with money. Money is not evil. It all depends on how you use it. Most of us honestly do not care much at all about money; however, we care quite a lot about what money provides. Money itself is the cornerstone, the brick, if you like. What you choose to do with it will determine your ultimate outcome, good or bad.

Develop a Respect for Money

Money is powerful. It motivates people. Its abundance can make life easier; its absence can make life troublesome. It can make a family or break a family. It is one of the most powerful ingredients for balance on the planet. If you do not look at money under this kind of magnifying glass, there is a chance you will be negatively impacted by money for the rest of your life.

If you desire financial abundance, you must develop a deep level of respect for money and the role it plays in your life. Now, you might be saying, *Look, Todd, I really do respect money. Honest.* But let me ask you, are your daily actions an accurate reflection of what you tell me you believe? Only you know the answer. Here are some examples of how we often disrespect money:

- We throw away clothing because we are tired of it, when, in fact, we could easily get more wear out of it.

- We throw away a twenty-dollar pair of socks that have a hole in the bottom when we could mend them and wear them for another year.
- We throw away food that isn't bad; we're just tired of it.
- We spend two dollars per shirt for laundry when someone would gladly iron it and all our other clothes for seven to ten dollars per hour. (Five minutes per shirt is twelve shirts an hour—or twenty-four dollars at the cleaners.)
- We buy a new pair of shoes when the older pair could be resoled less expensively.
- We buy something that is more expensive than an equivalent product that is cheaper and has the same function.

I am not suggesting your attitude toward money should be altered so that it has a negative impact on you and on those you love. A dent in a new car door—when your spouse was driving it, of course!—may not necessarily be a demonstration of his lack of respect for money. It most likely was an accident or something that could not be helped. However, overall, it *is* this governing thought process that makes people wealthy.

I heard a story once of a millionaire who was leaving the country for two weeks. So he went to his bank to get a loan. Upon receiving the five thousand dollars, he asked the bank employee to take his Bentley for collateral. Because he was a good customer, they happily parked it for him in their underground parking structure. Upon his return, he went to the bank to pay his loan back, plus interest and charges. His check was for $5,021. The bank asked him why he borrowed the money— after all, he was rich. His reply: "Where else can I park my Bentley in downtown New York for two weeks for only twenty-one dollars?"

Let Money Work for You after You Have Worked for It

Let's face it. You have worked hard for your money. It should also be working hard for you. I recently talked with some friends who would be considered "rich." They have a million-dollar home and a profitable dental practice. I was talking to the wife at a party recently about wealth building, and she told me they had one hundred thousand dollars in their checking account. Their living expenses are nowhere near that much, and yet she said that it is common to have that kind of money in their checking account.

"How much interest is it earning?" I asked.

"None," she admitted.

At the very least, everyone should have short-term funds in an interest-bearing account, such as a money market. Once a month, you would then write a check from the money market to your regular checkbook to pay your bills. Otherwise, let it earn interest. Money-market accounts are safe and good investments for your short-term cash and reserves.

Long-term, your money should be in residential real estate and stocks. Owning a home should be a major goal, if you do not already have one. Government agencies, such as Fannie Mae, Freddie Mac, and FHA, are making it easier to purchase a home of your own. We are not necessarily talking about great— or immediate—returns here. In fact, primary residences have averaged about 6-percent growth during the last twenty-five years. However, one of the great benefits, in addition to a home's security and relatively good returns, is the tax deduction. As of this writing, 100 percent of your mortgage interest, or roughly 95 percent of every payment in the early years of your loan, is tax deductible.

As for stocks, over time, they are likely to outperform most other investments. For example, during the last twenty years, large-cap stocks (the stocks of large companies that are well capitalized) gained an average rate of return of about 15 percent. The smaller companies did even a little bit better, although they carried more risk. Be a long-term thinker when it comes to your money.

Give Money Away and Watch It Come Back

Proverbs 11:24–25 tells us, "There is one who scatters, yet increases all the more, and there is one who withholds what is justly due, but it results only in want. The generous man will be prosperous, and he who waters will himself be watered."

I have seen it happen hundreds of times. There is a difference between frugality and hoarding. In fact, the law of reciprocity says that when you help others with money and/or services, you, too, will benefit. It should not be your motive to benefit except through personal fulfillment, but in many cases, you will have no choice. What goes around comes around. There is a reason that cliché has been around so long—it's true!

The church couple that has not been tithing 10 percent because they "do not have enough money" decides to adjust its lifestyle and give 10 per-cent of their income to their church. The Scriptures tell us that God loves this kind of cheerful giving and, in fact, says that if you give it all to God, He will open "the windows of heaven, and pour out for you a blessing until it overflows" (Mal. 3:10).

If you hold your money too tightly, it will slip through your fingers like sand.

The man who decides on Christmas to deliver ten dinners to people who are less privileged than he, benefits greatly. So does the software entrepreneur who donates $100 million toward the educational needs of our world's children.

There is a time where you will realize this reality: If you hold your money too tightly, it will slip through your fingers like sand. If you hold it loosely but intelligently, it will come back to you in ways you never imagined.

Chapter 26

Make Sense of Your Dollars

Have you ever made New Year's resolutions? Do you find yourself, like many, being "resolution challenged"? Are you on your fifth year of making the same resolutions about your money? Here is one man's story. In 1996, one of his New Year's resolutions was "Put more money in the bank." In 1997, it was "Kill all credit-card debt." In 1998, it was "Eliminate all credit-card debt." In 1999, it was "Reduce all credit-card debt." In 2000, it was "Use cash, not credit."

In seizing your personal financial freedom, you must progress to higher and higher levels of financial responsibility. I have yet to meet anyone who enjoys being in debt and living paycheck to paycheck. Yet when I evaluate how such folks use their money, it is clear that they are in the eye of the storm; *they* are the reason their external reality is wrapped in fear and uncertainty. They have not yet made sense with their money.

One of my favorite sayings is "The past does not equal the future." At least it doesn't have to. Yet habits are habits. The chains of habits are too weak to be felt until they are too strong to be broken. Common sense says, "Be responsible with your money." If that is true, then why are millions of people so irresponsible with it? Let me tell you the secret to personal financial freedom: Change your thoughts and beliefs

> **Change your thoughts and beliefs about money, and you will change the way you use it.**

about money, and you will change the way you use it. That's it. Sorry it's not more complicated than that. All breakthroughs toward financial freedom start with reinventing the way you think about money. Financial freedom is not about your bank account, your possessions, your freedom, the size of your house, or anything else. Those are the results of choices you are making or not making with your money. Financial freedom is when you make the mental shift that money can either be used or abused. Used appropriately, money creates pleasure and lifestyle. Used inappropriately, it brings on pain and frustration. Ultimately, it is your decision.

Are You in Need of a Financial Tune-Up?

It is time to come clean. Admitting that you are not all that responsible with your personal financial matters would be a large step toward your better fiscal health. To help you make progress, read the following questions and check the box if your answer is true:

- ❑ I say yes too often to easy credit-card offers.
- ❑ I am swayed by the enticements of advertising that stimulate my desire to buy more things.
- ❑ I try to keep up with the Joneses.
- ❑ I make spontaneous, last-minute purchases rather than plan ahead.
- ❑ I rely on fast food, restaurants, and coffeehouses, rather than making the same thing at home.
- ❑ I am not aware of whether my mortgage is the best one for me financially.
- ❑ I only save if there is money left over.
- ❑ Money and its availability typically stress me out.
- ❑ I spend money with the expectation that my income will go up or a commission will come in.
- ❑ I take cash advances on credit cards to pay off other cards or bills.
- ❑ I spend more than 20 percent of my take-home income on credit-card bills.
- ❑ I pay only the minimum balances on credit cards.
- ❑ I live without a budget.
- ❑ I collect cash from friends at restaurants and then put the bill on my card.
- ❑ I shop at the grocery store without a list or a budget.
- ❑ I often hide my purchases from my spouse.
- ❑ I have more than two credit cards.
- ❑ If I have a choice between cash or credit, I find it easier to opt for credit.

❑ I live paycheck to paycheck.
❑ I would like to stop this insanity.

How did you do? If you checked fewer than five of those questions, you are not in much financial danger. However, I still want you to consider why you have said yes to those five, and move to improve on them in the chapters to come. If you answered yes to between six and sixteen of the questions, you are living in the danger zone. It is time to draw up a budget, pay off your bills, and reevaluate your spending and lifestyle habits. If you answered yes to more than seventeen of the questions, you simply must stop, take a deep breath, and begin thinking more intelligently about your financial future. You would be wise to seek help from a financial planner or a credit counselor to draw up a recovery plan. Please do that as soon as possible—for your sanity and for your financial well-being.

Learn Your Lessons Only Once

It doesn't make sense to learn the same financial lessons more than once—unless you enjoy pain. As a child, I learned several powerful money-management techniques. I did not choose to live them all as I grew up, but I am happy to say that every one of them is in place today. I am especially grateful to my father and mother, mostly because of their role model behavior and the financial lessons they taught me early in life. You may have had the same experience. Perhaps you did not. The key is simply this: If you are not applying these lessons, start using them today.

Here are the lessons I learned from my parents:

- Spend less than you make.
- Don't buy it unless you can afford to pay cash for it (except for a home).
- Pay off your credit cards every month in full.
- Put at least 10 percent of every dollar into a savings account.
- Give at least 10 percent of every dollar you make back to God.

I thank my parents for these lessons. They have been part of my financial plan for years and have provided both financial and spiritual abundance for my family and me.

Chapter 27

It's a Matter of Interest

In later chapters, we will begin to discuss specific strategies to help you build your personal financial freedom. Before we do, however, you must understand a powerful factor in all investing—the power of compounding your interest. Compounding is one of the greatest secrets for building wealth, and it ranks as a serious motivator in getting your money to work for you. It makes no difference if you invest five cents or five dollars, the law of compounding interest works.

One of the greatest examples of compounding is found when Jesus prepared to speak to more than five thousand people and asked one of His disciples where to get the food to feed the crowd. Andrew told Jesus all they had were five barley loaves and two fish. Jesus told the people to sit down. And when He gave thanks for the food, He broke the loaves, gave them to the disciples, and all were fed. Wouldn't it be great if we could increase our personal investments in one day? Chances are it will not happen that quickly, but over time, you would be amazed at what will happen to your money.

The Principle in Action

Compound interest is the return generated by interest earned on both your money invested and the interest earned in previous times. It is *interest earning interest* and *profits making more profits*. Instead of removing the earnings on your investment, you leave them in and add them to your initial investment, thereby allowing your money to grow more quickly. If you keep adding the same amount, soon your earnings outpace your contribution. For example, if you invest five hundred dollars per month and earn 8 percent on it, this six-thousand-dollar annual investment will equal your interest earned in the ninth year.

That's right, six thousand dollars per year at 8 percent, and in the ninth year you will earn a few dollars less than that on the whole, about $5,994.

Here is an illustration, in simple terms, that demonstrates the power of this principle. Save one penny per day. Every day, add another penny. Let it compound daily for thirty days at 100 percent. At the end of one month, you will have $5,368,710.

Now you might be asking, "Isn't 100 percent an unrealistic rate of return?" Yes. But here's a question for you: "Isn't one penny per day an unrealistic investment?"

Choose Investments That Compound Daily

One of the distinctions you should be aware of is the difference between simple interest and compounding interest. Simple interest is calculated annually. Depending on the investments you choose, your interest can be compounded annually, semiannually, quarterly, monthly, weekly, or daily. Look at the chart below to see the effects of compounding:

Compounding Period	True Rate of Interest
Annually	5.000 percent
Semiannually	5.063 percent
Quarterly	5.095 percent
Monthly	5.116 percent
Weekly	5.125 percent
Daily	5.127 percent

Therefore, if you took ten thousand dollars, did not add any principal, and earned 8 percent simple interest for ten years, that investment would be worth $21,589. If you compound the interest daily your true rate of interest would be 8.328 percent and at the end of ten years, you would have $22,253. Compounding is the way to go.

Three Keys to Using the Principle of Compounding

Here are three keys to using the principle of compounding interest to your advantage as you build financial abundance.

Reinvest your dividends. Compounding has its greatest impact when you leave your earnings alone. Instead of taking your mutual fund's distribution in cash, instruct your fund to let those dollars remain in the account to purchase additional shares. Most mutual-fund companies will allow you to do this without paying an additional sales charge. Whenever and wherever possible, leave your investment earnings intact instead of taking them out.

Develop a regular investment strategy. Develop the habit of paying yourself first by using the automatic cash-allocation plan with your payroll deduction or by simply writing a check to "your

> **Compounding has its greatest impact when you leave your earnings alone.**

future" in the form of an investment. The more consistently you invest, the better. By investing consistently and regularly, you take advantage of a strategy called dollar-cost averaging. This strategy is the smart alternative to "lump-sum" investing or "fixed shares purchase." The goal is to buy the same dollar amount of stock monthly. Since the prices of the shares change, depending on whether they are up or down, you would buy more or less shares. Over time, this method generally allows you to accumulate more shares, on average. As the investment's performance improves, so does your value, because you have acquired more shares.

Let us say you made a one-time annual investment in a mutual fund of twelve hundred dollars in November when the shares were fifteen dollars. You received 80 shares. On the other hand, if you invested one hundred dollars per month, and over the year, the fund averaged eleven dollars per share, you would have received 109 shares. By investing this constant dollar amount monthly, you take advantage of the market's gyrations and lower your acquisition cost, which improves your returns.

Want to get started? Here's how. Select the company or fund you think you would like. (If you need help, see chapter 41, which lists some of the best Internet tools to help you with this decision.) Sign an authorization allowing the company to draw the money out each month. The rest is automatic. When you have reached your financial goal, you can stop the automatic process and allow the investment to go to work for you.

Make time work for you. The longer money can work for you, the better. That is why we push for starting early. The "Rule of 72" tells you how long it will take to double your investment, while the "Rule of 115" tells you how long it will take to triple it.

To find the number of years, simply divide 72 or 115 by the rate at which the investment is growing per year. If you know the number of years in which you would like your initial investment to double or triple, divide 72 or 115 by the number of years. This will give you the interest rate this investment must earn.

Thus, if an investment is growing at a rate of 6 percent a year, it will double in value in 12 years (72÷6=12). It will triple in 19.2 years (115÷6=19.2). Notice how much more quickly the original principal was earned the second time—only seven years instead of twelve. This is the power of compounding interest.

Since investments do not grow at steady rates, these rules should be used strictly as a guide in setting your long-term investment goals and strategies. Talk with your financial professional to determine the plan that is best for you.

Chapter 28

Pay Now; Play Later

I n chapter 24, I introduced you to the law of delayed gratification. In this chapter, I want to go much deeper into this subject.
I can say from personal experience that this is undoubtedly the
single biggest key to developing financial freedom. And it all starts
with the deepest core belief we have—our self-image.

How Much Is Enough?

If you once thought that a newer car, larger home, bulging
portfolio, or a new spouse would bring you lasting contentment
and came up short, then you know that *enough is never enough.*
According to *Fast Company* magazine, the answer seems to be
that there is no such thing as "enough." The more
people have, the more they want. Their research led
them to conclude that for high-income respondents
(those making more than one hundred thousand
dollars per year), the feeling is "the more money
people have, the more likely they were to view expensive cars,
bigger houses, and dinners at fancy restaurants as their just
deserts." At the other end of the financial spectrum (those making less than forty thousand dollars per year), people "agreed
that learning to live on less money, and stuff, is an important
factor in achieving balance in their lives."[1] Whether your income
is high or low, I believe the lower income thought process is the
true pathway to a life of riches.

There is no such thing as "enough."

The Law of Contentment

As you look at money, one of the big questions you should
ask yourself is, *Why?* Why do you want money in the first place?
If it is solely to be content, you are in trouble. Contentment is a

learned behavior. It does not happen when you have enough stuff. In the pursuit of *enough stuff,* your life will become increasingly complicated. A well-known first-century preacher once said, "I have learned to be content in whatever circumstances I am. I know how to get along with humble means, and I also know how to live in prosperity; in any and every circumstance I have learned the secret of being filled and going hungry, both of having abundance and suffering need" (Phil. 4:11–12). First century or twenty-first century—the truth of the message remains the same.

You need to be content for two reasons. First, contentment takes tremendous stress off your life. Second, and perhaps more important, the money you spend on the stuff you do not need can never be invested properly for your long-term fiscal health. The lack of this fiscal health ultimately can cause strain, stress, divorce, overeating, drinking, and in the worst-case scenario, suicide.

There is nothing wrong with making a lot of money. There is nothing wrong with having nice things. However, if the accumulation of things comes before the responsibility of delayed gratification, then you are adding years, perhaps decades, to that time when you will be financially free.

Lifestyles of the Wealthy

Wealthy people generally share four core strategies that allow them to arrive at their current level of prosperity. What do you think would happen to your financial picture if you were to follow their lead? Here is how the wealthy do it.

They are frugal, and they live below their means. Every person I know who is financially free has had an attitude of frugality. The wealthy realize that every dollar invested wisely will bring more happiness, security, and peace of mind in the future than any short-term pleasure they may receive from buying something they either do not need, or that is more than they actually need.

They have a plan, and they follow it. A solid financial plan is at the foundation of the fiscal strategy of the wealthy, and they are consistent in following their plan. They are diversified in their investments, with a mix that goes from the risk or growth side when they are younger, to the safe, "wealth-preservation" income side as they get older. Their plan is backed by solid estate and tax planning. Their insurance needs for today and the future are set in place as major priorities.

They are vocationally aligned. The wealthy love what they do. Whether they have done it for a lifetime and created wealth that way or are the new breed of Webpreneurs who have followed a dream and become instant multimillionaires, these wealthy people enjoy getting up every day and working. Their work ethic is solid, and they do not take shortcuts. They do what the masses have not fully committed to doing.

They are not trapped by social status. The wealthy own their homes and drive older cars. The poor rent and drive expensive cars. The world's average millionaires are rather simple people. They do not live in extravagant houses, drive ultraexpensive cars, buy overly expensive suits or clothes, wear abnormally large diamonds, or display their wealth on their sleeves. They refuse to fall into that trap.

One Man's Sad Story

In the end, you must love people and use money. You must become secure with yourself, your heart, and your motivations. If you display a hollow spirit, all the possessions in the world will not make you happy. In Section Three, we will talk in greater depth about how to obtain spiritual abundance. For now, however, take your lead from the following story:

> All he ever wanted in life was more. He wanted more money, so he parlayed inherited wealth into a billion-dollar pile of assets. He wanted more fame, so he broke into the Hollywood scene and soon became a filmmaker and star. He wanted more sensual pleasure, so he paid handsome sums to indulge his every sexual urge. He wanted more thrills, so he designed and piloted the world's fastest plane. He wanted more power, so he dealt political favors so skillfully that two U.S. presidents became his pawns. All he ever wanted was more—he was absolutely convinced that more would bring him true fulfillment. But history shows it differently. This is how

this man ended his life—emaciated, colorless, sunken chest, fingernails in grotesque, inches-long corkscrews, rotting black teeth, innumerable needle marks from his drug addiction.[2]

The man was Howard Hughes. He died believing the myth of more. He died a billionaire junkie. One more deal, one more billion, one more thrill would not have given him enough. Howard Hughes missed it. There is nothing wrong with goals, with being financially responsible, with wanting a nice car and a comfortable home for your family. However, if you feel they will provide ultimate contentment, none of these "good things" will ever be enough.

The pursuit of contentment usually pushes life out of balance. Balance is not something that happens over time. It is not something you suddenly enjoy when life settles down. The only time life settles down is when you decide to settle it down. There is a time for balance, and that time is now. *Balance is a priority problem.* It comes down to making a choice. You can have it if you want it.

Success and significance must never be linked to wealth, power, and more stuff. Success and significance are functions of excellence and fulfillment. True wealth is about who you are, not what you have.

Learn from the Best

Chapter 29

Building the Financial Plan

The statistics are overwhelming. You must initiate a workable plan, or you are likely to fail financially. You cannot build anything that will last without a plan. Here is why this is so critical. If you were to follow any one hundred people from age twenty-five to sixty-five, here, according to the Social Security Administration, is what you would find:

- Nineteen people will have died.
- Fifteen people will have incomes exceeding thirty thousand dollars.
- Sixty-six people will have incomes less than thirty thousand dollars.[1]

Here's a simple question: In which group would you rather be? If it is the middle group, which I suspect it is, then it is time to get serious about your financial planning.

The statistics above reflect the overall lack of knowledge most people have about the power of getting and using financial advice. In addition, most have not put the proper wills, trusts, and estate-planning documents in place to protect their estates from unnecessary and excessive taxes. All this advice has to come from someone. So the question is, Do you have a trusted advisor?

One of the most powerful books I have ever read on building wealth—and one I have already mentioned—is *The Richest Man in Babylon*. Contained within its covers are "The Five Laws of Gold." The third law is, "Gold clingeth to the protection of the cautious owner who invests and manages it under the advice of men wise in its handling."[2] This is the greatest time in more than one hundred years to be actively investing. The forecast for the future is good. Some forecasters speculate that the Dow Jones Industrial Average could rise to 20,000 by 2005. Maybe it will;

maybe it won't. Whatever the future holds for you, now is *not* the time to fail financially. Let me help you put a plan in place.

In this chapter, I will talk about the overall philosophy of investing. In chapter 36, I will give you a specific checklist on what to look for when selecting a financial planner. If you choose to go this path alone, then this and the next thirteen chapters are your framework for some of the most important decisions you will ever make in your life.

According to the Lincoln Financial Group, three of the top five reasons people fail financially are:

- They have no financial plan.
- They make poor investment choices.
- They procrastinate in starting a savings plan.[3]

Since there will be a time when you cannot work and, I am sorry to report, a time when you will die, it is paramount that you put and keep your financial house in order. A trusted advisor not only knows what he or she is doing, but also has the record of accomplishment to back it up. Such an advisor is also interested in you as a person. Your financial advisor knows your goals; he or she knows what is important to you now and in the future. Your advisor is your financial lighthouse, helping you to chart your course through what can be rough seas of financial planning.

Asset Allocation

You should follow some basic guidelines as you begin to think about the financial planning process. The essential idea is this: As your assets grow and as you get older, you build your foundation and then move from low-risk, to moderate-risk, to high-risk investments. During your wealth-building life, you will have different percentages of your portfolio in each of these categories, depending on your goals. You will probably be more aggressive in your earlier years; then as you approach retirement, you will become more conservative. Following are some of the general guidelines you should be aware of when building your plan and working with a financial advisor.

Age 16 to 30. Build your foundation. You should start a savings program, identify your long-term financial goals, train for a career that includes college, determine your life and disability insurance needs, protect belongings with automobile and personal property insurance, and consider opening an IRA or retirement plan to maximize tax-deferred income. You will be accumulating cash in low-risk investments, such as CDs and mutual funds. You should first have at least six months' reserves for expenses as your cash foundation and safety net, a small percentage in low-risk investments for short-term goals, and the balance in medium- to higher-risk investments for maximum growth.

Age 30 to 45. Your assets are starting to grow. If you have not yet done so, open an IRA or start a retirement plan. During this period, you will invest for capital growth, write a will, explore retirement goals, and, if you have children, add insurance to provide for a growing family, provide for expanding house needs, name a guardian for your children, and begin to build an education fund. Your investments will more than likely be in stocks and equity mutual funds. Your asset-allocation model, outside of cash, for long-term objectives would be 25 percent in low risk, 50 percent in moderate risk, and 25 percent in high risk.

Age 45 to 60. Your earning power is now at its peak. Your kids are out of the house or will soon be out (or you *wish* they were out!). You are beginning to shift from growth to income with your portfolio. You should diversify your investments, develop an estate plan, think seriously about retirement planning, review and revise your will as necessary, explore a living will—remembering to arrange for a power of attorney—reevaluate homeowner's, life, disability, and umbrella liability insurance policies, and consider deferred compensation plans with your employer. Your asset-allocation model, outside of cash, for long-term objectives would be 35 percent in low risk, 45 percent in moderate risk, and 20 percent in high risk.

Age 60 to 70. You should reevaluate your budget to meet retirement needs, reduce taxable estate, shift a portion of assets to income producing, and investigate part-time employment or volunteer work for retirement. Additionally, ensure that long-term care needs are met, put health insurance in place to supplement Medicare, review any will and trusts, convert group term life insurance. If applicable, consider plans for transitioning the family business. Update your living will and power of attorney, and share financial decisions with other family members. If you have children, investigate gift and insurance plans for children and grandchildren, explore charitable giving plans, and plan for shifting business interests, if applicable. Your asset-allocation model, outside of cash, would be 60 percent in low risk, 30 percent in moderate risk, and 10 percent in high risk.

The bottom-line goal of these objectives is long-term security. With asset allocation, you want to find the right mix of investments to give you the best overall return and that will be a reasonable hedge should your assumptions about what certain types of investments will do are wrong—or if the asset fails to perform as expected.

How Much Will You Need?

There are some rules about how much you will need to retire. Your primary goal is simply *don't run out of assets.* That is why the sections in this book that speak of frugality, delayed gratification, and respect for money are so important. It is very simple. You need to balance your enjoyment of life with responsible investing, which will allow you to live consistently at the level you have chosen. Sadly, many people live it up during their income-producing years and do not have enough to live on later. There are three basic sources your money is going to come from when you retire: Social Security, pension, and your personal investment portfolio. If those sources do not produce enough cash for you to live on, you will end up having to supplement your lack of money with a job. That's J.O.B.—Just Over Broke. Is that why you have been working so hard? As a rule, you will need 70 to 80 percent of your last year's salary during your first year of retirement. In your planning, decide the lifestyle dollar amount you will want when this occurs, try to factor in inflation, and then build the plan. If today you would be comfortable with fifty thousand dollars per year in your retirement years, and you are twenty years away from retiring, you need to do a few calculations. First, factor inflation at 3 percent. Then factor in your overall return on your investments, say 8 percent over the next twenty years. If you would like to retire in twenty years with an income of fifty thousand dollars per year, in today's dollars, you would need to save $1,904 per month, based on assumed inflation of 3 percent and a return of 8 percent.

Retirement Snapshots

Here are some of the most important things to consider as you build your retirement plan:

You will live longer than people did in the past, so plan accordingly. Your longevity will affect you in two ways. First, you will need more assets to produce income in your retirement years living to age eighty than if you lived only to seventy. Second, since Social Security was not built around the "live longer" model, it will not be as reliable in the future unless the government takes drastic measures.

You can be truly wealthy if you are consistent with the information you are learning.

Focus on building your retirement wealth. Use your 401(k), or if you work for a nonprofit organization, your 403(b). The rules of these plans all operate much the same, generally allowing up to 15 percent or ten thousand dollars for the 401(k) and 403(b) plans.

Supplement your retirement wealth with an automatic cash-allocation program. This is designed to put additional cash away every month into stocks, bonds, and other investment vehicles that are part of your asset-allocation plan.

All the above are fabrics of your financial future. Please do not end up being one of those alarming statistics who simply cannot make it and will be forced to work for the rest of their lives, whether they want to or not. The good news is that *you can be truly wealthy if you are consistent with the information you are learning*. Your assignment is to take the law of averages, bend it to your financial advantage, and enjoy your financial rewards.

Chapter 30

Who Says Plastic Is Fantastic?

More than 75 percent of Americans have at least one credit card. Credit-card companies know that merely putting a card into your hand will lead you to spend 34 percent more than you would without a credit card. Consumer credit outstanding in the United States has reached the unprecedented level of $1.23 trillion. Credit-card debt alone amounts to $528 billion of that total. How much of that debt is yours? Roughly two-thirds of Americans who have credit cards do not pay off their monthly balance. If you are making minimum payments on your credit-card balances, you are going through maximum pain—whether you realize it or not. If you cannot write a check right now to pay those balances off in full, there is a good chance you are having, or will have, problems building wealth.

For most people, one of the greatest challenges in building wealth is debt. Debt is like an anvil around your neck. The Scriptures say that if we owe money to a lender we become a slave (see Prov. 22:7). Again, history reveals clear patterns of misunderstanding that lead to misuse. Since money has no emotion, it could care less how much you pay for it. Credit cards and department-store charge cards carry the highest interest rates among all types of consumer credit. Since most of this debt is accumulated over time, it often seems insurmountable when the task of paying it off hits home. Most people with credit-card problems are living a lie. They would be wise to implement one of the steps from a Twelve-Step recovery program: Admit to the problem, come clean, and face the debt head-on. With the help of a higher power, of course.

Escape the Credit-Card Jungle

If you are weary of your balances never going down, and if you are abusive with this type of high-cost lending, your first mental shift must be long-term. You must figure out how the debt was created in the first place before you can begin to reduce the overall amount of what you owe. Here are five keys to escaping the credit-card jungle.

Make a list. You must know where you are before you start down this path. List all credit cards, department-store charge cards, and personal loan creditors, along with balances owed and the interest rates—the highest rate being on the top of your list.

Pick your number. Use the concept of *lifestyle adjustments* discussed in chapters 23 and 24 and decide the maximum dollar amount you can "pledge" to debt reduction each month. Stretch. Most people can adjust their lifestyles short-term to produce between one hundred and two hundred dollars per month in extra cash to focus on this process. If your monthly minimum payments total five hundred dollars, and you free up an extra two hundred dollars, you can now allocate a total of seven hundred dollars to debt reduction. How do you disburse it?

Accelerate your payments. Pay more than the minimum. Except for the highest-interest-rate card, pay your minimum balance plus an extra five, ten, or twenty dollars to the rest of the cards. Then allocate what is left over to the highest-rate card. If you have an extra two hundred dollars per month, and you paid a total of forty-five dollars extra on your other three cards, you will have one hundred and fifty-five dollars to pay to the highest-rate card. Continue this process until the highest-rate card is paid off and then start on the next-highest-rate card. The "plus" method is the only way to chip away faster at the total balance, assuming there is no other way to pay it off.

Here's what would happen if you paid the minimum, or more, every month on a $2,705 card balance, with an interest rate of 18.38 percent.

Payment Rate	Time to Pay Off	Interest Paid
2 percent of balance	27 years, 2 months	$11,047.00
4 percent of balance	8 years, 5 months	$2,707.00
8 percent of balance	2 years, 1 month	$94.00

Destroy all credit cards. When you are paying off a credit card, refuse to use it. If you must use a card, use the lowest-rate plastic in your possession. Cut up the high-rate card the moment you start accelerating your payments. If you have been following the first three steps, you are now beginning to enjoy financial momentum. Your resolve is higher than it was when you were staring at your debt mountain from the valley of pain below. Now, do the really big thing. Switch to a cash mentality. Here is how it works. Use only one low-interest, no-annual-fee credit card, decide on its preset limit, and *charge nothing* unless you have the cash equivalent to pay for it now—unless, of course, it is an emergency. Most important, *do not carry the card with you.*

Consider alternative options. If you cannot do the above, you have two other options. First, you can transfer your balance from a higher-interest-rate card to a lower-interest-rate card. When the transfer is completed, call the creditor on the higher-rate card, and close the account. The second option comes into play if you own a home and have equity in a line of credit. Most lenders today will finance 100 to 125 percent of your equity to take money out of your property. In addition to the benefit of a much lower interest rate, the interest is tax deductible. After you take out an equity line, close your high-interest-rate accounts. This may even be a condition the lender will give you as part of getting the loan.

Final Principles on Credit-Card Use

In addition to the five steps I have discussed, consider the following principles to help you reduce and, hopefully, eliminate your credit-card debt.

Determine how your credit-card company computes interest. You want a company that calculates interest based on your average daily balance rather than the less favorable two-month average daily balance. In the case of the latter, your interest expense can be more than 50 percent higher, even if you do not carry a balance from month to month.

Factor in the cost of interest on any items purchased on credit cards. Interest starts the moment you make the purchase, if you carry a balance.

Do not use a cash advance unless it is an emergency. Credit-card companies can charge a 2- to 3-percent fee for that advance, up to twenty dollars. Many do not charge a fee if you use the checks they send you periodically.

Do not pay annual fees. There are too many companies out there with no annual fee programs. Find them!

Remember that introductory rates will go up. Read the fine print before you ever accept a card, and scrutinize each bill for hidden charges.

If you need more help, contact Consumer Credit Counseling Service at www.nfcc.org, or call 1-800-388-2227 and check out www.consumercredit.com for a wealth of related information on this topic.

Chapter 31

The Ticker-Tape Parade

You have now made the commitment to build wealth. You have paid down or paid off your high-interest-rate debt by making lifestyle changes. You have also accelerated your payments and have started a cash-saving plan. The most probable next step you will take in implementing your plan is to begin investing in stocks or mutual funds. The stock market captures the screens of our televisions every day. The Dow goes up, NASDAQ goes down, new record gains are made, and new record losses are absorbed. The financial epicenters report the day's results with short- and long-term predictions, along with a difficult-to-understand explanation of what is happening. As confusing as this may be to the average investor, it is what makes the financial world go round.

One of the reasons for the compelling nature of stocks is their impressive history. For decades, stocks have consistently outperformed all other investments when looking at total return.

- The Standard and Poor's 500 Index, representing five hundred stocks that make up the bulk of the value of stocks traded on the NYSE, has seen an annualized return of 14.7 percent between 1978 and 1999.
- For the last ten years, the Dow Jones Industrial Average, the collective movement of thirty large-cap stocks, has produced an annualized return of 15.04 percent. For the last five years, the return has been 23.01 percent per year.
- The NASDAQ Composite Index, the average price of about five thousand stocks, which measures the newer, riskier stocks, has enjoyed an annualized return for the last ten years of 24.50 percent. For the last five years, the return has been 40.17 percent.

By contrast, U.S. Treasury bonds averaged 8.6 percent, and U.S. Treasury bills averaged 6.8 percent. During this same period, stock performance has nearly tripled the average annual rate of inflation during the last twenty years. Historically, it appears that stocks are the way to go. Forecasting their future also looks good. Right now, we are in the midst of one of the greatest economic periods in history. In the long run, stocks offer the best hope you have of making your money work toward building your ultimate wealth. How do you use this information to start building your plan? Maybe you should buy some stocks.

What Are Stocks?

Stocks are one of the primary tools a company uses to raise capital to fund growth and expansion. A share of stock represents ownership in the company, along with the right to share in the future financial performance of that organization, whether it is good or bad. The company's current and future earnings forecast determines how much a "share" of its stock is worth. If earnings are up and the forecast is good, the value of each share rises. If earnings are down and the forecast is not good, the value of each share declines. This is the cycle. Stocks do two things for you. First, they are the foundation for capital growth. Second, they help you set up a hedge against inflation. Generally, they are a safe parking place for your money.

What Kind of Stocks Should I Buy?

There are two types of stocks: growth and value. The first is stock in less mature companies, in which growth is driven by the sale of existing product. The second is in mature companies, in which growth is driven by both ongoing sales of current products and product expansion.

> **There are two types of stocks: growth and value.**

There are two ways to approach the purchase of stock in these companies. One is to choose a company and simply buy shares of its stock; the other is to buy shares in a mutual fund, where this individual stock may be pooled with other companies like the one you are interested in. For example, you could buy individual shares of Microsoft, or you could buy shares of a mutual fund that has shares of Microsoft as well as other companies. I will explain mutual funds further in the next chapter.

When Should I Sell?

Whether your stock is in a single company or a mutual fund, there are two basic ways to manage your portfolio. One method is the passive, low-risk approach, based on the theory that equity markets are efficient and well managed and that all information available is already factored into the stock's price. You now have a long-term plan, and if the growth on your money is equal to the average performance of that index, you are happy. This methodology is the safer way to go. Keep in mind, however, that although you may be a passive investor, if your stocks are in a mutual fund, the manager of that fund is going to take a more proactive approach.

The other method is active and has a higher risk. This means you believe that information not reflected in the current price of the stock will have a positive impact on the stock in the future. You seek out this information and make decisions accordingly, your goal being to outperform the average of that index. For example, although the Standard and Poor's 500 has averaged 14.7 percent during the last twenty years, there are stocks within that index that have done better, and others that have performed poorly. Active management means you are researching that sector, gaining knowledge about a particular company and its future growth plans, and buying more of that stock. If you choose to be actively involved in managing this process, your goal is to buy shares of stock in companies that are undervalued and to sell shares of stock in companies if they ever become overvalued. The lay investor who tries to "beat" the average generally doesn't. The experienced mutual fund manager has a far better chance of beating the average, which is why mutual funds are an excellent investment, as you will see in the next chapter.

If you don't need the money, don't sell.

I think the best approach is one that is blended, in which the crux of your financial plan is based on dollar-cost averaging. Have your asset-allocation model in place for this stage of your life, but designate a portion of your extra funds to go into your active "stock-watch" program. Doing this, you have the security of your plan working well, while at the same time you are enjoying the chase and the possible victory of picking a winner.

My overall rule: If you don't need the money, don't sell. Trust your financial advisor and your plan, and then let your money work for you.

Don't Panic; It Will Come Back

As you have seen so far, it is critical to select stocks that are part of your asset-allocation plan. If you need more low-risk stocks, buy them. If your plan calls for higher-risk stocks, get them. However, whatever you do, especially if you are managing your portfolio passively, do not panic. Here's why:

If you were to look at the S&P 500, in the last forty years or so, it has closed lower, measured year to year, only nine times. On Black Monday, October 19, 1987, the Dow Jones Industrial Average lost 508 points in one day. The previous Friday, it lost 100 points. In October of 1997, it had a one-day loss of 554 points. In fact, since that drop, there have been nine other large drops ranging from 2.2 percent to 22.6 percent. However, the market has proved its ability to come back to levels even higher in terms of gains than any of the losses.

Remember, contrarians are those who buy when others are selling, and they sell when others are buying. They look for companies with new management, new vision, and a new future that they believe are undervalued and then buy that company's stock, patiently waiting for the rest of the world to catch up.

Calculating Your Return

Ultimately, buying stock is all about hitting your goals. You may remember from Accounting 101 how to calculate your Return on Investment (ROI). If your memory has faded somewhat, here is the short course.

Growth investors buy an investment, a share of stock, for a

lower price, and then later sell that same share for a higher price. Their profit is the difference between the capital they used to buy the stock and the capital they receive when they sell. Their return is not found in the pure gain on the investment only, but also on the appreciation the investment delivered. With that in mind, consider this short illustration for a one-year return on a single stock:

Price at time of sale	$30.00
Price at time of purchase	$25.00
Appreciation	$ 5.00
Dividends	$ 1.00
Total Gain	$ 6.00
Total Profit/Purchase Price	$6.00/$25.00
Total Return	24 percent

Welcome to the heartbeat of investing. The stock market is an awesome medium for wealth building. Whether you take a buy-and-hold approach or actively play the market, stocks will go up and stocks will go down. Serious investors make a commitment to understand what they buy, reflect on how this meets their goals, review their overall plans yearly, and adjust holdings where necessary, using their asset-allocation models. Like stocks, mutual funds will also go up and down. Knowing how they work is an important ingredient to your accumulation of wealth, as we will see in the next chapter.

Chapter 32

The Fund Is Mutual

Mutual funds are exciting. There is perhaps no better investment vehicle for investors today than a well-run, well-managed mutual fund. The benefits are enormous, a few of which are:

- Entry costs as low as fifty dollars
- Liquidity
- Professional management
- Instant information and forecasting tools
- Limited speculation
- A wide variety of investment areas and diversification

What Is a Mutual Fund?

A mutual fund is really nothing more than an investment firm headed by a fund manager that sells shares to investors. The money from the investors is then used to buy different investments. The decisions on what to buy are generally made by the fund manager and, in some cases, may include a decision team managed by the fund manager.

Each mutual fund has a different goal and therefore invests in different products. Some of them invest for the short term, some for the long term, some for income, and some for both. Certain funds focus on overseas emerging markets, some focus on global markets, some focus on technology stocks, while others focus on energy stocks. Because of the buying power of a fund, it will typically buy more quantity than the average individual could ever afford. The pooled money has but one goal: *to make more money for the investor.*

> **A mutual fund is really nothing more than an investment firm headed by a fund manager that sells shares to investors.**

One of the primary differences between owning stock and owning mutual-fund shares is that you have total control over when you sell or buy more of a particular stock. With a mutual fund, you have no say in the matter. You rely solely on the expertise of the fund manager. If you have a financial planner, he or she will monitor your fund's performance and will advise you accordingly.

What Types of Funds Are There?

As with any investment, mutual funds also have risk. As part of your overall financial plan, you will need different percentages of your portfolio in different risk categories, depending on your age, your total assets, and your financial goals. Here is a comprehensive summary of the types of funds categorized by risk:

Low risk
- Money-market funds, both taxable and nontaxable
- U.S. government income funds
- Life-cycle funds

Low to medium risk
- Long-term municipal bond funds
- Corporate bond funds
- Bond funds
- Equity income funds
- Utilities funds
- Growth and income funds

Medium risk
- Flexible portfolio funds
- Global equity and bond funds
- International funds
- Aggressive growth funds
- Small company growth funds
- High-yield bond funds

High risk
- Precious metals/gold funds

- Option/income funds
- Natural resources funds

In addition, there are scores of other types of funds. Funds such as energy, environmental, sector funds, and socially focused objective funds. It can all become quickly confusing, so do your research. For a complete description of these funds, see chapter 41 on Internet tools. Again, your selection and distribution of funds will be driven by your personal asset-allocation model. As a rule of thumb, you should visualize your fund portfolio in four different classes.

The Top Ten Rules for Investing in Mutual Funds

Here are ten things you need to know before investing in mutual funds.

Reinvest all dividends and capital gains. By simply checking a box or calling the fund manager, all your dividends and capital gains can be reinvested. This is critical to compounding. It also enables you automatically to buy more shares of that fund.

Use an automatic purchase plan. By consistently investing a fixed dollar amount, say monthly, over time you can grow your portfolio more profitably through lower average acquisition cost. This is the program explained earlier, known as dollar-cost averaging.

Know the operating costs. *Operating costs* are generally the management fees and the advertising costs. Management fees are charged by every fund, and they range from .5 percent to 1 percent of the fund's assets. The activity of the management of a fund drives the frequency of buying and selling; therefore, these funds have higher fees. Passively managed funds, typically index funds, have lower fees. Some mutual funds charge an exchange fee when you move your investments from one fund to another within a family of funds. If you reinvest your capital and dividends, which is rule one, some funds will charge a reinvestment fee. Finally, virtually every fund assesses a fee to cover the costs of advertising and promotion, which is generally .5 percent.

A *front-end-load mutual fund* charges a commission as high as 8.5 percent when the shares of the fund are purchased. These are typically referred to as "A" shares.

A *rear- or back-end-load mutual fund* charges a surrender charge if you redeem the shares too soon after purchase. This is generally a fixed amount or a percentage of the value of shares at the time of sale. In some cases, this fee goes down each year to encourage long-term investment with the fund, generally starting at a 7 percent penalty and going down 1 percent per year. This may also be referred to as a "contingent deferred sales charge." These funds are typically referred to as "B" shares or as a "12b-1" fund.

A *no-load mutual fund* does not charge you a commission. Instead of a fee, these funds rely on performance, publicity, and commissioned brokers to sell the product. With the proper research, a no-load mutual fund is usually the way to go.

Read the statement of objectives. This statement gives the objectives of the fund. For example, it may say, "The objective of this fund is to achieve long-term secure growth through capital appreciation." This gives you a snapshot of whether this fund is right for your plan and long-term objectives.

Read the fund summary. Every mutual fund has a prospectus. Read it. By law, the prospectus must be updated once a year. It will also include a supplement called "Additional Information." You should request this supplement by calling the fund so you can be up to date on the securities held in the fund, which shareholders hold more than 5 percent of the fund, what the fund's financial statement looks like, who the key managers, directors, and officers are, and what their roles are in the fund.

Learn the fund's investment strategies. This is different from the statement of objectives. This tells you "how" the fund intends to achieve this statement of objective; it is the heart of the strategy and the policies of the fund that drive the decisions the fund manager makes. It could include risk level, investment grade on bonds, how much cash the fund holds, and maximum percentages of any one stock. It is the fund's "philosophy," and it should be close to your own.

Never buy a mutual fund on someone else's "hot" tip.

Understand the fund's risk. This is big. Never buy a mutual fund on someone else's "hot" tip. There are no shortcuts to establishing your financial future. You work hard for your money, and if you do not know the risk of a fund, you may as well go to the blackjack table and try your luck building your wealth in a smoke-filled casino. Every fund has risk, and the ultimate issue is the relationship between risk and payoff. Check it out, and seek professional advice before you get into any fund.

Know the fund's portfolio turnover ratio. The more active a fund, the more it buys and sells, and, therefore, the higher the cost of managing it. The overall expense of a fund's operating cost is important to you because it affects your net asset value (NAV). The more expensive the fund, which can also include the loads, the less your NAV.

Know the fund's distribution policy. There are simple things you must know, such as how frequently you will receive dividends; how often the dividends are declared; whether dividends, profits, and capital gains can be reinvested; and when, for how long, and whether you can change your options.

Profile the fund's investment advisor. Finally, know the person who makes the decisions. How long has he or she been doing this? How long has he or she been with this fund? What is his or her personal performance record of accomplishment during the past ten years, five years, last year? If advisor turnover is high, be careful.

As you begin to explore the world of mutual funds, gather as much knowledge as you can. There is a comprehensive menu from which to choose, and it is important that what you choose meets your objectives. Rule of thumb: If you are young, you want growth; if you are older, you want income to supplement your Social Security and individual pension plan.

Chapter 33

Fill It Up with Premium

Insurance should be a part of every financial plan. However, mention the word *insurance,* and many cringe. Despite everything you may feel about it, insurance is unavoidable. There will be a time when you will need life, health, and disability insurance. If you still have a bad taste in your mouth about buying insurance, perhaps it is because you once bought a policy you either did not need or paid too much for. In either case, your single bad experience should not close your mind to the importance of this critical part of your financial plan. This is why I recommend that you engage the services of a financial planner whom you trust to talk about insurance.

The policy you purchased may or may not have been prudent at the time. Further, the insurance salesperson may not have had a good idea of your financial plan or goals if, in fact, you had any. However, let the past be past, and move on to a more realistic view of your needs. The insurance you have *that you don't need* and the amount you will pay for a policy, *whether you need it or not* ultimately have bearing on your investments in general. Prudent investors have only the policies they need and pay competitive premiums for those polices. That is why for wealth building, you will need three kinds of insurance to protect you, your investments, and your estate: life, health, and disability.

What Is Insurance?

Before I give you specifics, here is a general overview of insurance. Insurance is a way to manage risk by spreading the costs of an expected future event over a large pool of people for an extended period. The premium payments from this pool, plus income derived from profit-making investments in stocks, bonds, real estate, and loans typically from thousands of insured, are used by the company to pay yearly operating costs, meet claim obligations filed by policyholders, build surplus funds to meet emergencies, and reinvest profits.

Six Important Questions to Ask before Buying Insurance

The insurance business is huge. The problem is that millions of people each year buy the wrong type of policy, buy too little or too much coverage, and do not recognize how deductibles or copays affect the policy. Often, in looking for the best deal, people end up with a firm that is financially unstable, which can lead to disastrous results if the unexpected actually happens and you don't have the right policy or company in place. Here are six questions you, your agent, and/or your financial planner should be asking:

- Does Standard and Poor's, Moody, A.M. Best, or Duff and Phelps rate the insurance company superior or higher (A+ or AA)? Never buy a policy from a company that does not have this rating from at least two of the above companies. They may not be around when you need them.
- What is the risk of the event the insurance may impact? Consider the risk and then arrive at a reasonable deductible. Coverage from the first dollar of loss is more expensive than insurance with deductibles or copays.
- Do I need this insurance now?
- If so, how much do I need?
- If there are different variations of this insurance, which type is best for me?
- How long will I need this insurance?

A Short Course in Life Insurance

Life insurance provides vital protection for you and your family and should be a major part of your wealth-building strategy. It affects your financial plan, your retirement, and your estate planning. There are essentially three types of life insurance: term, whole, and universal life. All other forms are variations of these types. A general rule is that if you have no dependents or no one who relies on you for income, you probably do not need any insurance at all. Otherwise, one of these types, or perhaps a combination, will be right for you.

Term policy. This type of insurance provides protection over a set number of years. At the end of that "term," the policy expires and protection ends. Usually, there is no cash value when the term ends, unlike whole-life insurance. Term insurance is usually the least expensive way to become insured, and in many cases can be converted to whole life at any time during the term of the policy. Term insurance can also be the most economical way for someone to get the kind of insurance that provides adequate protection for a family or for a single person to cover any debts or expenses in case of death.

> There are essentially three types of life insurance: term, whole, and universal life.

Whole-life policy. This type of policy provides protection for the lifetime of the buyer, and at the buyer's death the amount of the policy will be paid to a beneficiary. These policies are driven by two components: (1) the cost of providing the benefit on your death, which is funded by your premium payment, and (2) the excess amount of your premium payment, which is invested by the insurance company on your behalf and compounds over time. With every premium payment, the balance of this excess cash grows, and, if need be, you can borrow against it. When you reach a certain age, part of this cash balance will be used to keep your premiums level, even though the risk to the insurance company increases. If you outlive the time it takes to fund the death benefit in full, you can cash out the policy.

Universal. A universal policy is similar to whole-life insurance, but the premium payments can be flexible, and the cost of the death benefit is deducted from the cash value created by the premium. For more aggressive investors, you may consider using variable life products to better complement your long-term financial objectives. These policies can be complex, so please consult a financial advisor for more details.

Two more thoughts on life insurance. First, pay your premiums annually. This can save you as much as 8 to 10 percent. Second, review your policy every year to make sure your coverage type and amount are adequate.

The Health-Insurance Game

While the insurance industry is becoming increasingly bureaucratic, healthcare remains one of the most important types of insurance you can own. Most employed people have a health plan that is offered through their employer. The employer generally pays for the cost of the coverage and, depending on the arrangement, may cover add-ons. If you must provide your own health insurance, however, it quickly becomes a different game. In either case, the goal of health insurance is to obtain optimum care at an optimum price. Here are two keys to achieving maximum mileage from your health insurance:

Increase your deductible. For example, if under a typical policy you and your spouse were to increase your deductible from $250 to $1,000, your monthly premium would drop $116 per month, or $1,392 a year.

Manage overlapping coverage. Overlapping coverage occurs when two working spouses each have a policy and the provisions of those policies overlap or provide the same benefits. Most providers of these plans will coordinate the payout of benefits with one paying bills up to the limits of the policy, and the other picking up shortfalls. Therefore, you will not receive the same level of protection from the second provider, although you are paying the full premium. Compare the plans, restructure coverage, and go with the best.

Disability Insurance

One of the most overlooked insurance vehicles is disability insurance. Here's the test question: Could you survive today if you were not able to earn any income? If your answer is yes, how long could you live before your resources dried up? Until your assets are large enough to produce the revenue you need to live without working, disability insurance could be the most important insurance you will ever need. Here are some essential facts to review as you explore your disability insurance needs:

1. Fewer employers offer disability insurance than life insurance. If you are self-employed, you need to pursue this on your own.

2. It is more difficult to qualify for disability than for life insurance.
3. You will receive up to 50 to 75 percent of your monthly earned income before taxes and generally no more because the insurance company wants you back on the job.
4. You may have some disability insurance now through either Social Security or workers' comp. Go to the Social Security Web site to review your possible benefits. Know that workers' comp only provides benefits if you were disabled on the job. Neither of the above, however, will be nearly enough to give you what you will need to survive.
5. When selecting a policy:

   • Get the highest monthly benefits for which you can qualify.
   • Get "own occupation" coverage for life. "Any occupation" coverage can force you into a new line of work.
   • Get the shortest waiting period you can afford—generally a ninety-day period is sufficient.
   • Get coverage for the longest benefit period possible.

Disability insurance is vital for you and for your family. Without it, there could be enormous financial and emotional pressures, leading to unimaginable pain.

These three types of insurance are essential to your overall wealth-building plan. However, be sure you seek professional advice before making any of these decisions. Navigate the insurance waters with caution. Whatever you do, do not ignore the value of insurance simply because of a past bad experience. Financial advisors are very well educated in the area of insurance and will help you integrate your insurance needs into your overall financial plan.

Chapter 34

The Great American Dream . . . and the Mortgage That Comes with It

Your home is your most important financial asset. If you do not have one, it should be one of your primary goals. Buying a home for the first time is undeniably one of the most exciting things you will do in your lifetime. It can also be the most terrifying. In this chapter, I want to give you some keys to help you not only buy the right house, but also to demonstrate the role your mortgage must play in your overall financial plan.

The Dream

Whether you own your first home or are getting ready to "move up" to your second, third, or fourth home, there are some important strategies that when known and used will make a tremendous difference in the overall deal. For example, do you select a new home or a resale? What are the keys to negotiating the best deal? What type of mortgage should you select? Your real estate is part of your financial plan, and, although your home is a slow-growth investment, it can provide great financial and emotional security and stability for you and for your family.

Should I Buy a New Home or an Existing One?

This question has a lot to do with your personal, professional, and family goals. There are pros and cons to each, and it is up to you to decide what will work best for your long-term needs.

New homes. Developers have upgraded new homes substantially over the years. The competition among builders and developers to sell their homes is fierce, and therefore the way the homes are designed and the amenities offered have improved greatly.

However, the downside to a new home, in most cases, is twofold. First, during the past several years the lots have become increasingly smaller. Some developments sell homes so close to each other that you really can "reach out and touch someone." If you have a growing family and want a lot of elbowroom for your kids, a new home might not be your best option. One way developers are battling this issue is by building homes around central recreation areas strategically located within the development. The second downside to most new home developments today is quality. With the push for higher and higher profits, homes are being built faster and with poorer-quality raw materials, thus reducing the overall quality of the home. This will generally not affect the current homeowner as much as it will impact future buyers. Bottom line: New homes are simply not built like they used to be.

One other consideration in buying a new home is that roughly 5 to 15 percent of your purchase price will be needed if you want to landscape your new dwelling. This additional cost is often not factored into the purchase of a home by first-time buyers.

Existing homes. Buying an existing home makes sense for many people. In some cases, this may be a home that needs little work, if any. If this is the case, it is important only that your home meets the needs of your family and that it can be purchased for a fair and reasonable price, comparable with the prices of other houses sold within the surrounding neighborhood. If you can get the right deal on a "fixer-upper," you will enjoy the greatest amount of appreciation once it is fixed up, especially if you include some of your own labor. In either case, be sure you never buy an existing home without getting a thorough home inspection before signing your purchase contract or having the purchase contingent upon a satisfactory home-inspection report. Depending on how much information you want, these inspections can run from $150 to $1,500. As you make improvements to this type of home, get the information you need to see that you set yourself up to receive the greatest return when you sell it and that you don't inadvertently overimprove the property. "Economic Obsolescence," the term used by appraisers when a

> **Never buy an existing home without getting a thorough home inspection.**

property has been overimproved for an area, minimizes your improvement dollar. So be cautious. Whatever you buy, choose a home with maximum growth potential. In the last twenty-five years or so, homes have averaged an annual appreciation of 6.2 percent. Combine this with the enormous tax advantages a home offers, and you will discover it is difficult to beat a home as an investment.

Negotiate the Best Deal You Can

You do not need to be an expert negotiator to get a good deal on a home. Just be patient and follow these key rules:

Leave out the emotion. This is tough. The purchase of any home is highly emotional. However, the less emotion—and the more patience you demonstrate with the seller—the better deal you will probably get. Keep a poker face, and do not reveal your excitement.

Get preapproved. One of the best strategies to use while in negotiations is to be 100-percent approved for the mortgage you will likely need in the price range you are looking for before making any offers. This gives the seller the confidence of knowing that the deal is less likely to fall apart. In this case, you can often get a 2 to 6 percent reduction in the price of the home compared to someone else who might be interested but not yet approved.

Do your homework. Is the house being actively looked at by other prospects? Your agent will probably say yes, but do not be fooled by his or her salesmanship. Go slow. If you are interested in a property, tell your agent that you want to be notified if any other serious offers come in. Second, find out why the seller is selling. How motivated is he or she? How fast does he have to move? What additional concessions would she be willing to offer if you bought today? Get a comparative market analysis from your agent before you make your offer. This will tell you the value of the property relative to other homes in the area.

New home negotiation. This is quite a bit different from negotiating on existing homes. Generally speaking, there are a couple of ways to get a better deal when buying a new home. First, buying from "plan" can save you up to 10 percent. This means you do not need to see the finished model home before you sign a contract. Second, at the completion of a phase, you can buy the model, which usually has tens of thousands of dollars of upgrades that come with your home for a fraction of what it would cost for your own upgrades. Third, closeout deals of a subdivision are also good choices and can offer you even further savings. Finally, many builders today have their own mortgage company. If you use them, the builder might offer you additional discounts. Check them out and compare them to at least one other lender before using this option—especially when you factor in the information that follows.

The Mortgage for the Dream

Your mortgage is your largest debt. Most people who own homes are paying between 25 and 35 percent of their monthly paycheck toward their mortgage. Here is a question that about 95 percent of Americans who own homes fail to ask: *Am I treating my mortgage as part of my financial plan?* In other words, are you working for your mortgage, or is your mortgage working for you?

Your Mortgage Is Part of Your Financial Plan

The mortgage is the most critical aspect of the entire process. You should work with a mortgage professional who understands this. There are hundreds of options for mortgage financing today. There are thirty-year and fifteen-year fixed loans; there are one-, three-, five-, and ten-year adjustable-rate mortgages; there are loans that can negatively impact your equity; and there are loans and payment strategies that can positively impact your equity. You want a relationship with a mortgage professional in which your long- and short-term financial objectives are clearly understood so a mortgage can be designed to meet those objectives. You should find a "lender for life" who is interested in and capable of helping you *forever* with your real-estate financing needs. The best deal is not always the lowest rate. The best deal is the balanced package of rate, fees, points, term, prepayment options, adjustment periods, and loan index.

After You Are in Your Home

Millions of people are paying more interest than they should and are enduring higher rates than they should, all for longer periods than necessary. This can result in tens of thousands of dollars going to repay unnecessary interest rather than using the money as part of a financial plan. If you have never had a mortgage review, and if you are not sure your loan meets your overall financial objectives, here are some proven ways to help you close the gap.

Before you do anything, have a professional mortgage consultant conduct a mortgage review. Few lenders actually provide this no-cost process. The top professionals, however, do this annually for their clients as they lead them through a series of questions to help them determine if the present loan is best. The questions asked usually deal with long- and short-term financial goals, how long the person will be in the home, what the family dynamics will look like in the next one to ten years, and the nature of the person's real-estate goals. Such a conversation will be highly beneficial to you and will get you an overall lower cost for your mortgage. Keeping this conversation in mind, here are three important strategies for mortgage management:

Refinance for a lower payment or an overall lower cost. Which is more important to you, the *rate* or the *overall lowest cost* for the loan? If it is rate, there is a good chance you can lower it through a refinance. During the last eighty years, interest rates have been higher than 10 percent only 15 percent of the time. Depending on when you negotiated for your last mortgage, it may or may not make sense for you to refinance now.

On an ongoing basis, you should have a relationship with a lender who believes in keeping her clients for life. This means that she is interested in *always* working with you to help you with your real-estate lending needs. Part of her focus would include a "rate-watch" strategy, in which a target rate would be established when it would make sense for you to refinance. When the market closes in on that target rate, your lender would call you and let you know that it may be time to refinance.

Accelerate your payments. This strategy is one of the greatest financial management tools available to you. A home loan is still one of the most fiscally sound ways to borrow money. However, because of the size of the loan, many people still feel panicked at having a mortgage. If that is how you feel, work toward paying off your loan more quickly. Here's how. Pay one extra payment a year, or pay twenty-six biweekly payments instead of twelve monthly installments, or pay your thirty-year mortgage as if it were a fifteen-year loan. Pay a fifteen-year mortgage with a ten-year schedule, and pay your adjustable-rate mortgage as if it were a thirty-year or fifteen-year fixed. Although your equity will earn only the percentage of appreciation within your real-estate market, you will add great peace of mind.

If you are not in a state of panic, and if you anticipate stable employment for years to come, you can use this strategy to channel "additional payments" into your "mortgage balance account." This account is a secure monthly investment that pays you a safe 10 to 15 percent. You then let this build as your safeguard so that if you ever do panic, you can reduce your mortgage dramatically with one payment. With this strategy in place, you earn an interest rate differential of 3 to 7 percent. That is the advantage. The disadvantage is that your principal does not decrease as quickly, thus your interest payments remain higher for longer.

Pay your property taxes and insurance payments yourself. In many cases, your lender collects these yearly expenses each month from your mortgage payment. This means you do not earn interest on that money. Instead, tell your lender you want your payments to be *principal and interest only*. Then open a "taxes and insurance" account with a money market or CD rate, and make deposits into that account each month as you would to the lender. When you pay your real-estate tax and homeowner's insurance bill, draw from that account and keep the interest, which, depending on your real-estate taxes and insurance premiums, could be between $250 and $500 per year. With these overall savings, you and your family can experience more enjoyment in life and endure less overall financial stress.

Owning your own home is such a wonderful feeling! Having the mortgage managed to meet your financial goals makes the experience even that much better. If you don't own a home today, call a lender and see how easy it might be. If you are renting, there are more and more programs designed for you to be a homeowner too.

Chapter 35

School's Out Forever

The average cost of attending public colleges now exceeds ten thousand dollars per year. For private colleges and universities, it is a staggering twenty-five thousand dollars—or more—annually. The rest of the bad news is that the cost of a four-year college education climbs about 7 percent annually. If you have a son or a daughter who will soon be ready for college, do you have enough money? What about five, ten, or twenty years from now—will you have enough then? If you have a one-year-old right now, your cash requirement to send your boy or girl to college seventeen years from now will be a whopping $285,000.

If you question whether you want to provide a college education for your children, you need to know that according to census data, the average person with a bachelor's degree earns 73 percent more money during a lifetime than a person with only a high-school diploma. Economists tell us this gap is growing.

The average person with a bachelor's degree earns 73 percent more money during a lifetime than a person with only a high-school diploma.

In addition to the thrill of watching your children walk across the stage, the benefits of a college education are without measure: self-esteem, personal confidence, self-discipline, and the accumulation of knowledge—all things most parents want for their children. What a gift an education can be. Do not neglect preparing for graduation *today!*

My friend Barry Habib, a financial advisor featured on CNN, explains it like this:

> A mortgage affects a family's tax planning, investments, retirement planning, and can be a vehicle to fund a child's college education. Using a mortgage to tap into

the equity in your home can help in financial planning. A family with a three-year-old child may have concerns about how it will meet future college expenses. A family that draws equity from its home today and invests those dollars with the help of a financial expert should solve the problem. Historically, money invested in mutual funds has yielded an average return of 15 percent per year over periods of ten years or longer. This means that your investment should double every five years. An example of twenty thousand dollars invested today—when the child is age three—should double in five years to forty thousand dollars when the child is eight. This amount would grow to eighty thousand dollars during the next five years when the child has reached thirteen years of age. Finally, by the time the child is eighteen and ready for college, the total value of the fund should balloon to about one hundred and sixty thousand dollars. This return on investment ensures that the child will be able to have a solid college education.

Often, this type of cash out can be combined with a lower interest rate or debt consolidation plan that actually reduces the family's overall monthly payments while funding the college education plan. This type of scenario can also have favorable tax consequences since the interest paid on the mortgage is more than likely to be tax deductible.[1]

Tips on Funding a College Education

The earlier you start, the better. As with any investment, it is smart to begin with the end in mind. When you are pregnant, you know you are going to have a child who, in eighteen years, will be ready for college. This eighteen-year window gives you adequate time to get enough money going to cover the investment. If you wait too long to start a funding program, your monthly contributions will be higher, and you will not enjoy the full benefits of compounding interest.

Talk to your parents. Parents, yours and mine, today hold most of the nation's wealth. Certain gift allocations provide this growing segment of the population with substantial benefits when they help their children with their education.

Consider financial aid and scholarships. Financial aid and scholarships can be tremendous help in assisting with college expenses. In January 2000, the Free Application for Federal Student Aid (FAFSA) document became available and has become the base document for federal aid. For most schools, it is also now the starting point for institutional aid. The three best Web sites to research financial aid are www.fastweb.com, www.college-board.org, and www.finaid.org.

Consider a Roth IRA. A Roth IRA is better than an educational IRA, even though both are funded with your aftertax dollars. Here is a quick comparison:

Educational IRA	Roth IRA
Limit of $500 per year	Up to $2,000 per year
Penalty if money is not used by the time your youngest is 30	Withdraw contributions at any time without penalty or taxes
May not use federal tax credits	May use federal tax credits such as: The New Hope Scholarship The Lifetime Learning Credit

Your children's financial future starts today. Your job as a parent is to teach them the lessons of fiscal responsibility early in their lives and to prepare yourself and your children for the investment opportunity of a college education. Go for it.

Win with Wealth

Chapter 36

Selecting a Trusted Financial Advisor

At this point, you are probably aware that you must make some decisions about your financial planning. You may need to put one in place—something I recommend you do before you finish this chapter—or yours may simply need fine-tuning. In either case, a relationship with a trusted financial advisor could be one of the most important financial decisions you will ever make.

You may be asking yourself if you really need a trusted financial advisor. My advice is yes, you do, as long as he or she is a *trusted* financial advisor. There are many "advisors" in the marketplace who represent themselves as reliable, but who are not. That is why you must ask yourself two questions: (1) Does your intended advisor have your trust? and (2) Does he or she possess the knowledge, experience, and past performance to help you execute your financial plan?

> A relationship with a trusted financial advisor could be one of the most important financial decisions you will ever make.

Bear in mind that investing is not the same as gambling. Few people have extra money sitting around to gamble away. Yet, one of the biggest gambles is with people who fall into a relationship where the "advice" they receive on when to buy and sell comes from a person who is paid every time they buy and sell. It is this kind of commission-driven broker they infers that you are not smart enough to make your own investments.

The Financial Advisor Profile

Remember, people usually fail financially because they do not have a plan. To build wealth we need three things: (1) money to invest, (2) a plan to follow, and (3) sound advice on how to follow the plan. A trusted financial advisor can help in all three areas. We do not have the time to become the experts, and when we try, we invariably find it difficult to separate emotion from logic. There are thousands of investments and opportunities available, each with its own impact—good or bad—on your financial future. A trusted financial advisor can help remove the emotion and retain the logic, both essentials to serious, long-term wealth building. Harry Dent, in his book *The Roaring 2000s,* says that if only 20 percent of the professional money managers can beat the stock averages over time, it is highly unlikely that you or I ever will. I don't know about you, but it's enough of a challenge for me to stay focused on being my best as a husband, father, and business professional. I do not have the time to gain the expertise necessary to see that my family is secure financially. I need help. And, I would suggest, so do you.

> **People usually fail financially because they do not have a plan.**

If you needed a heart, lung, or brain operation, you would surely go to a trusted physician advisor. You certainly wouldn't do it yourself, and I'm sure you would go only to someone you could trust, and who had invested the long hours necessary to become an expert in that field. Yet, millions of people continue to put their "financial health" at risk by failing to seek the professional advice of a financial expert.

A financial expert is not someone who simply has done what she does for a certain length of time or who has expertise in only one area, such as insurance. A financial expert is someone who has comprehensive knowledge of her subject, a well-qualified team behind her, and who, in my opinion, is a Certified Financial Planner. To attain this level of expertise, she must study diligently and pass a series of exams that address all aspects of finance, including insurance, taxes, estate planning, risk management, and retirement planning. It generally takes years of study to pass this exam, not to mention the many hours of continuing education to make sure she stays up to date with current financial trends.

How Much Does a Trusted Advisor Cost?

Here are some statistics to help you see the value of hiring a trusted advisor. During a twenty-year period, funds and stocks managed by fee-based financial planners outperformed the same investment vehicle made by individual investors. For example, no-load mutual funds without an advisor returned 98 percent, while load funds recommended by advisors returned 114 percent. Fixed-income investment vehicles without an advisor returned 131 percent, while the same investment vehicle with an advisor recommendation returned 162 percent. It seems to me that if your investments do better with the right advisor than they would on your own, it would be worth something to have that guidance.

A trusted financial advisor is paid in four primary ways:

- Charging you a fee to do your plan
- Earning commissions when he or she implements your plan; when you buy insurance, stocks, bonds, and mutual funds, you pay a commission
- Hourly rate of fifty dollars to three hundred dollars per hour
- A percentage of your money managed, usually between 1 and 3 percent, which provides the additional incentive for your advisor to *grow your portfolio*

Beware of the "advisor" who provides free consultations; this is usually a lure to hook you for your money, and it is a marketing ploy that often portends a lack of confidence in the advisor's ability. It is also a hint that the relationship may become more transactional than relational.

What to Look for in a Financial Advisor

It's your money. How it is invested is your responsibility. When you select the right trusted financial advisor, you help guarantee a positive outcome. Let me suggest several things for you to look for in selecting such an advisor:

- A trusted financial advisor will always put your interests ahead of his or her own. Your trusted advisor should be more relational than transactional. Your trusted advisor will put people in front of profits and reputation ahead of revenue.

- A trusted financial advisor will encourage you to talk with their other clients before you sign on.
- A trusted financial advisor focuses on helping you close the gaps between where you are and where you want to be in every area of your life that is important to you.
- A trusted advisor will never do anything without requesting your permission or telling you in advance.
- A trusted financial advisor will be proactive, not reactive, always calling you before you need to call her.
- A trusted advisor will know your life's core values and align all actions to help you get more of what is important to you.
- A trusted financial advisor will prepare quarterly and annual reports and will meet with you regularly to show how you are doing and what changes you may need to make.
- A trusted financial advisor will do extensive research for you before recommending a course of action.
- A trusted financial advisor will be the liaison between you and the brokerage firm that holds your money.

You must be dogmatic about the advisor-selection process. Besides making the decision to build wealth, this could be the most important financial decision of your life.

What a Financial Advisor Should Know about You

You will know whether your relationship with a trusted financial advisor is beneficial to you largely based on how much time he or she spends with you before recommending a plan of action. Depending on the size of your estate, this initial meeting, along with the meeting where the plan is presented, should last between four and eight hours. Whether it happens in one sitting or over the first several weeks of the relationship is irrelevant. However, you must spend considerable—and unhurried—time upfront with your advisor. For this, there is no substitute. Your trusted financial advisor should know everything about you that may have *any* bearing on your financial plan. No secrets! You should respond to a thorough-going questionnaire that, at best, would be three to five pages long that goes into depth on the following issues:

- Personal information (address, phone, e-mail, Web site address, DOB, etc.)
- Spouse information
- Information on all dependents
- Sources of income
- All debt obligations and monthly expenses
- Details on locations of "parked" money (savings, CDs, money markets, etc.)
- Details on all real estate owned (mortgage balance, rate, payment, etc.)
- Details on all insurance policies owned (life, health, and disability)
- Vision of real-estate goals
- Vision of "retirement lifestyle"
- Vision of education for dependents
- Relationship between you and your parents on inheritance and general money matters
- Current status of wills and trusts
- All anticipated changes that may affect your financial plan

> **The more your trusted advisor asks you meaningful questions, the more convinced you can be that he or she has your best interests at heart.**

If a meeting with a trusted financial advisor prospect does not include *at least* these questions, tread carefully. The more meaningful questions your trusted advisor asks you, the more convinced you can be that he or she has your best interests at heart. A final note: Make sure that you shape the relationship expectations by setting up times for regular communication where you can inform your advisor how you perceive things are going. Do this as soon as possible, have fun, and watch your money grow.

If you still choose to go it alone, please go to chapter 41, "www—World Wide Wealth." I have provided an array of Web sites that you will want to navigate on your own, while still having the option of receiving electronic help from the experts.

Chapter 37

May the Financial Force Be with You

In the last fifteen chapters, you have heard me use two terms repeatedly: *asset allocation* and *dollar-cost averaging*. I have already offered brief explanations of the nature of each one of these investment principles. In this chapter, however, I want to give you more information on how you can use these two powerful investment principles for wealth building, and how each can help you work smarter and more efficiently with your trusted financial advisor.

The Force of Dollar-Cost Averaging

Let me repeat the simple definition of this powerful concept. According to *Money* magazine, dollar-cost averaging is the practice of continually investing a fixed dollar amount at regular and consistent intervals over a fixed period of time. The strategy is designed to reduce the average cost of the investment, since the investor buys more shares when the price is low, and fewer shares when the price is high.

Dollar-cost averaging will ensure that your out-of-pocket expenses are as low as possible. You can do this through your trusted financial advisor. In addition, many fund companies will also arrange to make automatic withdrawals from your checking or savings accounts to help you make regular purchases. Before you commit to this, however, make sure you know your budget numbers. A fund that requires an initial investment of $250 will most likely have a minimum subsequent purchase level of $50. In some cases, a fund will waive the minimums if you elect this automatic purchase plan.

The Force of Asset Allocation

A mutual fund generally has one of two objectives: growth or income. It will spread its capital among a wide variety of particular investments. If you are in that fund, then your investment is diversified, which helps to reduce risk. When you invest your money in several funds with different objectives, this diversification further reduces your risk. By being in three or four different funds, you have now effectively diversified into hundreds of investments. When you own many different funds, each with its own objective, you begin to form a personalized approach to building wealth. The continuation of this process over time, based on your goals, direction, and individual needs, is an investment strategy called asset allocation.

According to most financial planners, there are five basic investor profiles. If you fit one of these profiles, there is a recommended asset-allocation model for you to follow until your profile changes. The five basic profiles are:

- Aggressive growth
- Growth
- Growth and income
- Moderate growth income
- Income wtih capital preservation

Aggressive growth. This type of portfolio allocation is designed for the investor who has both a long-term vision of, generally, ten years or more, and some high risk tolerance toward market fluctuations. Receiving income now is not as important as building a portfolio for maximum growth. These types of investors are willing to accept market volatility while they aggressively pursue higher returns. Generally, the more risk tolerant they are, the more aggressive their allocation toward aggressive growth. They will likely focus on both small cap and large

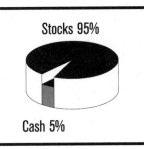

Stocks 95%

Cash 5%

cap companies with a promising future and some global and sector allocations. Their goal is to see their plan for retirement come to fruition.

Growth. This type of portfolio allocation is for long-term investors who are looking for strong growth and appreciation in their portfolios. Their time horizon is at least ten years, which means they are more interested in building future wealth than in receiving immediate income. They automatically reinvest all dividends and earnings. Their portfolio is aggressive and generally represents a family with anticipated future needs, such as their children's education and/or their own

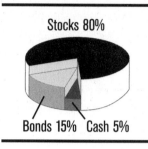

retirement. This profile suggests a higher tolerance for risk; therefore, their asset allocation would mean a larger portfolio percentage in small and large cap growth and global and sector funds, followed by a smaller percentage of fixed-income funds.

Growth and income. This type of portfolio allocation is for medium-term investors who are looking for capital appreciation and who do not need immediate income. Their time horizon is four to eight years. These individuals are willing to endure market fluctuations in exchange for modest but solid growth and capital appreciation. Most of their asset allocation would be in large cap blend or blue-chip stock funds followed by a smaller percentage of fixed-income funds. If this type of

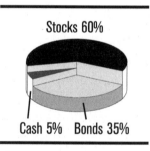

investor had more risk tolerance, he or she would add some small cap and global and sector funds. This profile most likely would be a family with needs, such as saving for a home or for a child's education.

Income with moderate growth. This type of portfolio allocation is for an investor who wants a strong, steady cash flow and some growth and appreciation. Because this investor will need this income flow within the next five years, he or she will take some modest risks in building the value of their portfolio. A

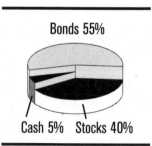

likely asset allocation of funds would be diversified bond funds with a moderate balance of some high-risk and low-risk stock funds.

Income with capital preservation. This type of portfolio diversification is for investors with immediate financial needs who have low tolerance for risk and market volatility. Their primary objective is to stabilize income; growth and appreciation are secondary. The time horizon—when the income will be needed—drives this investor and, therefore, does not follow the pattern of a "retirement" profile. It could also be a younger person who needs income for specific short-term

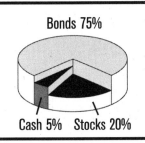

Bonds 75%

Cash 5%   Stocks 20%

goals, such as education or a business start-up. Their asset allocation will be mostly fixed-income funds, followed by a smaller percentage of stock funds and cash.

A Final Thought

As you can see, this investment strategy has much to do with your individual and family needs. The decisions on how to allocate your investment dollars should not be taken lightly. In choosing your investments, you will want to provide for possible adverse economic conditions by creating a diversified portfolio that gives you a comfortable rate of return, regardless of the market's gyrations. You will want to determine the right mix of stocks, bonds, and other investments to help you achieve your goals, while still providing the safety you seek.

As your goals and conditions change, so will your diversification strategies.

As your goals and conditions change, so will your diversification strategies. This allows you to achieve a maximum return on your investment dollars and to build true wealth.

Chapter 38

The Seven Habits of Acquiring True Wealth

A s you near the end of this section on building wealth, I want to help equip you for excellence as you start or continue your journey toward financial freedom. I hope you are excited about this, because there is so much opportunity available to you to live a richer and more rewarding life. In your pursuit of these worthy goals, one of your primary objectives should be *no money problems.*

In the health section, I introduced you to some research from *Fast Company* magazine. In the July/August 1999 issue, they asked their readers two questions: (1) "How much is enough?" and (2) "If money were not a problem, what would you do relative to your job?" What they discovered was startling but, from my perspective, predictable. Eighty-three percent said they would quit or reduce their time dramatically. While most people have to show up at a job, the pressures of money are not allowing them to work in the way they want to, where they want to, or within the time lines they would like to work.

Financial stress is one of the main reasons for marital or relationship problems. When money becomes the central issue, especially when it is couched in a negative environment, like not having enough of it, we often take out our frustrations on the people we love and care about. Let's get one thing clear: While money may not be of ultimate importance, it still ranks up there with oxygen in giving you life. With that in mind, let's look at seven habits that will help ease your financial pressures and allow you to do everything you have read up to now.

Develop a Positive Attitude about Money

Success with your money comes in "cans," not "cannots." Attitude is important when it comes to money. In fact, attitude is the driving force in your subconscious mind. Attitude shapes your self-talk and, ultimately, your financial reality. If you constantly say to yourself, "I'm broke; I'm broke," your subconscious mind hears these negative words and sets up your actions to be consistent with the message. If instead it hears, "I'm building wealth; I'm building wealth," it sets up your actions to become a wealth builder. The messages we send to our brains are heard as absolute truth, whether they are true or not. So, if you want to be wealthy, you must constantly engage in positive self-talk. I wonder what would happen, for example, if you repeatedly sent these messages to your fertile brain . . .

- I can save one hundred dollars per week.
- I can go out to dinner one less time per week.
- I can get by without a new car.
- I can tell what time it is with this old watch.
- I can live in this house another five years.
- I can start my own business and develop true freedom.
- I can; I can; I can.
- I am a financial success.
- I am achieving my ambitious goals day after day.

Develop a Written Plan

Dave Jensen of UCLA researched the people who attend the Peter Lowe Success Seminars. They included everyone from psychiatrists to truckdrivers, civil service workers to entrepreneurs, household executives to CEOs. He discovered that those with a balanced goals program earned more than twice as much money and were happier, healthier, and got along better with the folks at home. Here's why: People who know where they're going and have a plan of action to get there don't "sweat the small stuff." They have bigger objectives in mind.

If there is a "secret," it is this:

Without objectives we won't know what to do;

> Without deadlines we won't know when to do it;
> Without priorities we won't know what to do first.

Live below Your Means, and Live from a Budget

The opposite of the above headline can create tremendous financial pressure on any one of us. In fact, most wealth builders say that *living below your means and living from a budget* is the number one strategy for financial freedom. Their motto is "Spend less than you make, and know where you spend it."

Spend less than you make, and know where you spend it.

The only way you can be in the "black" instead of in the "red" is to determine your bottom-line profit. A business cannot stay in business forever if it continues to lose money month after month. Neither can you. However, you can stay emotionally healthy if every month you play the game "shuffle the payments." Here are two simple rules to doing this: First, write down where every dollar goes for one month. At the end of the month, determine how much you did not need to spend. Then the next month, don't spend it. Invest it.

Pay Yourself First

If you have ever been trapped in the nightmare of living paycheck to paycheck—where you pay everyone but yourself—you know how frustrating life can be. It can flatten your spirit, destroy your energy, produce negative stress, and, in some cases, push you to the edge. It doesn't have to be this way. The idea of "paying yourself first" is a way to develop the regular discipline of making your money make money for you.

Yet, people continue to tell me they can't do this because they do not have any money left over after they have paid all of their expenses. "But Todd," they tell me, "there's always too much month left over after my money runs out!" Please understand there are only two ways to change that sorry plight: Earn more or spend less. If you started an automatic investment program of fifty dollars per paycheck, you would be fifty dollars short in meeting your expenses. This only has to happen once or twice, if you are serious, before you begin to make some lifestyle adjustments to help free up that fifty dollars.

If you are already responsible with your finances, have no unnecessary expenses, and receive an IRS refund each year, fill out a new W-4. For every $2,000 in tax deductions to which you are entitled, add one additional allowance to the W-4. You may claim up to nine allowances before your employer is required to send a copy of the form to the IRS. As your allowances go up, so does your paycheck. Be responsible with this extra money and start your investment plan. Since your tax refund has been an interest-free loan to the IRS, it makes no sense to give the agency more money during the year than necessary.

Get to Know *The Richest Man in Babylon*

You are probably asking, "What is he saying?" You want to have more wealth, right? Then I encourage you to read *The Richest Man in Babylon* by George Clason—a book I have referred to already on several occasions. This 1955 book is a masterpiece that uses a series of parables about a fictional citizen of ancient Babylon. These stories explain the principles of building prosperity.

This book describes the seven cures for lean purses, the five laws of gold, and an effective strategy for getting out of debt. They work. I, along with millions of others, have used the principles in the book to build wealth, and so can you. This classic offers hope and good news to everyone who wants to build prosperity and live a life of abundance and fulfillment. The truth is this: Most people already have access to everything they will ever need to build great wealth. *The Richest Man in Babylon* will teach you how to harness it for your maximum benefit. Buy the book today!

Pay As Little Tax As Legally and Ethically Possible

There are three basic ways to lighten the federal tax bite, which can range from 15 percent up to 39.6 percent of your income. These are tax-free investments, tax-deferred investments, and tax credits.

Tax-free investments. These include government bonds, which give you a wide menu of diversity and a high level of safety. Some of these allow for federal tax relief, some for state, and some for both. Check with your trusted financial advisor for details.

Tax-deferred investments. These include U.S. savings bonds and growth stocks. As these investments grow, the equity, dividends, and profits are reinvested. You pay taxes only on their growth when you sell your shares.

Tax credits. A tax credit reduces your taxes one dollar for every one dollar of credit. This dollar-to-dollar pairing is ideal. This credit, offered by the government, is stimulated when it wants to see some form of social change take place: housing or city restoration, for example.

Don't Be a Gambler

If you gamble with your investments, you will probably never become a wealth builder. The similarity between the two is that they both have risk. It is risky to invest in a particular stock; it is also risky to put those funds on the blackjack table and tell the dealer to cut the cards. But there is also a difference between the two "strategies." When you invest, you are in command; when you give it to Las Vegas, you abdicate control to another human being and you cannot control the deck. When you gamble, your entire "invested" amount is at risk; when you invest, your principal is protected by your own watchful eye, and the eyes of your trusted advisor and fund manager.

Let your money work for you long-term.

Here is the rule that will favor most investors: *Let your money work for you long-term.* The gambler, the investor who jumps in and out of the market on the latest "counsel" from Uncle Charlie, the addicted day-trader who is always trying to time trades, or a "friend" who thinks wealth can be built in a day will invariably miss it without this rule. During the last twenty years, the S&P 500 stock index has averaged an annual return of more than 17.5 percent. From 1983 through 1999, the Dow Jones grew from 1,046 to more than 10,000. A one-hundred-thousand-dollar investment in S&P 500 stocks in 1973 would be worth more than three million dollars today. So, what will it be for you? Investments or the casino table? There *is* a difference.

The bottom line to this whole section is *start now.* The cost of waiting is far too high for most people. Procrastination is to prolong your arrival at a higher level of personal financial freedom. The word *procrastination* comes from the Latin and means "belonging to the morrow." To procrastinate, according to Webster, is "to put off doing something until a future time; especially to postpone habitually." If you have read this far, do yourself a favor. Do something in the next ten minutes to break through the self-imposed dam that has kept you in check for too long. Go to the bank, write a check, and open a new money-market account; find a financial planner; start an automatic investment program. Do something; do *anything* to move yourself from where you are to where you want to be. If you do not do this, tomorrow, you will be where you are today. Answer this question: If you stay with your current course of financial management, will you become wealthy? If the answer is no, then today is the day to make a change.

> **The cost of waiting is far too high for most people.**

Chapter 39

Don't Get Scammed

Financial scams and risky investments have been around for years. They prey on the young, the old, and on every age in between. In most cases, these schemes are lucrative for the seller because most people have a burning desire to be better off financially. Unfortunately, many buyers of these scams are caught off guard.

Sixty million Americans get suckered into some kind of scam every year. How much do they lose? About two hundred billion dollars. (That's seventy grand since you started reading this chapter.) Given the shrewdness of today's swindle professionals, chances are one of them has found his way to your doorstep—and perhaps to your wallet.

One of the largest scam platforms is in the area of money and investments. We are promised huge returns and guaranteed—yes sir, guaranteed!—to "get rich and be able to enjoy the good life" and to get "everything we deserve." However, the quick, easy money, the mega dollars, and the enormous guarantees never pan out, do they? Life is still a series of plays where we grind out most of our yardage on the ground. Successful "Hail Marys" are rare indeed.

Smart investors do not take the bait. They follow the rules of sound investing and avoid get-rich-quick products. If you have ever looked for the quick buck and found yourself victimized by such schemes, you ignored the most solid advice on building wealth: If it sounds too good to be true, then it is probably too good to be true.

As the song goes, you work hard for your money. Does it not make sense, then, that you should work equally hard to keep it? There are no shortcuts to fiscal security. Financial success comes through hard work and smart investing, just as toned muscles and lean bodies are the result of proper exercise and intelligent eating. Both require a commitment to regular disciplines, carried out for an extended time.

Here is some reliable ancient wisdom: "The plans of the diligent lead to profit as surely as haste leads to poverty" (Prov. 21:5 NIV). Nothing worthwhile that lasts comes easy. The key to wealth acceleration is wealth preservation.

Four Keys for Not Getting Suckered

To avoid being victimized by financial swindlers, beware of the following four popular scams:

Direct telephone offers. Many so-called "hot tips" come via the telephone from "boiler rooms" of hundreds of well-scripted telethieves. These operations take billions of dollars every year from people through a compelling display of "buy-now" emotion. These scammers build your enthusiasm, lift your hopes, and encourage you to believe that this could be your ticket out of financial misery. They generally inflate the product's performance capability or value and often offer investments that are nonexistent. They come in the forms of "you have won," "priceless coins," "free property," "hot stocks," etc. The best policy on any telephone offer is "No, thank you," unless, of course, you know and trust the caller. If they ask for money, hang up.

> **If they ask for money, hang up.**

Mass financial mailings. The direct-mail financial business is hot, and the folks who run these frauds play the odds game; odds are that enough people will respond to make it a profitable venture for the scam artist. Some of the products may be legitimate and worth the investment, but most can be dangerous. Blind letters, envelopes that tell you to "open at once," and the piece of mail that looks like a check, all can be bait that takes you down. If you ever get anything you feel you may want to purchase through the mail, check out the source. Better yet, call the Better Business Bureau, request a prospectus, or place a call to the organization.

Magazine or newspaper ads. Anything you read that asks for a decision based on what is in print could be dangerous. Generally speaking, a print ad should convey detailed information, state clearly that there is no obligation, and ask you simply to call if you are interested in a conversation with a consultant. Any ad that asks for money upfront or has a processing or application fee is probably a fraud, and you should not fall for it.

E-scams and Internet sales offers. Never invest money in anything based solely on an Internet solicitation. Demand the sales litera-ture, a prospectus, and a phone number for you to return the call. If you have used the Internet previously and you have signed up for one of these "offers," chances are good you are now on a "hot" list. The provider of anything suspicious—gambling, pornogra-phy, or scam-based investing—wants you back. Bite once on one site, and before you know it, your e-mail is passed to other scammers and you will be inundated with other dubious offers.

> **Never invest money in anything based solely on an Internet solicitation.**

General Thoughts

Inherent within all scams is the procurement of your credit-card number by professional scam artists. They either wish to sell you something, or they want to use your number to verify you are who you say you are. These scammers range from unknown sources posing to be everything from your "bank" to a representative of some "hot investment" to the newest diet in town—guaranteed, of course, to help you shed thirty pounds in as many days. These thieves are smooth, quick, and persuasive, and they rip us off by the billions. While this might be some-what different since the scam artist is pursuing you, the "hooks" are generally the same: wealth and health.

A general rule to help avoid being scammed is simply *go slow.* Even if the deal looks and sounds good, never give your credit-card number, e-mail address, or private financial data to anyone who calls you. Ask the caller for his or her number and tell them you will call them back—at home! (That's an old *Seinfeld* ploy.) If it is a scam, the person on the other end of the line will prob-ably hang up. If they are legitimate, they will give you their number. However, that still does not guarantee the performance or quality of what you may be buying. In the end, the caveat "let the buyer beware" holds true.

Chapter 40

Bullets from Buffet

Here are some of his company's holdings and value as of December 1999:

Shares	Company	Approximate Market Value
50,536,000	American Express	$7.9 billion
200,000,000	Coca-Cola	$13.6 billion
60,298,000	FHLMC	$2.9 billion
96,000,000	Gillette Co.	$4.2 billion
1,727,765	The Washington Post	$418 million
63,500,000	Wells Fargo & Co.	$3.1 billion

The man is Warren Buffet, the great contrarian investor who has racked up billions of dollars in personal wealth and created billions more for others by following a simple philosophy: Think long-term, buy businesses you understand, don't overdiversify, and compound your interest. If you were around in 1956 and had invested only ten thousand dollars with this man, you would be worth more than eighty million dollars today. Here is his sage advice.

Think Long-Term

Take your time. Don't get caught up in the emotion of building wealth. Forget about the daily fluctuations, and simply understand that up and down are okay. If the business in which you are investing is likely to be around for a long time, fiscally sound, and run well, then buy it and let it fly. You, of course, will want to follow its progress, so pay attention to its average fifty- and two-hundred-day trends so you will know when to buy more. Read the annual report, and pay attention to its future leadership decisions.

Understand What You Are Buying

Take a while to decide what to invest in. Check the company out carefully. If it has stores, visit them and experience the "culture" of the company. If it has products, buy them, use them, and see if you like them. Do your homework and study as much print information as you can. One of the great resources for this is www.jagnotes.com—a highly informative Web site to help you look at a company before you buy its product.

Don't Overdiversify

Take an appropriate asset-allocation path. Unless you trust completely the advice from others, get as much knowledge as possible about a few industries or companies rather than end up with too little knowledge about many companies. This is the "more-from-less" philosophy—the kind of thinking that will serve the average wealth-building investor well.

Compound Your Interest

The only time Buffet allowed his company, Berkshire Hathaway, to pay a dividend was more than thirty years ago. Buffet would rather reinvest the money and let the miracle of compounding interest work to his and his shareholders' advantage. I am assuming you are now clear on the power of compounding and understand that it will work to your advantage. Every dime you spend, on anything, anywhere, is a dime *you will not have in your possession* to compound during your lifetime.

> **Every dime you spend, on anything, anywhere, is a dime you will not have in your possession to compound during your lifetime.**

Bullets from Buffet

Here are some of Warren Buffet's best ideas on wealth building. As you get your financial plan off the ground, this sound advice from the man from Berkshire Hathaway could be most instrumental in your wealth-building efforts.

On borrowing. "It's a very sad thing. You can have somebody whose aggregate performance is terrific, but if they have a weakness—maybe it's with alcohol, maybe it's susceptibility to taking a little easy money—it's the weak link that snaps you. And frequently, in the financial markets, the weak link is borrowed money."

On market predictions. "I have never met a man who could forecast the market."

On choosing investments. "It's like when you marry a girl. Is it her eyes? Her personality? It's a whole bunch of things you can't separate."

On why Coca-Cola is a great investment. "Coke is exactly the kind of company I like. I like products I can understand. I don't know what a transistor is, but I appreciate the contents of a Coke can. . . . Berkshire Hathaway's purchase of stock in the Coca-Cola company was the ultimate case of me putting my money where my mouth was."

On debt. "If you are smart, you don't need debt. If you are dumb, it's poisonous."

On when to buy shares. "A great investment opportunity occurs when a marvelous business encounters a onetime huge but solvable problem."

On credit-card debt. "Nobody's ever gotten rich in this world getting money for 18 to 20 percent."

On predicting markets. "The fact that people will be full of greed, fear, or folly is predictable. The sequence is not predictable."

On why he bought Gillette shares. "It's pleasant to go to bed every night knowing there are 2.5 billion males in the world who will have to shave in the morning."[1]

Even though it may seem like today's investment environment is incredibly fast paced, with Internet IPOs and wild trading days, Buffet's strategies have stood the test of time. In fact, one of the persons from whom Warren Buffet learned how to invest was Benjamin Graham, author of *The Intelligent Investor.* Graham was brilliant at understanding a company's basic value and knowing when to buy shares in that company, below what those shares were worth. The two were partners for many years until Graham retired. Warren then started his own firm and today is one of the wealthiest men in the world. Under his leadership, a single share of Berkshire Hathaway stock soared to more than thirty-eight thousand dollars. His advice is sound—follow it.

www–World Wide Wealth

As you are no doubt aware, the World Wide Web is here to stay. The Web is a phenomenal tool for just about anything. In fact, the Internet is a faster and more efficient way to gain information on areas of importance to you than any other research vehicle in the world. Four people, plus myself, researched this book primarily on the Internet in only five days. The world is at your fingertips, and while access to important information is a positive reality, too much information can produce a negative future. If in the area of building wealth you still want to go it alone, here are some of the top Web sites I have found that you can use for virtually any financial needs you may have.[1] You, of course, will have to decide how to use the information contained herein.

SUPERSITES
Yahoo Finance   www.finance.yahoo.com
MSN MoneyCentral   www.moneycentral.com
Quicken.com   www.quicken.com

INVESTING SITES
Directories
Superstar Investor   www.superstarinvestor.com
Dow Jones   www.businessdirectory.dowjones.com

Financial News
CBS MarketWatch   www.marketwatch.com
CNNFN   www.cnnfn.com

Stock Quotes and Research
Yahoo Finance   www.finance.yahoo.com
MSN MoneyCentral   www.moneycentral.com/investor
10K Wizard   www.10kwizard.com

Portfolio Tracking and Analysis

CNBC.com	www.cnbc.com
Quicken.com	www.quicken.com

Mutual Funds

Morningstar.com	www.morningstar.com
Fund Alarm	www.fundalarm.com

Screening Tools

MSN Investment finder	www.moneycentral.com/investor
Quicken Stock Search	www.quicken.com/investments

Charts

MSN MoneyCentral	www.moneycentral.com/investor
Bigcharts	www.bigcharts.com

On-Line Brokerages

Charles Schwab	www.schwab.com
National Discount Brokers	www.ndb.com
Datek Online	www.datek.com

Bonds

Investing in Bonds	www.investinginbonds.com
E-Trade Bond Center	www.etrade.com

Miscellaneous

Jagnotes	www.jagnotes.com
Bridge.com	www.bridge.com
Netstock Direct	www.netstockdirect.com
Investtools	www.investtools.com

SAVING AND SPENDING

Banking

Wingspan.com	www.wingspan.com
Bankrate.com	www.bankrate.com

Credit Cards

Nextcard	www.nextcard.com
Cardweb	www.cardweb.com

Taxes

MSN MoneyCentral	www.msnmoneycentral.com/tax/home.asp
Fairmark Press Tax Guide	www.fairmark.com

Calculators
Financenter   www.financenter.com
Lincoln Financial Group   www.lfg.com

Retirement Planning
American Express   www.americanexpress.com/401k
Thirdage   www.thirdage.com
Lincoln Financial Group   www.lfg.com

Insurance
Insweb   www.insweb.com
Quicken Insurance   www.quickeninsurance.com
Insure.com   www.insure.com
Lincoln Financial Group   www.lfg.com

Homebuying
Realtor.com   www.realtor.com
Owners.com   www.owners.com
Yahoo Real Estate   www.realestate.yahoo.com

Mortgages[2]
E-Loan   www.eloan.com
I Own   www.iown.com

Chapter 42

Someone Asked Malcolm Forbes

The late Malcolm Forbes, editor and chairman of *Forbes* magazine, the American business journal founded in 1917, was the overgrown boy of the boardroom, a playful leader of the establishment who took up riding a Harley-Davidson at age forty-eight. A war hero and political candidate who collected Fabergé eggs, he was a friend of presidents, prime ministers, and Elizabeth Taylor. Interesting mix! During his lifetime, he amassed an immense fortune and held a specific attitude toward what it means to become rich.

Forbes on Real Fortune

Here are some real truths on true wealth shared with the world from this great man:

- "Meaningful truths are never newly discovered; they're just uncovered anew."
- "Sometimes doing what's expected is more effective than doing the unexpected."
- "The hardest work of all—doing nothing."
- "It's always worthwhile to make others aware of their worth."
- "In the long run, a shortcut seldom is."
- "If you want understanding, try giving some."[1]

Bulging portfolios of wealth are effective only to the point of personal security. The greatest joy comes when you use wealth to minimize the sadness and pain that surround you. If amassing wealth becomes all consuming, it can filter out the satisfaction that comes from touching the lives of others. You will never be a complete success as a human being if you determine to keep your wealth to yourself. If you need a quick start in this area of phi-lanthropy, here are some ideas to help you ignite that passion.

Have you ever been asked a question that stopped you in your tracks, such as "How much is enough?" or "When you die, how much money do you intend to leave behind?" I don't know your answer to the first question, but here is how Malcolm Forbes answered the second one: "All of it."

Listen to this commentary from Suze Orman, best-selling author of *Nine Steps to Financial Freedom:*

> Money flows through our lives just like water—at times plentiful, at times a trickle. I believe that each one of us is, in effect, a glass, in that we can hold only so much; after that, the water—or money—just goes down the drain. Some of us are larger glasses, some of us smaller, but we all have the capacity to receive plenty more than we need if we allow it.[2]

The Bible teaches this principle throughout its pages, and it is best represented by what is known as the *law of sowing and reaping.* Here are some examples that should encourage us to see a world that is beyond ourselves:

- "The generous soul will be made rich, and he who waters will also be watered himself" (Prov. 11:25 NKJV).
- "It is more blessed to give than to receive" (Acts 20:35 NKJV).
- "Do not be deceived . . . for whatever a mans sows, that he will also reap" (Gal. 6:7 NKJV).

My friend and mentor Zig Ziglar says, "You can have every-thing in life you want if you will just help enough other people get what they want." This principle, based on the Golden Rule, is as reliable as the law of gravity. Squeeze your money and, like a handful of sand, it slips through your hands; share it with others, and your abundance multiplies.

How much you earn is not important. How much you give is. Surprisingly, a recent government survey stated that those earn-ing less than ten thousand dollars give away 5.5 percent of their income to charitable causes, while those earning more than five hundred thousand dollars give less than 3 percent.[3]

Here are a few questions that may prompt your thinking on how to let go of some dough:

- How can I give more of the money God has blessed me with to my church, synagogue, or other place of worship?
- On whom can I bestow my money so that it makes the greatest difference?
- What charitable organizations have the kinds of goals and objectives that are in sync with my own?
- What could I do today to give something away that would fill a void in another's life?

While everyone knows that money cannot buy happiness, it *can* buy a sense of peace, security, and comfort, and it can also help buy it for those less fortunate than you. If you want to feel good, *use your wealth to make others feel good.* It is a profound way to live your life.

Final Thoughts on Wealth Building

You can have it all—a portfolio, security, and a large future income, all while you are leaving your own legacy. All you need is the plan, and I encourage you to begin one today. It is my hope that your life has already been impacted by the six steps we have addressed so far in this book. I also hope there have been a few special steps that are already moving you to action. If that is the case, I encourage you to send me an e-mail today and let me know of your progress. Write me at tdg@toddduncan.com. I will return the favor.

If you want to feel good, use your wealth to make others feel good.

Remember, the successful person who attains true, long-lasting significance and abundance does not focus only on being physically and financially fit. Such a person also works to become spiritually fit, sensitive to life, to people, and to the world that surrounds him. When these three dynamic elements work together, people begin to live richer, fuller lives. Is that what you want? If so, then let's go!

Part
Three

Spiritual
Abundance

Breathe Life into Your Relationships

Chapter 43

Making Time for What Counts

ere is something you already know. However, it is so important, I am going to remind you of it upfront: *One of the greatest ways to start your journey to spiritual mastery is through the art of time usage.* How good are you at time management? Do you honor your commitments to your family, friends, and associates? Are you organized to deliver on what you promise to others and what you promise to yourself? When you say to those around you, "You can count on me," can they? Are you able to look in the mirror at night and say, "I used my time to the fullest today"? If you struggle with managing the greatest resource you own—time—it is possible that one of the things taking a backseat to other "urgencies" of life is doing what is important.

> One of the greatest ways to start your journey to spiritual mastery is through the art of time usage.

Time Management Is a Waste of Time

For most people, time management is like raking water: lots of activity and no results. We are limited not by time, but by how we use the time we have. Time management is life management. Time management is values management. Time management is event control. You and I will never be clever enough to control our time, but we *can* choose the events with which we *fill* our time. If there is not enough time at our disposal, it is because we are failing in our priorities and our focus. To change course, we must focus on our productivity. To develop spiritual abundance, our productivity must be based on priorities that will lead to productive behavior.

Life-Productive Behavior

I love the idea of *life-productive behavior*—the art of making time for what counts. It is ordering your life so that what is most meaningful, that which feeds your spirit, gets accomplished intentionally. One of the heartbeats of this spiritual completeness is feeding the relationships that are most important to you.

Here are some steps to help you in your journey toward spiritual abundance.

Clarify your values. If you don't know what's important to you, you will spend time doing what's not. To know what is important to you, and to commit to those things as a priority, is to create the environment for a more effective use of your time. When your activities align with what is significant to you, you will find inner peace. High levels of inner peace reduce stress; they calm you throughout your day. We all need to have a full grasp of those things that mean the most to us. I suggest that we spend at least fifteen minutes a day—in one sitting—to see how we can discover fulfillment in either one or all of those areas. Roy Disney said, "When values are clear, decisions are easy."[1] The decision on what to do with your time should be an easy one *if you are clear on your values and if you spend time reviewing them on a daily basis*. Once your value areas are clear, you can then move from behavior to habit.

> **When values are clear, decisions are easy.**

Block the time. Managing time is deciding in advance what your day will look like and then disciplining yourself to live accordingly with the time allotted. Managing time is not Post-it notes, scribbled "to-do" checklists, or even those things backed by electronic gadgetry such as a PalmPilot or other organizers. *Time blocks* are planned segments of time that help you complete your most important predetermined activities. In the context of this chapter and this book, there would be blocks of time for physical, financial, and spiritual abundance. Within the latter, you would allot time for your most important relationships, which would include time for you to connect with God. Because your activities are "life events" and each event is linked to what you value, not only will you develop a clearer, less cluttered schedule, but you will also enjoy increased levels of motivation to *do* the events. Schedule your priorities rather than merely prioritizing your schedule.

Form the habits. Why aren't people as productive as they might be? Mostly because they miss the connection between "trying" to be productive and "committing" to be productive. There *is* a difference. Habits are formed only when the attempted behavior becomes permanent.

Be proactive. The only alternative available is to be reactive. People who move toward more productive lives do not wait for life to come to them. They go out and make it happen. The Scriptures tell us that "faith without works is dead" (James 2:26). You can hope for as long as you like that life will get better. However, unless you do something to back your greatest hopes, not much will change. Change must come from within. Here's a great question: If you continue on the path you are now on, will your life take you to the level of your dreams?

> **If you continue on the path you are now on, will your life take you to the level of your dreams?**

Start at the end. My friend Dan Trinidad carries out an interesting exercise each year. He stops long enough to answer these questions: "What will my life look like when I am eighty? What will I have accomplished? How will I have affected those most important to me: my wife, my children, and their children?" So my question to you is, Do you know what your life will look like when it is over? Have you spent time starting at the finish line and working backward to see how you will have run the race?

Rank your value areas. To achieve true fulfillment, you need to experience personal momentum. I define this momentum as the feeling you get when you have done the most important things so long that they have become easy for you to do. Yes, the bicycle analogy would work well here. You will never forget how to ride a bike. The best way to experience this momentum phenomenon in your life is always to do the most important things first. This is a "do-first-things-first-or-they-won't-get-done" mentality. Generally, the first things, the most important things, are the most difficult, and that is why they usually are not done. Procrastination is a direct route to spiritual flatness. Give up procrastination, and you will get some momentum going.

Do a regular checkup. My father-in-law was visiting us recently. I look forward to his visits for many obvious reasons, but also for a few of the not-so-obvious reasons. For example, he is a great knife sharpener. After he leaves, our knives are sharper than they have ever been, and they again perform the role for which they were invented: They are sharp and efficient. There's a life lesson here: If we are not sharpening life by stopping long enough to evaluate where it is dull, boring, ineffective, and inefficient, chances are good we are missing out on the excitement of what life is supposed to be.

Your use of time is the measure of what is important to you. Is it a reflection of what you feel? Spend conscious time on those things that will feed your spirit. Get close—very close—to those who make your life worth living.

Chapter 44

Suffocate Stress; Experience Joy

One of the things that saps our energy, and therefore our ability to live life more fully, is stress. We *tranquilize* when we need to *energize*. We do ourselves a disservice whenever we use pills, potions, excuses, spending, and excess food as "narcotics" to prevent us from facing the challenges of the real world. This only depletes our energy. When we learn to reduce stress, we gain energy and don't have to escape from reality! We look forward to it!

I love the following quote—one I memorized years ago. Sir Thomas Buxton said:

> The longer I am alive, the more convinced I am that what makes the difference between one person and another, between the great and insignificant is energy. That invincible determination, a purpose once formed, nothing can take away from it. I am convinced that anything on this earth that was meant by God to be done requires energy, and no training, talent, opportunity, or circumstance will make any man without it.[1]

Without Energy, Life Loses Its Excitement

Without energy, we will miss life's many opportunities. Energy is vital to overcome inertia. Energy is perpetual: The more you work at getting it, the more you will receive. In the first three steps of this book, I outlined how you can have more energy through good nutrition and a regular exercise routine. In the next three steps, I outlined how responsible financial management will also allow you to live right and give you more energy. If you don't work on the physical and financial areas, chances are your life is loaded with "bad stress" and will get in the way of your experiencing abundance in the spiritual areas. As I mentioned in chapter 7, bad stress is one of the primary reasons for low levels of energy and high levels of frustration. By contrast, good stress provides energy because it produces healthy internal responses to outward circumstances.

Twenty Guaranteed Stress Busters

1. Do more of the things that inspire you and give you positive feelings.
2. Say no more often to tasks and people to whom you know you should say no.
3. Manage "on-the-job" responses and efficiency with a healthy sense of time management.
4. Practice random acts of kindness.
5. Strive for direction, not perfection.
6. Ask yourself, *How important will this situation or event be three months from now?*
7. Practice patience.
8. Write a personal note every day to someone you care about.
9. Get comfortable with silence, and spend some time in solitude.
10. Don't worry about winning an argument.
11. Live for today.
12. Listen to soft music and relax in front of the fireplace.
13. Spend an entire day with your spouse doing nothing you have to do.
14. Spend an entire day with your children doing something you don't have to do.
15. Go the speed limit, and slow down for yellow lights.
16. Look for the eye of the hurricane—the serene place in the midst of chaos.
17. Take responsibility and stop blaming others.
18. Spend one hour in the garden or at the beach or on a rock, alone.
19. Don't worry about keeping up with the Joneses. Learn to be content.
20. Tell everyone you love, every time you talk with them, that you love them.

A Final Stress Buster: Give Up Worry

It is amazing that what we really want—*happiness*—and what we normally experience—*anxiety*—can be neatly contained in one short phrase: "Don't worry—be happy." For millions, worry is a way of life. However, worry is a dead-end street. It creates stress, destroys relationships, causes physical imbalance, and limits our personal and professional growth. God says in His Scriptures, "For this reason I say to you, do not be anxious for your life, as to what you shall eat, or what you shall drink; nor for your body, as to what you shall put on. Is not life more than food, and the body clothing?" (Matt. 6:25). God is all-loving, all-knowing, and all-powerful, and His words are meant to encourage you and me.

> **If you have faith in your future, you will have power in your present.**

Four Steps to Worry-Free Living

Seek God's plan. If you have faith in your future, you will have power in your present. This power helps you tunnel through the challenges that create the worry. This power comes to you when you realize you need to learn something from what worries you. When you realize your worrying is simply telling you your life is out of alignment with God's plan, you are suddenly *on the grow.*

Align your actions. The best way to eliminate worry is to put your plans in sync with God's plans. The only way to do this is to seek His guidance through prayer and His Word as you scroll through the important decisions you must make each day of your life. When what *you* do and what *He wants for you* are congruent, you will have His power to achieve your goals.

Be responsible with what God has entrusted to your care. There are two kinds of worry that trouble us most: (1) things we can control and (2) things we cannot control. Worry about relationships, money, health, and vocation is usually tempered when we take responsibility for growing in those areas.

Pray. When we come across situations beyond our control, we can replace our worry with prayer. We are told in Scripture to pray about everything and worry about nothing (see Phil. 4:6).

In the center of our worry, we must learn to be silent and listen to God's counsel to us. Begin small, by sitting quietly, perhaps meditating on a psalm or other scriptures, and listening for God's reassuring voice.

Have you ever worried and later learned that it was a colossal waste of time? I can see you smiling Yes! We have all been there more often than we would like to admit. So, what is the answer? Remove the stress, develop a faith-based life, and move forward. If you remove the distraction from your life that separates you from experiencing God's love, you will discover a peace that goes beyond all human understanding.

Chapter 45

"I Do"

It was a beautiful August day in 1987. I remember standing in the Gazebo at the Ritz-Carlton Resort in Laguna Niguel, California, overlooking the Pacific Ocean as I stared into the blue eyes that I would look into for the rest of my life. Then came the moment when I said, "I do." I have learned every day since that marriage is a matter of commitment, not a matter of convenience.

Marriage is a matter of commitment, not a matter of convenience.

To make a marriage work is exactly that—work. Let's take a quick inventory. How alive is your relationship with the one you love? Do you block time on your calendar to be with your spouse? Is he or she the most important person in your life? If so, do your actions show it, or do your words ring hollow?

Let's Go Down Memory Lane

Have you ever gone camping? If so, you remember all the work that went into building your evening fire. Long before the flames were crackling, you had cleared the ground and sought out small twigs for kindling. You then put the twigs on top of a piece of newspaper while you carefully laced a few larger branches among some smaller twigs. To top if off, once you got the fire going, you gingerly placed one or two logs on the top, hoping they would ignite from the fire below. Then you struck the match, touched it to the paper, and *whoooom!* . . . you had a fire. If the plan was to use this fire for several hours, you watched the fire with a careful eye, constantly adding more fuel, stoking the fire, and nurturing the flames. Then—and only then—would you have a fire for the night. Love is a lot like that campfire: We are either stoking it or soaking it.

Do you remember the first time you and your spouse saw

each other? That look. That special smile. Those are the memories and emotions that love songs are made of. Do you remember how your heart raced at the thought of the next time you would see each other? You were so in love that you physically could not eat. I hope you are starting to feel those feelings again. Because while those emotions may be long in the past, you can still rekindle them into an exciting present—if you want to. Both the today and the future with your spouse have much to do with returning to the "mode of yesterday."

Are You Too Late?

If you are still married, it is never too late to rekindle the love you once had. It is hardly front-page news that marriages are disintegrating at an alarming pace. In 1900, there was one divorce for every ten marriages; today, there is one divorce for every two marriages. Do I need to labor the point that divorce is painful for everyone within the family unit? The wounds of divorce run strong and deep. Other marriages, while still intact, are barely surviving.

Marriage is tough work, and a healthy marriage does not happen accidentally. That is why we must ask ourselves, How can we demonstrate our commitment to our spouse day in and day out? What guidelines have we set forth to keep our marriage healthy and strong? The answer, I would suggest, comes in *demonstrated love*. The Scriptures tell us, "Let all that you do be done in love" (1 Cor. 16:14). There are hundreds of ways we can make sure our spouse knows and fully experiences our love, rather than just routinely hearing, "I love you."

Dating says, "I love you."

Remember when you were dating? This is the "mode of yesterday." Dating your spouse says, "I love you." Think for a moment of the top five things you did when you were dating, when your only goal was to fan the early flames of your relationship. You spent time together, you asked questions, you listened, you were courteous, you were patient, you were kind, you weren't rude, you were unselfish, you expressed hope, and you were polite. You certainly did not spend your time just talking about yourself. Imagine what your relationship would look like at this moment *if you did those same things today*.

The good news is that because you did it once, *you can do it again*. If you do not have a healthy relationship with your spouse, you will not enjoy spiritual abundance. It just isn't going to happen! Okay, enough theory. Let your spouse know that you love him or her today by doing any or all of these things:

Ten Ways to Demonstrate "I Love You"

1. Spend meaningful time together.
2. Ask questions that demonstrate your interest in your spouse.
3. Listen when your spouse talks—make eye contact.
4. Be courteous when you are together.
5. Be patient with your spouse.
6. Be kind to your spouse in both word and deed.
7. Put your spouse's needs before your own.
8. Leave your ego at the door.
9. Hold true to your time commitments.
10. Forgive, forget, and move on.

Alone and Feeling Unloved

"This is all great," you say, "if you are married. But what about those of us who are single?" Eleanor Roosevelt wrote, "One must never, for whatever reason, turn one's back on life."[1] Great counsel if you do not have a mate. The God who loves you has created you for a divine purpose. Yet, if you are without a partner, you may feel some of that God-inspired purpose and abundance has lost its edge. That is when you simply must believe that you are not here by accident.

Let me tell you a story. My dad's mom, Ellyene Enault, passed away at the age of ninety-six. She enjoyed a rich life, but for the last twenty years of it, she was without a mate. My mom's mom, Kathryn Burgess, is ninety-three and has been without a mate for more than fifty years. Both of these women have led wonderful lives, and both have made a deep impact on mine. Do you think it is possible that being without a mate right now could be a good thing for you? Is it possible that *your being single* may be part of God's plan for your life?

When I was twenty-five, I was engaged to be married. I still remember the excruciating pain I felt when my fiancée initiated the breakup. I felt empty, hollow, and hurt. Then I was engaged to another woman a couple of years later. Although I broke off that engagement, it was still painful. Throughout this entire process, Nana Ellyene kept saying, "Todd, when it is right you will know it. When the woman you will spend the rest of your time with appears, you won't have to force anything." She was right. I had to wait on God's timing. I did, and I finally found a wonderful wife, Sheryl, and we have two beautiful boys, Jonathan and Matthew. I cannot imagine living my life without them.

Here's the good news: God has a tremendous, one-of-a-kind plan for your life. His ways are always right, although at times they may feel anything but right to you. So take heart. If you are single today, there is hope. And that hope is in trusting God for His plan. It may be tomorrow, next year, ten years, or even longer before you find a mate. Or it may be never. The key is this: Do not put your life on hold while you wait for Mr. or Miss Right to come along. Hey, they may not show up. Take the initiative on becoming whole. Take care of you, pursue your purpose, go for excellence, relax, and reach out to others. Add value to everyone you meet, and never, for whatever reason, turn your back on life.

Whether you are married or not, you simply must say, "I do" to life. Relationships make the world go round, make our spirits thrive, give us meaning, and create memories more lasting than a Kodak moment, which are the source of what gives us the passion and energy to keep going. Say "I do" to everything around you, and begin to enjoy life's richest rewards.

Chapter 46

The Circle of Life

When the timer went off, Sheryl and I ran to the bathroom, looked into the window on the little white tool, and to our absolute joy, we saw a little red "+." If you have ever experienced this, then you know the joy when you find out you and your spouse are going to have a baby. Wow! What a joy, and what a responsibility.

Did you see the movie *Lion King*? As the film began, Elton John sang the words:

> From the day we arrive on the planet
> And blinking, step into the sun
> There's more to be seen than can ever be seen
> More to do than can ever be done
>
> Some of us fall by the wayside
> And some of us soar to the stars
> And some of us sail through our troubles
> And some of us live with the scars
>
> In the circle of life . . .

As I sat in the darkness of that theater, I kept thinking of the role we parents are designed to play in the raising of our children, and how we are responsible to equip them for excellence. Long after his dad, King Mufasa, had died saving him from the wildebeest stampede, Simba returned to the pride and used the lessons his father had taught him, for he was now the leader, and on his own. Good lesson for us who live in the human jungle! During your life as a parent, have you made the commitment to share life's enduring lessons with your children, young or grown? Are you actively leaving them a positive legacy that will shape their lives forever—long after you have gone?

Lessons from the Leader

If you are a parent, you are the leader of the pack, and your age or the ages of your children do not matter. Life is all about learning lessons, and you, the parent, are the one to provide that guidance. From the time your children are young to the time they are grown, to the time when you or they die, life is only about lesson learning. I have experienced the power of this truth both by being the father of two young boys, and by being the son of a father who is committed to helping his three sons until the end.

There is a difference between merely being part of our children's lives and being actively involved *in* their lives. The difference is often only "inches." The distance from the couch to the carpet is only inches, but what a difference a few inches make in a child's life. The distance between passing in the hallway and hugging in the hallway is only inches, but what a difference it makes in your young boy's or girl's life. The difference between telling your children to pray and getting on your knees and doing it with them is only inches, but how important those inches are. Here are some of the most significant things you can do to get even closer to your children.

> There is a difference between merely being part of our children's lives and being actively involved in their lives.

Don't wait. Demonstrate your love for your children by giving them your time, energy, and resources from the moment they are born, through their toughest years, and when they become your friend later in life.

Invest time. Spend time with them on their "level," seeking to be with them at "their age" while maintaining your own.

Love them. Without hesitation, let them know you love them through words and deeds. My mom and dad have a positive effect on me every time I see them. When they arrive and when they leave, the two constants are a hug and the words, "I love you."

Be "in the moment." Be accessible to your kids. This does not just mean being available; it means being *with them* when you are available, concentrating on them, *being there*. Let them know you are approachable. Make sure they know that you are their coach. Give your kids the freedom to ask you tough questions.

Have nonnegotiable dates. The importance of this is priceless. As a young boy, I looked forward to the one-on-one times with my dad. Whether it was hiking, fishing, attending a baseball game, or going to the park, he kept those dates as priorities for my brothers and me. My friend Bob Shank did the same thing with his two girls, showing them through modeling the kind of man they would one day marry. This is strong food for thought. Today, I look forward to the one-on-one times with my sons. And with equal enthusiasm, I can't wait for the times when our family gets together with my folks or with Sheryl's dad. These moments are what life is about.

Journal the lessons. All the lessons you learn in your life should be cataloged so your kids can have a look at them later. I would recommend you write a "living document" titled "Lessons I Don't Want My Kids to Learn Twice and Hopefully Not Have to Learn Once." Journal the lesson, the date, the impact it had on you, and what your life is like after learning the lesson. This guidance is rich for those whom you love and who look to you for direction.

The Power of Leaving a Legacy

Most people do not think much about centering their lives on a purposeful plan of action that promises a legacy, especially with their children. What is the impression they choose to leave for their children? Will their legacy endure for the children's lifetimes and help them shape their actions as they go through life?

As I mentioned in my book *Closing the Gap,* I have a drawer in my office reserved for my kids. In it is the "treasure chest" I am leaving for them. I don't want my kids to have to learn lessons that are avoidable, and if they learn them once, I certainly don't want them to have to learn them twice. I plan to reach into this "treasure chest" often for the rest of my life. When it is appropriate, I will pass out the trinkets that are visual and emotional reminders to my children of what I believe in and what I stand for—the spiritual "pieces of eight," the core of what I want them to learn and remember from their father. Building a legacy for Sheryl and for my sons, Jonathan and Matthew, is part of my life plan. I am doing it on purpose and *with a purpose.* So can you!

What is in your "treasure chest"? What legacy are you creating? If you were to die today, how would you *not* want to be remembered? What should you be doing differently to leave a more positive, authentic impression on those you love? How does God want you to behave differently in those relationships that are most meaningful to you?

Three Steps for Creating a Legacy

Create the final frame. How do you want to be remembered by those you love most? I am not just talking about being a good spouse or parent. Those are givens. I am referring to the heart and soul of what you stand for, the lessons you have taught, and how you have demonstrated your convictions over the years. What does the "final frame" of your life look like? The good news is that you still have time to reshoot the scene and to begin living a life consistent with your final picture.

Commit to daily discipline. Build a list of what you stand for. Include the attitudes you want to display and the things you know you want to communicate. When you do this, you can hone your discipline to do these things more consistently.

Make an eternal impact. Make a difference—forever. You may never know the full impact of your spiritual decisions on your life and on the lives of those you love. But exercise those decisions anyway. You might as well, because the bad news is that life has a 100-percent mortality rate. The good news, however, is that you *can* be certain of your next stop. When you finally depart this earthly scene, where will you go? What happens to those you love? Will they join you? It is something to think about.

An Amazing Moment

Isn't it amazing when you think back to that moment in time when you learned you would be a parent? Since that time, your journey has certainly had its challenges and its rewards. No matter what stage of parenting you are experiencing now, there is no greater way to create a healthy spirit within than to pour life energy into the hearts of those you love. Step it up a notch or two in the area of lesson teaching and legacy leaving, and see what happens. I know you will love the results.

Chapter 47

The Art of Adding Value

The call was gut wrenching. "Honey, we have been in an accident. Jonathan is hurt, and the paramedics are taking him to children's hospital. Meet us there right away." With that, Sheryl, my wife, then pregnant with our second son, was taken by ambulance with Jonathan to Sharp Memorial Hospital. She went to one emergency room, and Jonathan went to another. I am happy to say that God gave me another chance to make sure my family knew how much I cherished them. To this day, I neither leave home nor hang up the phone without telling each of them how much I love and value them.

In less than one minute, John F. Kennedy Jr., his wife, and her sister plunged from the sky into the ocean off Martha's Vineyard. Three days later, their bodies were found. I wonder if they said all they needed to say to their loved ones before they took off that fateful night . . . or if their loved ones had said everything they wanted to say to them.

> If we are not adding value to the people we live with every day, it is possible they will begin to look for value elsewhere.

In the blink of an eye, the game can change. Do the important people in your life know how much you care? Have you told them lately that you love them? Is your life so organized that you add value to their lives? Are you cherishing the moments with them in a way that reflects your knowledge that one day, they—and you—will be gone? How you answer these tough questions will have a dramatic effect on how you feel tomorrow if, God forbid, you were to lose them.

True Value: Coming Up with the Real Hardware

If we are not adding value to the people we live with every day, it is possible they will begin to look for value elsewhere. When this happens, it is the beginning of a family's disintegration. If you are not adding more to the family account than you are removing, you need to reevaluate your priorities. Here are ten strategies to help you add true value to your family.

Keep your promises—period. To add value to those you love, you must be reliable. Your integrity, character, and legacy are on the line whenever you make a commitment to your family. The rule is this: Appointments with your loved ones are nonnegotiable commitments. Not to honor your commitments to your children is to teach them to lie. Keeping your promises is the most powerful form of leadership you can exercise as a parent. How do you measure up?

Invest the time. Bond together by being together. With more families relying on dual incomes, it becomes increasingly difficult to pull this one off. However, at the heart of adding value is simply *being together.* Ask your spouse and your children how to spell love, and they will probably spell it *T-I-M-E.*

Plan regularly scheduled family time. In my book *The Power to Be Your Best,* I demonstrated the art of time blocking. Here's my counsel. Put your family on the calendar first, or you will never spend the time with them that you could . . . or should. Is your family part of your daily plan? I am talking about the intentional events that add value to the ones you love. These are the "appointments" that add true value to your life and far outweigh the other "urgencies" and "reactive obligations" we *think* are so important but in the end simply are not.

Develop a family hobby. I still have indelible memories of being with my family while I was growing up. For many years, it was the winter ski vacation, the summer at the ranch, and the ongoing weekend outings and camping trips we always took together. Guess what? I am now doing these same things with my own family. I can honestly say that having a "family hobby" is an incredible way to add value to one another. What's yours?

Be consistent; don't cram. You can't lose weight overnight. You can't get rich in a day. And you cannot make up for *not adding value* by dumping a whole bunch of it on the ones you love in one great gush of compassion. It won't work. Your family will wonder what you are up to and be suspicious of your intentions. Add a little value every day, however, and you will never need to make up for lost ground—or lost time.

Don't keep score. Adding value is not a game. It is the most important unilateral commitment you will ever make. If you give of yourself only partially, you will destroy one of the most important laws ever formulated: *the law of reciprocity.* Go 100 percent of the way, and you will be amazed at what you receive in return.

Demonstrate your love. Do not give your family half a loaf by just *telling* them that you love them. You must tell it *and* show it for maximum impact. Ask yourself this question: *Do my actions and words both say "I love you"?*

Teach your children well. Your house is a classroom. Where is your centralized platform for learning? My friend Mike Vance once told me, "All parents should have a 'kitchen for the mind' for their family." In this room is every imaginable learning tool: musical instruments, microscope, terrarium, talking globe, VCR, paint zone, Play-Doh zone, computer, encyclopedias, learning games, and a host of other things. Especially when they are young—children form knowledge that will last them a lifetime. Do yourself a favor, and step it up in the area of making learning fun for your children.

> Adding value is not a game. It is the most important unilateral commitment you will ever make.

Have fun. Kids love to learn and have fun while doing it. You cannot do Strategy 8 without a commitment to having fun. Become a child with your children. Get down to their level. Come alongside them. Be in the moment. Make learning enjoyable.

Praise their accomplishments. You cannot believe the pliability of a child's self-esteem. You must praise their most innocent—even feeble—attempts at doing *anything.* My friend Ken Blanchard once said to me, "People who feel good about themselves produce good results." The self-esteem of children is shaped from the word *go.* Praise them verbally. Praise them in public. Showcase their work on your refrigerator. Install a "Wall of Fame" where every one of your child's works is displayed. Give your children good reason to feel proud and to move on to the next task. Give them the miracle of a healthy self-image. They will thank you forever.

What Is a Family?

Is your family on a collision course with disaster? Are you a lighthouse that is shaping your course and your future as a family? I'm sure you want what is best for your family, so do I. However, most families are so busy doing "family" that they have not yet decided what the family is supposed to be. They haven't answered such important questions as, What is our purpose? What do we value? In those areas we value, where do we want to go individually and together as a family? What are the short-term goals and the activities today that will help us get there? Unfortunately, most families do not have a "lighthouse"—that bright and sure mechanism to keep them on the right course over time.

Parents must lead the charge as the co-CEOs of the family. In that capacity, you are responsible for facilitating the discussion, development, purpose, core values, vision, mission, and activities of the family. First, you must decide what you stand for and where your priorities lie. With those in check, you must share them freely with your family—and stick around long enough to hear their comments. When you integrate your objectives with those of your family, all members will begin to work toward common purposes and goals. As you do this, you form a bond that helps to keep your family safe.

The outcome of this dialogue generally results in a family creed or statement of conduct—a written set of standards and principles for which the family stands and on which all future decisions are made. Here are some practical ideas to help you get started.

Set up a summit meeting with your spouse. This will be the longest part of the process. During this time, both of you must address such questions as, Why are we here? What do we value? Where do we want to be individually and as a family in this area? What are some of the activities we must do, individually and collectively, to live out our purpose?

Set up a summit meeting with your children. I have seen this work with children as young as five years old. Share with them the findings of the summit with your spouse. Ask them to help you understand some of their own values and goals. Seek together to formulate these thoughts into a short working document.

Create the document. Draft the document, including all areas of importance: spiritual, financial, physical, relational, and vocational. At the top should be the *purpose of the family*. Then, for each of the areas just mentioned, write a brief "job description" for each family member.

Calendar the activities. Whatever activities the family decides on to help them live out the family creed must be scheduled and put on the family calendar. You must then review your calendar at your weekly "team meeting." I promise you that this powerful process will change your family forever.

A family is a unit—one with a future. And that future, and all the moments, memories, and legacy it leaves are predicated on the decisions, goals, and objectives set today. Get together with your family right now, and chart your course for the journey of a lifetime.

Chapter 48

The Power of Friends

Shaping your life's conduct by the counsel of a few close friends will play a major role in your living a life of spiritual abundance. Countenance is composure, and your friends and colleagues can help you enjoy more of it when you feel alone, abandoned, uncertain, or afraid. In the area of spiritual abundance, they can help you know things about God's love for you that you simply cannot see. Friends with spiritual discernment can provide you with wisdom and clarity. They can give you hope during your most troublesome moments. There is nothing more important during these times than knowing you have someone to turn to who will love you and understand you.

Are you growing through what you are going through?

Since this section of the book deals with the abundance that comes from a spiritual focus, let me share with you this comforting thought. The psalmist David said, "Even though I walk through the valley of the shadow of death, I fear no evil; for Thou art with me; Thy rod and Thy staff, they comfort me" (Ps. 23:4). All of life's challenges are transitional, *not permanent.* You will go through them. The question is, Are you *growing* through what you are *going* through? Enjoying maximum growth as you go through your challenges and decisions is a result of seeking and listening to the counsel of others.

Taming Life's Transitions

You go through many transitions on a regular basis. So do I. I probably have the same concerns you do about these transitions, most commonly about making the right decision on *how to go through it.* Again, there's the rub: We *will* go through it. In his book *Transitions,* William Bridges says that every transition begins with an ending.[1] We must let go of the old thing before we can pick up the new—not just outwardly, but inwardly, where we keep our connections to the people and places that act as definitions of who we are. One of the best ways to do this is by asking for the discernment, wisdom, and unbiased opinion of a friend. Here are the rules I live by during times of transition.

Don't go it alone. Everyone needs a friend during times of difficulty and transition. There is as much benefit in being a friend as in having a friend. There are times when we all need the support and counsel of others. There are also times when our friends will need us. Who are the top two or three friends you can count on to help you through difficult times? Do they know you have selected them as one of your circle of friends on whom you can rely in times of difficulty or transition? If not, call them today and let them know how special they are to you.

Find an accountability partner. Each Friday, I have a conversation with an accountability partner. He asks me six questions that have everything to do with how I am handling issues and transitions in my life. I create many "valleys" in my life, but I can have fewer of them when I perform well in these six areas. When I fail, my friend shows great compassion and helps me get back on track. There is no pretense. No ulterior motive. He simply cares for me and wants me to succeed despite the challenges and transitions I am facing. Where are your battles? Would your life be different if you had a friend who asked you some tough questions week after week? Get clear on your challenges—those things that keep you from the enjoyment of peak spiritual performance. Share them with a friend, and start being accountable.

Get involved in a small group. Small groups that meet regularly to discuss issues of importance to each other provide a forum for releasing pent-up emotions, for encouraging right behavior, and for promoting a love that transcends the boundaries of performance—all in a context of love and understanding. All difficulties are easier to handle when we have others to help us see the light.

Scribbles for Spiritual Sustenance

Throughout Scripture, God warns His people to remember Him. Still, it did not take long for the Israelites to forget the safe crossing of the Red Sea, the provision of their daily bread, and the reliable nightly guide in the form of a pillar of fire. God was serious when He instructed Israel to construct monuments and memorials to Him. His intention was not only to help them remember His mighty deeds from the past, but to inspire them to trust Him in the future. What in your spiritual life demands "stones of remembrance"? Are you making notes of your joys and struggles? Are you scribbling down the details of how God is working in your life?

Journaling is powerful. If we are to experience more abundance in our spirit, we must imprint life's events so we will remember them and use them for our benefit. Journaling is the personal history book of how God has worked, and continues to work, in our lives. Sometimes we like what He is doing; sometimes we question the wisdom of His actions. However, each time we learn a principle, we grow and are able to set off in a new direction. These moments of ideas, events, reactions, and insights are worth writing down, allowing for ongoing reflection and helping us see God's mighty hand at work in our lives.

When you write in your journal, you create intimacy with God. Journaling helps you become consistent in your walk with your heavenly Father. It helps you to remember His faithfulness more clearly and augments your capacity to trust.

My friend Daniel Harkavy, president of Building Champions, says that the motivation to begin journaling can be fueled by the following five benefits.[2]

Journaling increases thanksgiving. By writing down the lessons God has taught you today, you reap a heart of thankfulness because of what He is teaching you, of where He has brought you from, and for the blessings of today and of eternity to come.

Journaling ingrains the lesson. When we take the time to write out the lessons of today, we imprint the lessons on our mind and increase the impact of those lessons. We learn from our quiet time, from our prayer time, and from our life experiences. When we engage in a constant review of these lessons, we reduce or prevent the negative lessons from recurring.

Journaling enhances our lives. By journaling, we can better assess the progress of our lives. The process of writing brings about a clarity that enables us to make better decisions. It forces us to crystallize our thoughts, which leads to a rich and rewarding life.

Journaling quiets our hearts. Serenity is a by-product of journaling. Life is too short not to hear the quiet whisper of God. His voice is soothing and packed with compassion. To feel His presence while journaling is one of the most powerful forms of spiritual abundance.

Journaling leaves a road map. When we record the events, thoughts, lessons, and ideas that we have learned from God, we are creating a road map for our children and friends to follow. Whether we use this road map as a tool while we are on this earth or leave it behind, it is vital that we live a life that is worth learning from and reading about.

There is no question in my mind that journaling is one of the most powerful tools available for spiritual growth. When you write things down, especially those moments when you are learning your greatest lessons, you will shape your future positively forever and, I believe, experience more of the unlimited abundance life has to offer.

Chapter 49

The Power of Purpose

One of the most difficult, yet most powerful, steps to spiritual abundance is the idea of having a purpose. With it, life is one big, memorable event. Without it, life is confusing and filled with unresolved frustration.

Life Is a Journey; Mastery Is the Result; Purpose Is the Bridge

I'm convinced that the bridge between success and mastery is purpose. A purpose is ongoing and gives meaning to our lives. When people have a purpose in life, they enjoy everything they do more. People go on chasing goals, trying to prove something that does not need to be proved: *that they are already worthwhile.* The fastest way to achieve goals is to stay on-purpose. So the question remains: What is your purpose? Do you know?

Can you identify with any of these symptoms: stress, burnout, difficulty in making decisions, too many things on your plate, inconsistent goal achievement, defeat by comparison, not enough time, unhappiness, a sense that life is slipping by, lack of clarity on what's important, a sense that you're missing out? If you can, then it is time to close the gap between mediocrity and mastery by discovering your purpose.

Discover Your Purpose

The discovery of your purpose is your first requirement for achieving significance in life. Mastery is the result of living your life on-purpose. As I mentioned earlier, the alternative to living your life on-purpose is to live it off-purpose, or without purpose, which is how most people are living it.

A travel map shows you how to get from point A to point B. A life map shows you how to get from where you are to where you want to be. You would not take an automobile trip across country without referring to a road map; you would not trek the outback of Australia—or even climb the rugged Sierra Nevada chain of mountains in California—without a compass. Yet, we often live our lives without compass or map, without a moment's thought on how to design our lives.

If you did not answer the purpose-discovery question in chapter 15, I encourage you to go back and complete that exercise in order to determine your purpose.

Avoid the Fence

Many of us assume that if we career wildly off enough walls, hit enough fences, and make enough mistakes that somehow we will arrive at the place of our dreams. The truth is most people are so busy making a living that they forget to work on their lives. They are so busy being successful that they fail to achieve significance. They are simply traveling through life *as it comes to them,* making decisions as they go, rather than crafting the life they have imagined and moving with confidence.

> **Most people are so busy making a living that they forget to work on their lives.**

Here are some memorable words from Henry David Thoreau:

> If one advances confidently in the direction of his dreams and endeavors to live the life which he has imagined, he will meet with success unexpected in common hours. He will pass an invisible boundary; new, universal and more liberal laws will begin to establish themselves around and within him; and he will live with the licenses of a higher order of beings.[1]

Did you catch the key words and phrases in Thoreau's words? *Advances confidently. Dreams. Imagine. Endeavor. Success.* You can have it all—but you must first know where you are going. You must be in possession of a map.

Take Charge and Design Your Life

Here are the four steps that I share in almost every document I write and in every speech I give. They can make all the difference in the world to the person who heeds them:

Determine your "accounts." Accounts are those parts of your life on which you place great value. These accounts, like the ones at the bank, require your attention and focus—and they work much the same way. If you are not putting value into them, one day you may find yourself overdrawn. My research has revealed that the five most common life accounts are spiritual, physical, financial, relational, and vocational. How many of these are important to you?

Determine your vision for each account. In each of your account areas, there may be a gap. Here, however, you do not close the gaps; you simply take note of where the gaps lie. For each of your account areas, you must ask these two vision questions: (1) "Where do I want to go?" and (2) "In the next five, ten, or fifteen years, what will this account look like?"

Determine your actions in each account area. In each of your account areas, the gaps set up the equation and a plan of action that you must solve. What steps are you taking to close the gaps?

Schedule your actions. To advance confidently in the direction of your dreams is to do what will close the gap in any account area. This means you must schedule your prayer time, family time, workout time, financial management time, and vocational excellence time. The difference for you now is that your plan has suddenly become proactive. It is part of your larger vision. Best of all, it is backed by purpose. You now commit to a few doable changes. You turn new behaviors into solid habits. And the changes that matter most are the ones that create the habits for a lifetime. This is your map. Follow it!

In this step you have learned how to breathe life into your relationships. You are now embarking on one of the most important sections in this book, "Transform Your Spirit." In this important next step, you will learn how to let God breathe into you the power that only He can give. When this happens, your life will never be the same.

Transform Your Spirit

Chapter 50

The Law of Prayer

Archbishop Leighton said, "When God is the center of the soul, although disasters may crowd in on all sides and roar like the waves of the sea, there is a constant calm within. The world can neither give nor take away this kind of peace."[1] Prayer gives you light, and it gives you life. The Scriptures say, "Let him who walks in the dark, who has no light, trust in the name of the LORD" (Isa. 50:10 NIV). That is what prayer is all about—stepping out of the darkness, removing the web of uncertainty, and getting into the light of God's goodness where your decisions become clear. Prayer is the vehicle through which you experience God's light in your life.

As we navigate life's challenges, road-blocks, and tough choices, we can experience great assurance in knowing that a much greater force is in control. You may have experienced this power in the past, and now you want more of it; or perhaps this is the first time you are willing to give prayer a chance. Either way, only the power that comes from peace with God can calm your mind and put your anxious heart to rest. This power for living comes when you seek intimacy and guidance with the highest power in the universe, Almighty God.

> **Prayer is an individual choice that is the gateway to experiencing the strongest power in the universe.**

Spiritual abundance through prayer is available for all. It is not reserved for those who attend church any more than it is for those who do not. Prayer is not an automatic benefit of following dogmatic guidelines about a Sabbath ritual or a litany of "must do's."

Prayer is an individual choice that is the gateway to experiencing the strongest power in the universe. To enter that relationship with the Creator, we must be open to speaking to God as a friend. Pastor, author, and United States Senate Chaplain Lloyd John Olgilvie says it like this:

> Nothing is more important [than prayer]. It is the source of life's greatest joy. There is no power or peace without it. With it, we receive supernatural insight and wisdom. Our ability to understand and love people is maximized. We think more clearly and can act more decisively. Our problems shrink and we can tackle opportunities with gusto. Most of all, we fulfill the reason we were born: to know and love God.[2]

Recent surveys indicate that more than 90 percent of Americans believe in God and that nearly every citizen owns at least one Bible. Further, 86 percent of Americans call themselves Christians. Of 1,012 adults surveyed in a July 1997 study by Barna Research, two out of three (67 percent) said they believe God is the all-knowing, all-powerful Creator of the universe who rules the world today.[3] Most people I know want to experience the direction that prayer offers but say they either do not have the time to pray, do not know how to pray, or both.

The Platform for Prayer

Prayer is simply having a conversation with God. Prayer is a relationship, not a formal religious activity. When you have a conversation with another person, you not only speak, you also listen. Over the years, however, many of us have been conditioned to think that prayer is one-way communication. I would like you to think of your interaction with God as two-way. If you pray, you already understand how God speaks to your spirit in the silence of your prayers. You also know this happens only when you stop long enough to listen. The psalmist said, "Be still, and know that I am God" (Ps. 46:10 NIV). God wants you to be still, to be calm in the middle of the storm. He does not want you to be troubled or to tremble in the face of uncertainty. He wants to comfort you. That's why He promised He would prevail against

Prayer is simply having a conversation with God.

all that troubles or threatens you. You would be wise to place the storms and rough seas of your life in God's hands and let Him take over. He can do a better job orchestrating the direction of our lives than we can. Genuine prayer does not *lead* to an encounter with God; the act of prayer *is* the encounter.

As you prepare to pray, I would offer you these suggestions:

Pray constantly. You can pray at any time, at any place, about anything. Prayer is your personal dialogue with God.

Pray with purpose and experience God's purpose. How specifically do you want the power of God to help you in your life? God uses kingdom principles to accomplish His purpose. He reveals His ways to you because that is how He accomplishes His purpose for you.

Pray with passion. Realize that God loves you more than you can ever imagine. Love Him back with your words and your energy.

Pray for provision. God has said we are His most important creation. He tells us not to worry, for He will provide for us.

Pray for protection. There are great forces in our world that threaten us every day. Everything from addictions to other temptations have the other universal power of Satan behind them. God will build a wall of protection from these evils around you if you will only ask.

> Genuine prayer does not *lead* to an encounter with God; the act of prayer *is* the encounter.

Pray for people. You know people who need the power of Almighty God in their lives. They may be hurting, sick, or just struggling to make it through another day. Bring these friends and associates to God in prayer.

Pray patiently. The goal of prayer is to transport your joys and sorrows to God's level, not to bring God to your level. If you do not sense clear instruction from God in your prayer time, be patient and wait for Him. His timing is always right, and it is always best.

Three Powerful Parameters of Prayer

The Scriptures tell us that God is our strength and our shield, that He gives us power to live life well, freely giving us protection to tunnel through life's difficulties. However, to experience

God's power of strength and protection, we must become intimate with Him.

In July 1989, I was greatly impacted by a speech given by Zig Ziglar. He reminded me that the Creator of the universe looks out for us on a full-time basis. It is we who lack the same commitment. If we were as full time for God as God is full time for us, much of what confuses us about Him—and what He "allows" or "does not allow" to happen to us—would impact us differently. One way to become more in tune with God and His plans is to take the time for study and prayer. Here are the three most important lessons I have learned in the last twenty years about spending time alone with my heavenly Father. It is my hope they will also be an encouragement to you as you engage the power of this life-giving force.

Make the time to pray. Even though it is acceptable to pray any time, a focused session of prayer each day is essential to your spiritual health. Prayer is the foundation for peace of mind; there is no better way to begin the day. Have you noticed that we seem to worry about everything? We are often like strings on a violin—so tight that we are on the verge of breaking at the slightest provocation. What a waste of our bodies and our energies. God says that He did not intend for humans to live in a state of being constantly "stressed out." He once said that He would take care of the birds and the lilies of the field. If that is true, and it is true, how much more will He care for you and me? He tells us not to worry about today or tomorrow—to have no anxiety at all. Why? Because He promises to care for us (see Matt. 6:25–34). As you develop an effective prayer life, you will find yourself increasingly aware of the following: union with God, focus on God, experiencing God's plan for your life, daily provision, forgiveness for your wrong actions, protection from evil, and a celebration of His relationship in your life.

Listen for God's voice. When you set aside time for prayer, bring the great, important, and difficult issues of your life to God and say, "Father, speak to me. Tell me what You want for my life." Then listen, perhaps as long as five, ten, or even fifteen minutes—even though it may seem like an eternity. Just keep listening, because time will provide the answer. Soon you will feel God nudging you, saying, *This is the way you should go.*

Pray constantly. One of God's great men of history was a man named Paul. He writes that we are to "pray without ceasing" (1 Thess. 5:17). Why would he say this? And, we might ask, is this not impractical? Paul would say, no, it is not impractical. He would encourage us to pray *always* because we are not strong enough to carry out life's tough choices alone. Here's a way to get started: Pray what I like to call "situational prayers." Throughout the day, take every situation in which you need guidance from God and pray a short prayer, followed by a period of listening for His voice. You will make better decisions when you do, and you will enjoy more peace of mind.

As we close this chapter, it is important to know that prayer is a discipline. You cannot go from no prayer to a daily commitment to prayer overnight. As with everything we have discussed in this book, new behaviors take time before they become habits. In my life, to make prayer a habit has taken years. However, each time I hear the voice of God, and as He helps to shape my decisions and direction, I again reaffirm the power of prayer and my desire to stay focused on it daily. It takes time, but it is worth it. If prayer is already an integral part of your life, you know what I mean.

Frances de Sales said, "Do not look ahead to what may happen tomorrow. The same everlasting Father who cares for you today will take care of you tomorrow and every day. Either He will shield you from suffering or He will give you unwavering strength that you may bear it. Be at peace, then, and set aside all anxious thoughts and worries."

Chapter 51

The Law of Balance

The sirens came from all directions, and the little two-year-old jumped up and down with excitement. "Fire trucks, fire trucks, fire trucks!" he yelled. "Ambulance, ambulance, ambulance!" he shouted, as they screeched to a stop in front of the house. What the little boy did not understand was that they had come for his dad. As the paramedics attended to the boy's father who was sprawled on the ground, his demeanor changed. Suddenly he was afraid. What were these people doing to his daddy? As they loaded him in the ambulance, the little boy's eyes filled with tears. Minutes earlier they had been playing basketball together. Then, in the blink of an eye, the game was over, and Dad was on the ground.

As I lay in the hospital that Saturday night, I caught a quick glimpse of how fast the game can change. I was suddenly reminded that a busy life is not necessarily a productive life. A productive life pays attention to the important things. God had my attention.

How Much Is Enough?

It is great to be busy—provided we are busy doing the right things. Being busy can either add to or take away from our spiritual abundance. One downside of busyness often takes the form of work. If we are not careful, we can be driven by our schedules, become workaholics, and feed our fast-paced existence with more stimulus to get a little more adrenaline flowing. Have you bought into the myth that *more will be enough?*

Millions of people are becoming successful but missing the bigger goal of attaining significance. "Where are they missing out?" you might ask. In their relationships with God, their spouse, their children, and with those closest to them. They are missing the greatest lesson of all: Contentment does not just happen when you finally have enough stuff. Contentment is a learned behavior.

Living life fully requires balance. High-tech aircraft and space vehicles demand balance. The performer on the high wire lives and dies by balance. Our physical bodies cry out for balance. Overabsorption with work makes us lopsided and weakens our spirit. It is true that the average person on his or her deathbed will probably not say, "I sure wish I had spent more time at the computer or shuffling paper at the office." So, the question is, Where are you in the balance department? Are you too busy at the office to spend time with your spouse, your children, your neighbors, your friends—or with God?

It Could Be Worse

I love the Peanuts cartoon strip featuring good ol' Charlie Brown and his friends during Thanksgiving. Snoopy is perched on the top of his doghouse, looking sad, forlorn—even bitter. Inside, gathered around the table are all his friends. The turkey is in the center of the table, and surrounding it are all the other dishes we typically enjoy at this holiday: potatoes, green beans, cranberry salad, rolls, and gravy. You have the picture. Snoopy obviously would rather be inside, but instead, he utters a classic line of contentment when he says, "It could be worse. I could have been a turkey."

I think we can learn something from that lovable dog: No matter how tough your situation—it could always be worse. The fact that things are not as bad as they could be should give you peace. One of the keys to achieving balance is to be thankful. You already have more than most of the world will ever possess, although, at times, you may feel like a financial orphan. Get off the treadmill of trying to keep up. Start enjoying a life of serenity; begin living a life of balance.

Balance Is a Design Problem

Balance is a journey—a lifetime of striving for excellence. Balance is an ongoing process that happens when we reevaluate our priorities and actions and continually shape new behaviors into habits. There will always be a disparity between who we are and what we want to be. That is why we will always be subjected to the question of whether our behavior reflects growth. To help you get a better handle on your pursuit of personal mastery and spiritual abundance, let me share three laws I have found to be true.

You must change your beliefs in order to change your behavior. While I was addicted to cocaine, my belief was "This is cool." I quit using the substance when my belief changed to "This could kill me." My new behavior has now been consistent for more than fifteen years. I used to think that money bought me happiness. Now I believe that being happy makes me wealthy.

Results take time to measure. Growth toward balance is the process of measuring these results.

Repetition is the key to sustained growth and balance. I said, *Repetition is the key to sustained growth and balance.* I said, *Repetition is the key to . . .*

God's Short Course on a Life of Balance

People say they want to live a balanced life. They ask themselves, *If I am so wealthy, why don't I feel happier? If I am so successful, why don't I feel more satisfied? If I am so busy, why do I spend so much time on the things that are a waste of time?* The answer is locked in the secret of contentment. To be anything other than content is to live the existence of a fool. Here is a story that sums up this thought:

> Beware, and be on your guard against every form of greed; for even when one has an abundance does his life consist of his possessions . . . . The land of a certain rich man was very productive. And he began reasoning to himself, saying, "What shall I do, since I have no place to store my crops?" And he said, "This is what I will do: I will tear down my barns and build larger ones, and there I will store all my grain and my goods. And I will say to my soul, 'Soul, you have many goods laid up for many years to come; take your ease, eat, drink and be merry.'"

> But God said to him, "You fool! This very night your soul is required of you; and now who will own what you have prepared?" So is the man who lays up treasure for himself, and is not rich toward God. (Luke 12:15–21)

To attain true wealth is to follow God. God assures us that if we do follow Him, He will give us everything we desire, according to His plan. In the spirit of balance, here is God's advice. Heeding it gives us the power to live a life of serenity.

- Seek God first and love Him with all of your heart.
- Trust God's provision for your life.
- Love others as you love yourself.
- Go to God when times are tough, and thank God when times are good.
- Have faith in God's plan for your life.

Ten Ways to Enjoy More Balance

In my book *Closing the Gap,* I shared the following ten ways to help you enjoy more balance in your life—starting today.

Schedule balance. Balance is not something that happens after work and on weekends. It is something that must become routine. Work hard and smart, and keep your edge by scheduling those things that make you feel whole. Get up earlier and stay up a little later, but do the things that refuel you before you burn out.

Delegate activities. You have many lost hours you could capture for "balance activities" because you do not delegate effectively on the job. Your most important tasks are people related. What are you doing that an assistant could do so you would have the luxury of working on your balance? Start off-loading everything that is dulling your edge.

Pray. Don't look down; look up. Pursue spiritual harmony and peace—two critical components of the balanced life. For me, this is private time with my Creator. I feel more in tune with life and the workplace when I am in tune with Him.

Date your spouse. A leader I coached recently told me he dated his wife recently for the first time in twenty-one years. I think such a revelation provides one clear indicator: that what has taken us *off balance* are the very things we once sought to *ensure balance*. My friend told me that dating his wife again was an incredible experience, one that rejuvenated their relationship.

Hang out with your kids. Recent statistics show that dads spend as little as thirty-seven seconds a day with their kids. *Thirty-seven seconds*. Not even one minute. While moms might be there more, surveys show that the time moms spend with the kids is less one-on-one and more just "being there," usually with considerable distraction in the background. More on this in the next section.

Walk on the beach. Take time to be tranquil. Fill your lungs with fresh air.

Work out. Feeling balanced has a lot to do with your energy level and mental and physical health. Working out enhances both. Take time to make sure that you get at least three days a week of good, solid exercise. You will be on your way to balance.

Take a vacation or a day off. Sharpen the saw. You must be sharp to lead and to develop a sharp team.

Get a massage. Relax to recharge. Every month, get a good massage to release the stress and toxins that have built up in your body.

Read a good book. Put your brain in neutral on occasion. Fill it with a story that makes you feel good.

You can live a balanced life, starting today. I encourage you to do it with passion!

Chapter 52

The Law of Faith

You already live with it, and yet you may be taking it for granted. It is faith. You have faith in your car that it will start and stop. You have faith in your TV that it will turn on and turn off. You have faith in your computer that it will not lose data. You have faith in your heater and air conditioner that they will keep you warm in the winter and cool in the summer. You live with faith every day, whether you realize it or not. While these everyday demonstrations of faith may not seem important, they actually are reminders that spur you to ask the bigger question: Do you have faith in your future? If not, then how can you expect to demonstrate energy and power in your present?

The Hour of Power

Let me tell you a story. I was only five years old at the time. Several years after moving from Cincinnati, Ohio, to southern California, my parents decided that they would visit some local churches and see if that might add a positive dimension to their lives. I remember how excited they were when they finally found a church—a congregation that later changed my life forever. It started as a little church in Garden Grove, California, simply named Garden Grove Community Church. It was, as the name implied, a church for the community. From as far back as I can remember, the pastor was a man of faith and a man of vision—a God-sized vision. Now, thirty-five years later, on any given Sunday, this church reaches more than twenty million people worldwide with its international and national TV presence. It is now called the Crystal

> Do you have faith in your future? If not, then how can you expect to demonstrate energy and power in your present?

Cathedral, and the man God used to build it is Dr. Robert Schuller.

On the first Sunday of the new millennium, Dr. Schuller invited me to be a guest on his television program, *The Hour of Power.* His goal, and mine, was to share with the millions of viewers the power of God's plan for their lives and the importance of trusting our heavenly Father as a faithful, loving Lord. In this chapter, I want to do the same for you.

Lessons from God

Over the years, God gave some powerful teachings to Dr. Schuller, and Dr. Schuller, in turn, impressed them on me from the age of five—potent lessons on how to become a person of faith. I have never forgotten these teachings, and I want to share a few of them with you for your benefit and for God's glory.

The lesson of belief. Robert Schuller has belief—more than most people can comprehend. Perhaps it is because he has seen the mighty hand of God at work in his life for more than seventy-three years. One of his favorite scriptures is, "All things are possible to him who believes" (Mark 9:23).

> **All things are possible to him who believes.**
> **—Mark 9:23**

Dr. Norman Vincent Peale, longtime friend of Dr. Schuller and author of the international bestseller *The Power of Positive Thinking,* wrote,

> The most powerful force in human nature is the spiritual-power technique taught in the Bible. Very astutely the Bible emphasizes the method by which a person can make something of himself. Faith, belief, positive thinking, faith in God, faith in other people, faith in yourself, faith in life. This is the essence of the technique it teaches. . . . "If ye have faith . . . nothing shall be impossible to you." (Matthew 17:20) "According to your faith be it unto you." (Matthew 9:29)[1]

You need to believe in yourself. You need to have faith in your ability. Dr. Peale says, "Without a humble but reasonable confidence in your own powers you cannot be successful or happy."[2]

The lesson of positive thinking. To this day, Dr. Schuller begins every telecast with the same words he used when I was only five. With passion and enthusiasm he says, "This is the day that the Lord has made. Let us be glad and rejoice in it." These are powerful words. You and I really *do* have a new day, every day, to awaken to and to be happy about. Hey, we breathed on the mirror this morning, and guess what? It fogged up. That in itself is cause for celebration. We are alive. We have breath! So there is no reason to be anything but joyous! If you already know and experience God in your life, your past is forgotten, your present is secure, and your future is guaranteed. How can you be anything other than excited when you think of life in those terms?

The lesson of vision. When I attended Dr. Schuller's church for the first time, I learned that just years earlier he had been preaching from atop the snack bar at the Orange Drive-in Theatre. Then in a beautiful sanctuary with glass windows that slid open so he could also address those worshiping in their cars, Dr. Schuller spoke of his next vision—building the Tower of Hope. Soon after came yet another vision—the building of the Crystal Cathedral. And on January 2, 2000, he stood before twenty million viewers and said his new vision was to see *The Hour of Power* broadcast to every television set in the world on Sunday, January 3, 2100. What vision! What incredible vision!

If you truly want to turn your life around, I hope you will learn a lesson from Dr. Schuller about vision—and your need to have an absolutely clear picture of your better future. To discover your vision, however, you must seek the counsel of Almighty God. God already has an enormous plan for your life. You simply need to let Him tell you what it is and then go about the task of getting it done. To *listen* during your times of prayer is the best way to know what visions you should be about.

The lesson of persistence. The final lesson I want to share with you is the power of persistence. Dr. Schuller keeps reminding me that "tough times never last, but tough people do." What you believe about God, particularly in the area of faith, will determine what you do and how you live, whether you go forward or whether you give up. What you do with your life reveals to others what you believe about God. It is far easier to be persistent when times are tough if you understand the following truths:

- God loves us, and His plan is best.
- God is smarter than we are, and His direction is accurate.
- God is more powerful than we are, and His power will help us through the tough times.

With the knowledge of these three attributes of an Almighty God, it is easy to see how we can be more persistent in our pursuits.

The Power of a Rubber Band

Several years ago, my wife and I were vacationing in northeast Australia in the little seaside town of Port Douglas. I had just finished a speaking tour through the country and we were unwinding before heading home. After a week of travel, we were heading for the airport, when out of the right window I saw the sign: *A. J. Hackett Bungee.* I had always wanted to bungee jump, but for some reason had not. However, the time was now.

After a quick lesson, I climbed the fifteen-story tower, proceeded to have a super sized rubber band wrapped around my ankles, and within seconds was perched 150 feet off the ground on an eighteen-by-eighteen-inch platform. Then just about as quickly, I heard, "Five . . . four . . . three . . . two . . . one!" Then I leaped, by faith, and fell to the water below. As I neared the bottom, my hand grazed the surface, the rubber band pulled me back up nearly one hundred feet, and I fell again back to the water. Without faith, I would not have jumped.

Faith is hard to get your arms around, but it is a very real thing.

What is the point to telling you this crazy story? Simple. Do not take faith for granted. It is easy to put your faith in things human, but how much more powerful it is to put your trust in a heavenly being—the One who has control over all, who causes the sun to rise and set on demand, and who puts the universe into motion in a way that initiates life. He is the One who created you and me for greatness.

Let Faith Change Your Life

Can you think of a situation in which you or a loved one has struggled to the point of despair? Perhaps it was with work, a financial setback, an illness, or even a death. Maybe your experience of God in that moment was tainted, and you kept asking God, Why? Perhaps your own experiences with church and religion have been hollow and empty. As you were growing up, you may have developed some negative opinions of faith in general and about God in particular.

Faith is hard to get your arms around, but it is a very real thing. God is impossible to get your arms around, but He is a very real being. Millions of people have used the powerful principle of faith for living life well, and so can you. The Scriptures define faith as "the assurance of things hoped for, the conviction of things not seen" (Heb. 11:1).

Let me close with this. In a recent television interview, I heard a famous actor say that in his attempt to understand faith, he took the word itself and turned it into this acrostic:

Fantastic
Adventures
In
Trusting
Him

If you have been trusting in yourself too long, give God a chance. You will be pleased.

Chapter 53

The Law of Uniqueness

You may not be aware of this but, if you are a man, during your lifetime you will produce about 1.7 trillion sperm. If you are a woman, during your lifetime, you will produce some two million immature eggs. By age seven, most of these have been reabsorbed back into the body, and you will have about three hundred thousand left. Out of those, you will produce between three hundred and four hundred mature eggs. When your mom and dad decided to have you, some six hundred million sperm were immediately released, and the race to the finish was on. *The fact that you are reading this paragraph means you won that race.* There are millions of other ways you could have turned out, but that didn't happen. You are a winner because you are you. You are a unique, one-of-a-kind human being . . . with the DNA to prove it.

> **You are a unique, one-of-a-kind human being . . . with the DNA to prove it.**

You Are a Miracle from the Start

Genesis, or "the book of beginnings," says, "Then God said, 'Let Us make man in Our image, according to Our likeness; and let them rule over the fish of the sea and over the birds of the sky and over the cattle and over all the earth, and over every creeping thing that creeps on the earth.' And God created man in His own image, in the image of God He created him; male and female He created them" (1:26–27).

Where's the miracle? In the next chapter, we are told, "The LORD God formed man of dust from the ground, and breathed into his nostrils the breath of life; and man became a living being" (2:7).

One of the most powerful pathways to high levels of spiritual abundance is found in understanding and believing the story of creation. If you study these scriptures, you will see that everything with a heartbeat was created on days five and six, and man was created after every other living thing was formed. Perhaps this was so man could never claim that he assisted God in the creation of the world—or the universe. Man himself was the last creation of Almighty God after the world, after all else had been finished.

The Greatest Miracle in the World

In his book *The Greatest Miracle in the World,* Og Mandino ends his story with "The God Memorandum." I want to share some of these truths that God believes about you. Over the years, these words have prompted me to create a list to remind me how unique I am. I call my list "Why I Am Unique," and I share this list with you, hoping that you will always remember your own uniqueness.

Why I Am Unique

I can think.
I can act.
I can love.
I can laugh.
I can talk.
I can create.
I can plan.
I can dream.
I can hurt.
I can feel God's presence in prayer.

You and I have been endowed with powers not held by another creature on this planet. You and I are one-of-a-kind winners. Og says, "Count your blessings, proclaim your rarity, go another mile, and use wisely your power of choice."[1] You are the greatest miracle in the world.

Three Ways to Celebrate Your Uniqueness

During the activity of the day, when the battle is fierce, it is often difficult to remember that we are made special. Yet, within us, there remains the flame of uniqueness that must be fanned into a roaring fire. How do we do this? By aligning ourselves with a loving God who has given us life in its abundance—and made us unique in the process. Here are some ideas that will help you celebrate your uniqueness.

See God in everything. If I look to see God in everything, He will add meaning to everything I see. If I see God in my spouse, I will see a deeper, more meaningful human being. If I see God in a project or an assignment, I will feel the power in how to go about that assignment. If I see God in a flower or a tree or in an ever-changing stream, I will see His uniqueness, and then I will see my own.

See God in your future. If I look to see God in my future, my present is more secure. If I see His plan for my future, I will realize my uniqueness in my present. In *Tried As by Fire,* these words captivate my soul: "It is said that springs of sweet, fresh water pool up amid the saltiness of the oceans, that the fairest Alpine flowers bloom in the wildest and most rugged mountain passes, and that the most magnificent psalms arose from the most profound agonies of the soul. May it continue to be. Therefore, amid a multitude of trials, souls who love God will discover reasons for boundless, leaping joy."[2]

See God in you. The Scriptures say that God stands at the door and knocks (see Rev. 3:20). If you invite Him in, He promises to stay with you. The Scriptures also say that the old you is suddenly gone, and the new you has arrived (see 2 Cor. 5:17). Talk about uniqueness! You were unique *before* God came into you. Imagine how you will look when you become *new!* That is why you must stop getting down on yourself. Quit thinking everyone else has it easier or better than you do. Start realizing you began as a winner (remember, you won the race), and you can finish as a winner. The choice is entirely up to you.

Chapter 54

The Law of Solitude

They had just returned to the room, and you could tell by the looks on their faces they had gone through a life-changing experience. The exercise was called "Go to Your Rock." I do this in my seminars to help busy executives realize the power of solitude. Years ago, I adopted this strategy as a tool for seeking quiet and feeling God's presence in my own life—something that never happens if I'm left to the distraction of the day. Every time I do this, it has the same calming effects on my spirit—solitude and peace. The Scriptures say: "God made us plain and simple, but we have made ourselves very complicated" (Eccles. 7:29 TEV).

Slowing down and finding solitude are the prescription for unraveling most of our self-imposed messes. The proverbial treadmill is such a paradox. If you are on it, why doesn't it feel healthy? Isn't a treadmill supposed to be a *good* thing? I guess it depends how you use it. The executives who came back into the room after being "on their rock" had many comments, all of which could be summed up with these words: "I need to make time for the things that are truly important, the things that will last a lifetime."

> **Slowing down and finding solitude is the prescription for unraveling most of our self-imposed messes.**

Three Steps for Experiencing Peace in Your Life

Spend time alone with God. Solitude leads to peace of mind . . . but only when what you discover in those moments is converted into the right kind of activity. Personal growth comes from those accumulated moments of self-reflection and new courses of action. Spiritual abundance comes from knowing that you are experiencing God in a meaningful way and that your life's actions are a reflection of those moments of solitude with Him.

Simplify your life. Chuck Swindoll says, "Without simplification we will find ourselves unable to be at rest within, unable to enter the deep, silent resources of our hearts, where God's best messages are communicated. And if we live very long in that condition, our hearts grow cold to God and we become objects of seduction in a wayward world."[1] The purpose of solitude is to reorder your life's priorities: to simplify. This process invariably centers you on the important issues of your life. To simplify, we must make new choices. To make new choices, we must reconnect with what is vital. As a foundation for this course of action, we need to realize that the only time life will settle down is when we take the initiative to *slow things down*. These questions will help you chart new courses of action.

- What activities or relationships would need to disappear for me to be able to slow down? How and when can I make these changes?
- What areas of my life do I value—but are suffering because I give them too little focus? What would my life look like if these areas received serious attention?
- If my life were a reflection of what I truly felt was important, what would it look like?

Enjoy the experience of serenity. I fear that too many people use busyness as the excuse for not having enough time to do what is important. If this is true for you, perhaps you need to reorder your life, take control of your time, and begin doing those things that are most important to you. If you are overly busy, you will miss what God is trying to say to you every day. He wants the best for you. That is why He tells us through the psalmist that He is our Shepherd: "The LORD is my Shepherd, I shall not be in want. He makes me lie down in green pastures, he leads me beside quiet waters, he restores my soul" (Ps. 23:1–3 NIV).

Right now, do you feel you are living life to its fullest? Are you drinking from the cool waters and enjoying the green pastures that life offers you? If not, spend some time alone with God. Trim your sails, and tack in His direction. This is ultimate rest—that moment in time when you set aside your needs and wants for the peace and tranquillity of "safe" waters. This is where your mind, body, and soul are rejuvenated.

Life by Design Checkup

Here are several questions designed to help you become more deliberate about your life. I recommend that you answer these questions in an environment free from distraction and that you spend at least sixty minutes on the questions the first time through.

1. Am I missing anything in my life right now that is important to me?
2. What am I passionate about that gives meaning to my life?
3. Who am I, and why am I here?
4. What do I value that gives me real happiness?
5. Where do I want to be, and what do I want to be doing in five, ten, or twenty years?
6. What gifts has God given me that I am perfecting? Which ones am I not using effectively?
7. What would I be willing to die for?
8. What is it about my job that makes me feel trapped?
9. What changes can I make in how I run my business to experience more freedom?
10. What steps should I be taking now to make sure that my future will be meaningful?
11. With regard to money, how much is enough? If I have more than enough, what purpose does the excess money serve?
12. Am I living a balanced life? Which areas are in need of more time or focus?
13. Where do I seek inspiration, mentors, and working models for greater significance?
14. For what do I want to be remembered?
15. What legacy do I want to leave for my family?
16. Where will I go when this earthly life is over?

Slow Down before It's Too Late

We must learn the habit of slowing down. It bears repeating: The best way not to go too fast is to move more slowly. Burnout and blowout are wicked realities for those who refuse to slow their pace. High-performance machines need care and maintenance. Without either, they sputter and fail to perform. You and I are also high-performance machines designed to last a lifetime. We will only stay the course, however, if we subject ourselves to regular maintenance and proper care.

Chapter 55

The Law of Wisdom

The Scriptures say, "If any of you lacks wisdom, let him ask of God, who gives to all men generously and without reproach, and it will be given to him" (James 1:5). Life is, well, life! It's one curve ball after another. One tackle after another. Life is tough. On balance, there are probably more challenges than slam dunks! Unfortunately, however, when we see all this as negative and not simply as reality, we can let it throw us. How about a new approach? Get wisdom before you attack any challenge. I promise you, this process works. During the last twenty years, I, like you, have needed wisdom in handling hundreds of touchy, complex situations. Here are a few:

> Get wisdom before you attack any challenge.

- Dealing with a major career move
- Having our first child
- Severing a business partnership with a friend
- Teetering on the brink of bankruptcy
- Dealing with the embezzlement of hundreds of thousands of dollars from my company
- Creating higher levels of intimacy in my marriage
- Reordering my life to serve God more effectively

How are you doing in the wisdom department? Have you had the need for any wisdom lately? Take a moment and jot down some of the things you are working through right now where a healthy dose of wisdom might be the thing you need.

_____

_____

_____

_____

_____

The Book of Proverbs is rich with wisdom illustrations. A proverb is a short, poignant nugget of truth that is practical in nature and often concerned with the consequences of behavior. Proverbs also make strategic use of parallelisms, especially in the pairing of opposites. Typically, you will get both sides of the behavior. For example, Proverbs 11:27 states, "He who diligently seeks good seeks favor, but he who searches after evil, it will come to him." Whether we seek wisdom from ancient counsel like this, or from our advisors and friends, there will always be two sides of the choice, and that's what makes wisdom so powerful.

Four More Lessons from a King

You may recall that in chapter 9, I shared with you the "Seven Laws of a King." Here I want to add four more lessons that pertain to wisdom. If you are willing to go deep into this topic, I would suggest reading the Book of Ecclesiastes, written more than three thousand years ago.

Seeking wisdom is not easy. Are you a wisdom seeker? If you are, then you know the difficulty of the task. That is why I encourage you to remain focused on the power of the *outcome* of applied wisdom. Having wisdom for a particular situation gives you the confidence to act. When your action meets with the outcome that the wisdom promised you would receive, you now experience fulfillment and wholeness. If this new outcome is behavioral, then that wisdom will equip you in forming a new habit. For example, if the element of wisdom is, "Turn away from evil. It will be healing to your body" (Prov. 3:7–8), and you struggle with an addiction to alcohol, then the more often you turn away from the bottle, the healthier you will be, and the more likely your new behavior will become a habit.

King Solomon says that "in much wisdom is much grief, and he who increases knowledge increases sorrow" (Eccles. 1:18 NKJV). We know this is true. However, the remedy for "too much" wisdom is offered by the words, "Trust in the LORD with all your heart, and lean not on your own understanding; in all your ways acknowledge Him, and He shall direct your paths" (Prov. 3:5–6 NKJV). Bottom line: Spiritual abundance comes from knowing that God will equip you with the knowledge to navigate life's uncertain waters if you will call on Him.

> **Spiritual abundance comes from knowing that God will equip you with the knowledge to navigate life's uncertain waters if you will call on Him.**

Pursuing pleasure and possessions is futile. King Solomon said that pleasure and possessions are vanity and that the joys of earthly accomplishments are ultimately unsatisfying. Solomon had it all—wine, women, money, and song. We are told he was the richest man who ever lived. All of the world's wealth flowed into Jerusalem, and it was all at his disposal. It is the same with you and me. Possessions and pleasure cannot be our gods. If they are, we will never experience lasting happiness.

Ask yourself right now if a new house, a new car, a new job, or a new mate would honestly bring you permanent happiness. Chances are you will reflect in that moment on times past when you did exactly that. What was the outcome? Not quite what you expected, was it? Why? Because lasting happiness is an inside job. It is about getting right with yourself and with God. It is about understanding that life is not about what you have, but about who you are. Whether you follow Mother Teresa or take King Solomon's approach, ultimately nothing matters unless your motives are pure and you move from self-esteem to God-esteem.

There is a time for everything. While I have touched on this in previous works, it will serve us well to see it again. The words ring in our memories as a melody that was made popular by the rock band the Byrds in the '60s with their musical hit "Turn, Turn, Turn." The message of the song is that there is a time for every purpose under heaven. That is the key: *under heaven,* or under God. God has made everything beautiful in its time. He has placed eternity on our hearts. Not one of us can see His mighty hand from beginning to end, but in that time, everything can happen, and it will. So the question is, Is what is happening in your life right? What changes do you need to make immediately? What fundamental life changes do you need to make to do the things God wants you to do? What do you want to accomplish before your time is up?

God has an enormous plan for your life. Wait on Him until He meets you there, for He always returns to your path, if you will allow Him to do so. One way to make certain you are on the same path as God is to order your time to be with Him. Horatius Bonar shares these thoughts:

> **What do you want to accomplish before your time is up?**

> Begin the day with God! He is your Sun and Day.
>> His is the radiance of your dawn; to him address your day.

> Sing a new song at morn! Join the glad woods and hills;
>> Join the fresh winds and seas and plains,
>> Join the bright flowers and rills.

> Sing your song first to God! Not to your fellow men;
>> Not to the creatures of his hand, But to the glorious one

> Take your first walk with God! Let him go forth with thee;
>> By stream, or sea, or mountain path,
>> Seek still his company.

> Your first transaction be, With God himself above;
>> So will your business prosper well, All the day be love.[1]

Use your time wisely. It is running out.

Sow your seeds today. One of the most profound lessons I have learned is the lesson of sowing good seed today. King Solomon said, "Cast your bread upon the waters, for you will find it after many days. . . . In the morning sow your seed, and in the evening do not withhold your hand; for you do not know which will prosper, either this or that, or whether both alike will be good" (Eccles. 11:1, 6 NKJV).

The lesson: Do not use uncertainty as an excuse for laziness.

You cannot bring in the harvest unless you plant the seeds. In life, seed planting takes place not only in the fields of your job, but also in the fields of your relationships. Reaping meaningful, productive results requires that you commit to the diligence of planting.

Og Mandino, in his classic *The Greatest Miracle in the World,* tells us the power of goal setting and seed planting:

> The prizes of life are at the end of the journey, not near the beginning; and it is not given to me to know how many steps are necessary in order to reach my goal. Failure I may still encounter at the thousandth step, yet success hides behind the next bend in the road. Never will I know how close it lies unless I turn the corner . . . I will be likened to the raindrop which washes away the mountain; the ant who devours a tiger; the star which brightens the earth; the slave who builds a pyramid. I will build my castle one brick at a time, for I know that small attempts repeated will complete my undertaking.[2]

God wants you to plant seeds in the "good soil" of your life. Watch, water, and invest in those seeds, and your harvest will be plentiful.

Step Nine

Live Life Powerfully

Chapter 56

The Law of Powerful Living

A re you living life powerfully? Are you committed to a life of excellence? These are big questions, because a life of excellence is not for everyone. In fact, it is not for most people. Most are looking for life's shortcut. The quick fix. They live their lives playing the lottery, hoping beyond reasonable odds that one day their ships will come in. Their lives are a start-stop, go forward–go backward routine of mediocrity. Their hallmark signature is, "I quit." They give up on God, give up on their bodies, give up on their relationships, give up on their jobs, and give up on the disciplines required for a life of excellence. I have a hunch that if you are still reading this book, you are *not* one of these people.

If Life Were an Olympic Event, Would You Make the Team?

And if you did, would you earn a medal? Life is a race that demands what every race requires—commitment. A commitment to run the course, not to be distracted, to overcome insurmountable obstacles, and to finish victoriously. The Scriptures say this with clarity: "Let us also lay aside every encumbrance, . . . and let us run with endurance the race that is set before us" (Heb. 12:1).

Running the "Race" Requires Commitment

My friend Dr. Ted Engstrom tells of a conversation he once had with his friend Art Linkletter, who related a story that personifies commitment:

> Last year she placed third, just 2½ points from first, in the
> Iowa girls' state diving championships. She'd worked two

hours a day for four years to get there. Now at the University of Florida, she's working twice as hard and has earned the number-two position on the varsity diving team, and she's aiming for the national finals. Wendy is carrying a full academic load, finds time for bowling, and is an accomplished water-skier. But perhaps the most remarkable thing about Wendy Stoker is her typing. She bangs out forty-five words per minute on her keyboard, with her toes. Oh, did I fail to mention? Wendy was born without arms.[1]

How did Wendy do it? She quit feeling sorry for herself. She knew she had potential for something better, and she acted. That is the commitment of a champion. Champions do not allow inconveniences to get in their way. They pursue purposefully. They realize they have the power to achieve anything.

The Lunch of a Lifetime

Since I have already mentioned him, let me tell a little more about Dr. Ted Engstrom. Ted is former president and chief executive officer (now president emeritus) of World Vision International. Also a popular management consultant, he has coauthored scores of books and has received three honorary doctorates. What is *not* in his résumé is this: Dr. Engstrom is one of the finest men on earth. I know, because on January 28, 1998, I joined him and my good friend and colleague Bob Larson for lunch at the Olympic Club in Pasadena, California. As I sat next to this man, I was humbled for two reasons: (1) He is a man of God, and (2) when it comes to attaining personal excellence, he is an icon. This man, now in his eighties, was rich with wisdom and guidance when he responded to my question, "What are the secrets to living life powerfully?" Here is what he told me.

- Stay humble, and lose the ego.
- Love and honor your spouse.
- Stay on your knees, and seek divine guidance each day.
- Use the gifts God has given you wisely.
- Let God work in you daily.

Good coaching from a man who has earned that right.

Five Principles for Living Life Powerfully

I have spent years studying and interviewing high-performance people like Dr. Engstrom, Robert Schuller, Zig Ziglar, Ken Blanchard, Glenna Salsbury, and Og Mandino, as well as thousands of students who go through my seminars. I have observed five common traits that enable them to live life powerfully. I am confident that if you put their five secrets for living into your active life, you will never be the same.

Discover the power of dreaming big dreams. Do you have any idea how powerful your mind is? It is far more capable of helping to chart your course in life than you perhaps give it credit for. If left to solitude for any period, your brain will come up with a new picture of how it—you—would like to see life. It is a very creative organ. That is why solitude is so important. It provides you with the environment to think and to dream.

Think of some of the great dreamers history has given us. Jonas Salk created the vaccine for polio. Henry Ford created the automobile. Thomas Edison gave us electric light. John F. Kennedy put us on the moon. Abraham Lincoln set the stage for the abolition of slavery. Martin Luther King Jr. saw desegregation. Elizabeth Cady Stanton and Susan B. Anthony pioneered the rights of women, including the right to vote. Ronald Reagan saw Berlin without the Wall. Walt Disney saw a place where a person could always be a kid. The list goes on, but more important

> **Nothing is impossible to the person who believes in his or her dream.**

than the list is the question, What do you see for you? For your family? For your future? How big are *your* dreams?

Nothing is impossible to the person who believes in his or her dream. If you have faith, you can move mountains. The idea of doing big things is part of God's plan for your life, and you come to know those plans best in an atmosphere of quiet, where you seek His divine direction. A peaceful mind generates power, and God alone provides that peace and serenity. In fact, He says that we can do all things through Him because He gives us strength (see Phil. 4:13). So what are you waiting for? God says that He is for us and not against us (see Rom. 8:31). Since that is true, how can you possibly fail? Start dreaming today, and see where it leads you. You could find yourself at a new level of living powerfully. "If you have faith. . . nothing will be impossible for you" (Matt. 17:20 NIV).

Become "silver-lining" oriented. As you might imagine, I spend many hours flying in airplanes. I also live near San Diego, where it is generally sunny. However, there are several months during the year when we have heavy cloud layers. On those days, the city is dark, damp, and cold. Amazing is the journey, however, when, after takeoff, we go through the clouds and suddenly discover a new world of glorious sunshine and warmth on the other side.

Positive people who live life powerfully realize that for every negative, there is a positive. When you put a battery in your tape recorder or radio, you have to know which side is up and which side is down to activate its power. The negatives in life also have a positive side. You simply have to choose the one on which you will focus. My counsel: Never surrender your power to the negative side of anything. Nineteenth-century preacher Charles Spurgeon said, "It is not difficult for God to turn night into day. He who sends the clouds can just as easily clear the skies. Let us be encouraged. Things are better down the road."[2]

> **Never surrender your power to the negative side of anything.**

Do not be afraid if a dark cloud is descending on your life. Remember that God is in it, and on the other side of the darkest cloud are His radiance, love, majesty, power, and glory. Your life in God's hands is much like the clay on a potter's wheel: It is not perfected until the piece is finished. However, the process for perfection demands that you remain soft, usable clay and that you stay in the hands of the potter—God Himself. As the psalmist said, "He who dwells in the shelter of the Most High will rest in the shadow of the Almighty" (Ps. 91:1 NIV).

Act like Curious George. The book weighs several pounds, and it is equally as heavy, if not heavier, with a profound thought for living life powerfully. It asks the question, "Are you curious?" As each story unfolds, Curious George, a little brown monkey who is friends with the man in the yellow hat, is let lose to experience the challenges of life. His curiosity, it turns out, is his greatest teacher. Curious George learns more by being curious than he ever would by being passive.

Contrary to popular opinion, curiosity did not kill the cat—being safe and staying stagnant did. You will have to act a lot like George if you want to live life powerfully. One of the greatest illustrations of this truth is when we become curious about the questions in our lives. "Why is this happening this way?" "What can I do to change my direction?" "What have other people done to tunnel through this challenge?" These are questions of observation, curiosity, and breakthrough. Only when we acquire new knowledge can we begin to live life more powerfully. Most of us have stopped being curious. We need to get in sync with Curious George.

The Scriptures tell us that a person who finds wisdom and understanding is blessed (see Prov. 3:13). I know of no better way to gain knowledge and understanding than by stepping up your CQ—your curiosity quotient. Make some new observations today, learn some fresh lessons, journal your insights, and review them regularly. Here's a worthy goal: Be curious and strive to learn life's lesson once, or through the wisdom of others.

> **Never give up on your dreams.**

Master the fine art of in-flight corrections. Never give up on your dreams. How foolish that would be for the person who is living abundantly in the presence of God. The Scriptures say that "the mind of [a person] plans his way, but the LORD directs his steps" (Prov. 16:9). What remains for you to do? I would suggest just one thing: Make minor in-flight corrections. Never, ever, ever give up on your dreams. If things are not moving in the direction of your worthy objectives, simply change your course or your actions. Inevitably, your dreams will come true. Failure is no longer an option for you. And failed actions in the process are nothing more than forward progress toward your desired results.

Here are some keys to make this principle work in your life:

- Know specifically what you are aiming for.
- Know which steps you must take to go in that direction.
- Evaluate your actions each day to see if your steps are leading you toward your desired results.

- If they are not, find out how you can make minor modifi-
cations to the steps to help you stay on course.
- Every day, seek wisdom and direction from God on how to
proceed.

Allow the Driver to sit in the seat. This final principle is the most powerful. When I heard Dr. Robert Schuller say this during one of
his sermons, it struck me profoundly. If the Creator can cause
the universe to operate without incident, how capable do you
think He would be if He "took over" your life on your way to
living powerfully? I would say, *Completely qualified.* Wouldn't
you? Think about it. Who would not want that kind of power in
the driver's seat?

In fact, God says to us that whatever we ask Him to do in His
name, He will do it, so that He will be glorified by the outcome
(see John 14:13). He also says that He will cause all things to
work together for good in the lives of those people who love
Him and do His purpose (see Rom. 8:28). So, if you are tired of
going solo, it might be a good idea to let God take over. I admit
it. Every major "collision" I have gotten myself into in this life
has been a result of my own driving. However, whenever I
would hand the "wheel" of my life over to God in those areas
and let Him be in charge, I received a power that could come
only from the force that built this universe. Just so you're crystal-
clear on this, He "drove" me out of an addiction to cocaine, alcohol, and cigarettes; out of an addiction to pornography; through
the challenge of financial ruin; through the stormy seas of being
a husband and father; and into an intimate relationship with
Him.

He can do the same for you.

Build a Plan for Excellence

Chapter 57

The Power of Life Planning

There is absolutely no question in my mind that one of the steps you need to take in your life is to have a plan. I ask people in my seminars, "Which is more important to you: this building or your life?" What's your answer? I then ask, "Then tell me why it is that more planning probably went into this building than has gone into your life?" The expressions are sad but true. If you don't have a plan for your life, you cannot determine how to live. A life plan is the filter through which every physical, financial, relational, and spiritual decision is made. Without a plan, you are living life accidentally!

Steven and Deanna's Story—January 2000

Hi, Todd!

I've been listening to the new Mastery tapes and feeling like I needed to send you a thank-you note for the unbelievable impact that you have had on my personal life. You have had the single greatest impact on my life.

Obviously, financial success is the most tangible measurement (although not the most important). When I first attended your seminars in 1992–93, my income was dismal. My tax returns reported income of $10,000 to $20,000 per year, slightly lower than a full-time McDonald's employee. Presently, I earn $700,000 to $900,000 per year and have over $1.2 million in cash and stocks. I get excited when I think that I went from heavily in debt six years ago to a personal net worth of over $2 million.

To me financial independence is only a small part of success. The true measure of success is being a loving husband and father, being physically fit, being happy and emotionally abundant, and constantly growing and learning.

With you as a mentor, coach, and role model, I have defied the odds and set a new standard for my life. My life feels balanced and I have a clear vision for the future.

Thanks to you, I feel like I have all the resources within me to live life to the fullest and to realize all of my dreams! With the momentum I have built over the past six years, the sky is the limit.

Tim and Sherrie's Story—December 1999

Dear Todd:

This is such a special time of the year for me. It is a time we celebrate the birth of our Lord. My family celebrates the births of our sons Tau and Windsor. And we also celebrate a life-changing friendship that began, first between you and me two years ago, then between our families this past summer in Kauai.

It was two years ago in Del Mar, California, when I met you for the first time at the Productivity School. That was my first exposure to you and your "Life Planning" ideology.

I heard your name for the first time just a few months earlier through a friend in the business, so I came to the five-day Productivity School with very high expectations. High expectations not only because of what I had heard about you and your program, but also because I had committed $2,000 for the seminar plus airfare and hotel. It was a tough decision to spend that kind of money in our situation. We had just transitioned from two incomes to one income with the birth of our first son, Tau, and were committed to Sherrie's being a stay-at-home mom. Spending almost $3,500 on a seminar did not seem the obvious best use of our money at that time, but I felt strongly about going and Sherrie supported me. Two weeks before the program I got cold feet because of the money outlay and decided not to go. Then, at the last moment I changed my mind, caught a flight to Del Mar and the rest, as they say, is history.

As a result of applying what I learned from you during

that week I now earn that $3,500 back every two to three business days. I get a chill when I think back on how close I came to not going!

You shared so many valuable principles that week but one that was particularly impactful for me was about how important it is to have our own personal definition of success. That was a simple but a profound statement. You said that if we let a general definition of success or someone else's definition of success become ours by default, then we are setting ourselves up for a lot of disappointment in life. Beyond that you helped me to understand that it is not *what* we want in life that is most important, but *why* we want it. Two analogies that you used continue to replay over and over in my mind to this day:

- The first was how the Space Shuttle uses 80 percent of its fuel in the first 7½ minutes of flight, representing the amount of initial effort it takes to effect significant change in our lives and the amount of resistance that we are likely to encounter.
- The second was about the sun and a seventy-five-watt light bulb. I am paraphrasing, but you said, "The sun is widely accepted as the most powerful energy source in the universe, but with a ball cap and a quarter size drop of sunscreen you can significantly reduce its effect. On the other hand, you can take the energy used to light a seventy-five-watt light bulb, channel it into a laser beam the size of a human hair, and cut through six inches of steel. This demonstrates that you do not need limitless ability, but absolute focus in order to accomplish incredible feats."

I followed your advice and one step at a time "went deep" with life planning, time blocking, business planning, action planning, strategic partnerships, stronger personal relationships, and systemization of recurring events, to name a few. I experienced incredible changes in my personal and professional life. Here are some of the results:

- Personal income increased from $75,000 in 1997, to over $200,000 in 1998, and nearly $300,000 in 1999.
- Business increased from 10 million in 1997 to 40 million in 1998 and is still climbing this year.
- I am in the top 1 percent of my industry, in terms of production.
- My position in 1997 was "Loan Officer," in 1998 was "Senior Loan Officer," and in 1999 is "Senior Vice President" of a half a billion dollar a year mortgage company.
- I worked most Saturdays and some Sundays in 1997. I do not work weekends now.
- I took a week and a half off for vacation in 1997. I took six weeks in 1999.
- I spend up to twenty more hours per week with my wife and children now than I did in 1997.
- I have less stress in my life than I have ever had before.
- I have more clarity in my life than ever before.
- I am living my life in alignment with my values.
- I am living my life on-purpose within my personal definition of success.
- I have a more intimate relationship with my Heavenly Father than ever before.

I keep a journal of events in my life that I call life markers. These are events that I feel have changed or shaped me in some way to become the person that I am today. I currently have seventeen of these events recorded. I want to share the top six with you so you can have an idea of how significant you have been in my life:

1. The day I received Jesus Christ as my Lord and Savior
2. The day my best friend Sherrie said she would be my wife
3. The day Sherrie accepted Jesus Christ as her Lord and Savior
4. The moment that I saw my son's face for the very first time and for the first time in my life cried uncontrollably with joy
5. Twenty-two months later when my second son was

born and for the second time in my life I cried uncontrollably with joy

6. Day four of the Productivity School when you released the potential that had, until then, lain dormant inside of me

Thank you, Todd, first for your commitment to God and to your family, but also for the impact you are having on so many lives as a result of your seminars and your books. I will continue to confidently recommend you and shamelessly promote your work. Keep changing lives! You are a hero to me!

Let's Write Your Story

What's your future look like? What do you want to see your life become? What are you no longer going to settle for? What do you want the end result of your life to look like? One of the greatest concepts you could ever learn in this area is the concept of "leverage." Leverage is what you gain when you go on record letting someone know what you are committing to as a course of action for your life. You could share the details of what you want your life to look like with your spouse, with a friend, with a partner. You could even share it with me! When you go on record, committing to this new course, there is an incredible power you receive to stay the course, to take the race of life to completion. So here's your assignment: Complete the story below, writing your future as if you were living it now. Then send your letter to someone who cares, and copy me on it at www.toddduncan.com.

As you look at it every day, you will start to move in some very powerful directions. You will sense the highest level of internal accountability that you have ever experienced. Now you will be on your way to living the life that you have imagined, one filled with opportunity and reward, happiness and fulfillment, excellence and excitement. Remember, you are a miracle, one of a kind, and there is no other person on this earth like you—never was, and never will be. Make life your masterpiece . . . now!

Dear _____.

I want you to know that I have made some profound decisions in my life—as a result, you would not believe how my life
is looking. I want to share with you my new commitments so
that in some way, I might experience even more accountability
than I already feel. And, if you are okay with it, each time we
speak, I'd like you to ask me how I am doing.

In the spiritual area of my life, I am committed to: _____

_____

_____

In the physical area of my life, I am committed to: _____

_____

_____

In the financial area of my life, I am committed to: _____

_____

_____

In the relationship area of my life, I am committed to: _____

_____

_____

I want to thank you for being my friend, and I look forward
to talking with you soon. This is the biggest commitment of my
life, sharing this with you. My signature below authenticates my
commitment to living life excellently, from this day forward.

Sincerely,

_____

(Your Name)

Awaken the Olympian Within

I asked you a question in chapter 56: "If life were an Olympic event, would you make the team?" And if you did, would you earn a medal? There is no better person to help you learn how to score a perfect "10" than a person who has done it. The same disciplines of an athlete preparing for an Olympic event can be the ones that help you prepare for life. I'd like to introduce you to Peter Vidmar, the 1984 Olympic gold medalist who scored a perfect "10" on the high bars.

How to Take Risks with Confidence

I fell nine feet, and that wasn't even close to the worst of it. The year was 1983, the country was Hungary, the city was Budapest, and the guy who was walking miles from his hotel and *not* hailing a cab was me. Teammate Bart Conner could have driven up in his Porsche and tossed me the keys, and I'd have tossed them back. Sometimes you have to walk. I had to walk.

Just moments earlier, I'd been in the Budapest Sports Arena, going through a routine on the high bar that I thought was going to turn me into a world champion. I was twenty-two years old at the time and competing in my third world championships. These weren't just any world championships. With the Los Angeles Olympic Games coming up in eight months, these Worlds were serving as a tune-up, a final preview of the upcoming Olympic medalists.

I was in second place going into the high-bar finals, close enough to the lead that winning the title wasn't out of the question. I wasn't the only one thinking along those lines. Between the preliminaries and the finals, word had spread to the broadcasting team from ABC's *Wide World of Sports,* which was primed to tape the finals. When the Japanese gymnast, who was leading the competition, fell during his routine, their cameras focused on me—Peter Vidmar, United States of America—all set to chronicle my ascent to the top. I thought I was ready. All I had to do was nail my routine, and I would be the new high-bar world champion.

The value of the TV coverage was not lost on me. I knew that *Wide World of Sports* had made Kurt Thomas the most famous American gymnast ever. I knew it was Kurt Thomas in the early '70s who forged a reputation as the best "gamer" in the history of gymnastics. He always saved his best for whenever they turned on the red light—when it counted. By using television, Kurt Thomas had easily done more for U.S. gymnastics than any American gymnast in history. He hadn't done too badly for Kurt Thomas either.

Now it was my chance to be the next Kurt Thomas, and I knew it. (And so, I suspect, did Kurt Thomas, who, along with Al Michaels, was handling the broadcast that night for ABC.)

There was one slight problem. I was suddenly having difficulty with a particular skill in my high-bar routine—a tricky maneuver that I'd managed to pull off without a hitch in the preliminaries, but which was now giving me problems. This was a skill that had gotten me into world championship contention in the first place. Indeed, this was the skill I needed to perform if I wanted to get my bonus two-tenths of a point for risk.

But, as I said, it was tricky. It called for me to swing around the bar then let go, fly straight up over the bar into a half-turn, straddle my legs, come back down, catch the bar, swing, immediately let go again, do a backflip with a half-turn in the pike position, come back down, and catch the bar. Trust me—it's hard.

As I warmed up before the finals, I kept messing it up, and as a result, I kept getting more and more frustrated. This was no time for things to go bad.

Of course, worry soon gave way to panic. I looked at my coach, Makoto Sakamoto, and pleaded, "Mako, you've gotta help me. I've got fifteen minutes until the competition starts, and I can't do this right! It's my only risky skill! What's wrong?"

Mako watched me.

"Oh, just pike more on your swing," he said.

"Uh, arch more at the bottom.

"Try letting go of the bar a little later."

All these insightful tips, followed by the ultimate coaching wisdom that we've all heard before: "Just do it right!"

But I wasn't doing it right, and for a fleeting moment, I decided I'd just bag it. I'd leave it out. Why not? I'd lose the two-tenths of a point for risk, but I could still score as high as a 9.8. That would put me on the winners' rostrum for sure. That would mean a medal, maybe even a silver.

But it wouldn't earn me the world championship, and I knew it. I knew others would take a risk. Someone else would make it count, and that person would become the world champion, not me. Someone else would get the gold medal. I also instinctively knew that it wasn't every day that I got a chance to be a world champion—in anything. Now that I had that chance, was I going to play it safe? Was I going to throw out the risk when I was so close?

No! That was my answer. I decided to stick to the game plan. I'd leave that risky skill in. With it, I would ride to the top of the world—or else.

When my name was called I signaled to the superior judge and jumped up and grabbed the bar. The risky skill came right at the beginning of the routine, so I swung around the bar, let go, came straight up over the bar, did a half-turn, straddled my legs, came back down, caught the bar, immediately let go again, did that backflip with the half-turn in the pike position (so far so good), came back down to catch the bar . . . and the bar . . . was . . . not . . . there.

That's when gravity, the supreme justice of gymnastics, prevailed. After dropping nine feet, I hit the mat face-first on a foam pad four inches thick. Now, the rules in gymnastics are adamant about one thing: You're only allowed one dismount in a performance.

I did the only thing I could do. I jumped up off the floor, grabbed the bar again, and finished my routine. But I was already out of the running. I landed my "second" dismount perfectly (big deal), saluted the judges, jumped off the platform, grabbed my bags, and left the arena. I was devastated. Destroyed. Inconsolable. I'd blown it. I'd choked, and I'd failed. And I'd managed to do it on ABC's *Wide World of Sports!* My teammates told me that when Kurt Thomas in the broadcast booth saw this "wannabe" crash and burn, he just flipped his pencil in the air in disappointment.

I finished eighth. And if you're thinking, *Hmm, eighth place in the world is not that bad,* I thank you. But there were only eight people in the competition.

Not being the world champion wasn't what bothered me most. It was that I'd had the opportunity, and I hadn't come through. I hadn't done a Kurt Thomas. And I really thought I would. That's what got to me; that's what I kept thinking about over and over again as I walked back to my hotel. I thought I would come through, and I hadn't! Doubts suddenly came creeping in from all corners. Deep down I wondered if I would *ever* be able to rise to the occasion under pressure. Did I have what it takes to deliver the goods when it came time for real world-class competition, or would I crack under the strain?

That's what consumed my thoughts as I walked head down through the dark Budapest night. A light snow began to fall. *How appropriate,* I thought.

It wasn't until I got to the hotel and was halfway through the front door that Mako caught up with me. I didn't feel much like talking to him, but we were in the space between the hotel's double-entry doors, which keep the heat from getting out and, in this case, was keeping me from getting in. He had me cornered. He said a lot of things. But this is what I remember:

"This is not the end. Everything is a learning experience," said Mako, "even competition. What you did tonight can be a valuable learning experience. You can benefit from this."

Mako didn't know it at the time—because I didn't tell him—but what he said struck a chord with me. This *had* been a valuable learning experience. I didn't want to hear it, but I knew he was right. That fall taught me something that I somehow hadn't completely learned until that night.

Never, *ever* take anything for granted.

Especially don't take risks for granted.

I realized that I had made the decision to take the risk, but I had forgotten to *really* prepare myself for taking it! Knowing how important that particular skill was . . . that I couldn't leave out that trick and still win the title, I should have been better prepared. I was certain to have to take the same risk at the Olympics, and no matter how the skill might feel in warmup, I had to commit *now* to taking it there as well.

I promised myself that from that day forward, if I were going to take a risk, I was going to be ready.

This time, there would be no more fooling around. I had known that the double-release move on the high bar was extremely difficult. I was the only person in the world doing it at the time, so that should have been my first clue. I received maximum risk points for it precisely *because* of its difficulty. It was a move that needed extra attention. It wasn't something I could take for granted. But every day in the gym I had treated it just like the two hundred or so other tricks I had to work on. I'd given it no extra care. And now I knew it needed that.

The Olympics were eight months away. I resolved that from that moment on, I'd go back to the high bar at the end of my workouts and work overtime on that risky double-release move. I was determined to learn my lesson. The next time the pressure was on, I would not fail.

So that's what I did. For the next eight months, there wasn't a workout between Budapest and Los Angeles that didn't include an extra session or two, working on that high-bar double-release. I practiced it twice as much as any other skill. Twenty times as much as some. I worked on it, and I worked on it, and then I worked on it some more. To be honest, I never really liked doing it because I frequently missed the bar and crashed to the floor. But I did it anyway—always with the memory of a missed world title.

By the time the Olympics came around, I was a lot more comfortable with that double release. Not quite eight months after the fall in Budapest, I jumped up and grabbed the bar in the All-Around finals at the Olympic Games. About one minute later I came back down—when I was supposed to. I scored a perfect "10" on the high bar.

Looking back (it's always easier looking back), I can say I'm glad I failed in Budapest. And you know what? I really am. Sometimes it's necessary to fail. That's how we learn. It wasn't fun when it happened, but it taught me how important it is to focus on what we need to focus on, not what we would like to focus on. Respecting a risk is every bit as important as taking one. Maybe more important. If I hadn't fallen off that high bar in the world championships, I might have fallen off when the pressure was even greater.

When I talk to corporate audiences about risk, I like to begin with that story about my fall in Budapest because it combines so many of the important elements of taking risks—and because it has a happy ending.

The point is that I needed that risk. I never could have realized my potential without it. But I also needed to respect it. We all need risks. The challenge is to know how to control them, instead of letting them control us.

Risk taking goes beyond just a necessary step, beyond just a requirement to reach the perfect "10." Risks—sensible, calculated, prudent, rational risks—are the obstacles that make reaching the destination worthwhile. Without them there would be no struggle and no satisfaction.

I'm not saying *all* risks are good, and I don't recommend that we take every outlandish gamble that comes our way, but progress in business or sports occurs only when we risk going someplace we've never been before. A new product or a new territory or even new packaging can be risky, but it's also more rewarding when the risk pays off. To awaken the Olympian within, we should look for those hidden risky opportunities, places to go, and ways to stretch our abilities. These daily challenges and events outside our comfort zone can be a valuable part of our journey through life, and we should resolve *in advance* to prepare for them in order to meet them and to beat them.

Triumphs that are truly meaningful are triumphs that require effort. If there weren't a "rough" on the golf course, could we appreciate driving a golf ball dead in the middle of the fairway nearly as much? If the marlin just jumped in our boat, would catching it be as satisfying? If not for risks, rewards would lose much of their value.

I currently ride a mountain bike both for the exercise and the thrill of careening down a mountainside. The risk of danger is real (and I've crashed more than I care to admit), but I have done my homework there as well. I train hard for the uphill climbs, and I keep my bike's brakes and shocks prepared for the dangerous downhill descents. As a result, I feel better physically, and I can't begin to describe the personal satisfaction I get from being on the mountaintop, the thrill of dodging the trees and boulders, and the adrenaline rush I get from racing to the finish line.

Risks give life its zip. Why else would people bungee jump, climb mountains, jump out of airplanes, or run with the bulls? Approached sensibly, risks can bring excitement. They bring exhilaration, zest, and inspiration. And when one prepares for them, they can bring deep satisfaction and impressive results.

My fall in Budapest taught me the lesson well. It didn't teach me to avoid risks, but rather it taught me that a life without risk, a life of safe mediocrity, hurts more than a "face plant" from nine feet.

Notes

Chapter 1: Are You in Shape?
1. Centers for Disease Control Web site, www.cdc.gov/nchs/fastats/deaths.htm.
2. Ibid.

Chapter 3: Confessions of a Couch Potato
1. Nanci Hellmich and Joe Urschel, "Surgeon General: Inactivity Is Bad for USA's Health," *USA Today,* 10 July 1997, 18.
2. Nanci Hellmich, "Hour of Exercise Keeps Weight Off," *USA Today,* 1 June 1999, 1A.
3. "Barriers to Physical Activity," www.cflri.ca/LT/92LT/LT92_07.

Chapter 4: Lessons from a Sumo Wrestler
1. "Nurses Health Study," *New England Journal of Medicine* 337 (20 November 1997): 1491–99.

Chapter 5: Sugar and Spice and Everything Bad
1. Author's personal notes from Hyrum Smith's keynote presentation at "Sales Mastery '94" conference.
2. Kenneth Cooper, *Regaining the Power of Youth* (Nashville: Thomas Nelson Publishers, 1999), 168–69.

Chapter 6: Let's Don't Do Lunch
1. Barry Sears, *The Zone* (New York: HarperCollins, 1999), 15.

Chapter 7: On a Scale of One to Four Hundred Pounds
1. Cooper, *Regaining the Power of Youth*, 72.

Chapter 10: A Funny Thing Happened on the Way to the Fridge
1. FDA Web site, "The New Food Label," www.fda.gov/opacom/backgrounders/foodlabel/newlabel.html.

Chapter 11: Eat, Drink, and Be Merry For Tomorrow We Die(t)
1. "What Should I Eat?", www.healthyfridge.org/choose.html.

Chapter 12: Feasting on Fast Food

1. John Ortberg, audiotape of speech given at St. Andrews Presbyterian Couples Retreat, 1996 at Forest Home Conference Center.
2. onhealth.com.

Chapter 13: Let's Go Swimming

1. Robert L. Pela, "Water Works," *Men's Fitness,* n.d., 74.

Chapter 16: Hooked on a Feeling

1. Nanci Hellmich, "Hour of Exercise Keeps Weight Off," *USA Today,* 10 July 1997, 1A.

Chapter 17: Jump in Heart-First

1. Covert Bailey, *The New Fit or Fat* (Boston: Houghton Mifflin Company, 1991), 70–75.
2. Sears, *The Zone,* 60.

Chapter 19: Do It a Few Hundred Times, and You Have It Made . . . Almost

1. Source unknown.
2. Source unknown.
3. Source unknown.

Chapter 20: My Wake-up Call

1. Zig Ziglar, "Creating Professional Presentations," speech given at National Speakers Association Annual Conference, 1989.
2. William Barclay, *The Letters to the Galatians and Ephesians* (Philadelphia: Westminster, 1976), 100.
3. Source unknown.
4. Source unknown.

Chapter 21: Smell the Roses and Other Nice Scents

1. Gordon MacDonald, "Rest Stops," *Life at Work,* July/August 1999, 43.

Chapter 22: Ladieees and Gentlemen

1. Thomas Stanley and William Danko, *The Millionaire Next Door* (Atlanta: Longstreet Press, 1996), 3.

Chapter 24: Start Acting Your Wage

1. George S. Clason, *The Richest Man in Babylon* (New York: Penguin Books, 1988), 63.
2. "100 Steps to Wealth," *Money* magazine and Time Inc., Financial Network learning tool, 1999.
3. Stanley and Danko, *The Millionaire Next Door,* 3.

Chapter 28: Pay Now; Play Later

1. "How Much Is Enough?" *Fast Company,* July/August 1999, 108.
2. Ortberg, audiotape of speech given at St. Andrews Presbyterian Couples Retreat.

Chapter 29: Building the Financial Plan

1. Social Security Administration, Office of Research and Services, "Report on Income," May 1994.
2. Clason, *The Richest Man in Babylon,* 63.
3. Jeff Duncan, interview with author.

Chapter 35: School's Out Forever

1. Barry Habib, interview with author.

Chapter 40: Bullets from Buffet

1. All quotes from Simon Reynolds, *Thoughts of Chairman Buffet* (New York: Harper Collins, 1998).

Chapter 41: www—World Wide Wealth

1. *Money,* December 1999, 188.
2. See chapter 34 for the benefits of using a mortgage professional in this category. Typically, the e-mortgage sites do not have the consultant who can guide you in integrating your mortgage into your overall financial plan.

Chapter 42: Someone Asked Malcolm Forbes

1. Source unknown.
2. Suze Orman, *9 Steps to Financial Freedom* (New York: Crown Publishers, 1997), 266.
3. Ron Blue, "How Much Is Enough?" *New Man,* May 1996, 62.

Chapter 43: Making Time for What Counts

1. Hyrum Smith, interview with author.

Chapter 44: Suffocate Stress; Experience Joy

1. Thomas Buxton quote.

Chapter 45: "I Do"

1. John Bartlett, *Bartlett's Familiar Quotations* (Boston: Little Brown & Co., 1980), 786.

Chapter 48: The Power of Friends

1. William Bridges, *Transitions* (Reading, Mass.: Addison-Wesley, 1980).
2. Daniel Harkavy, interview with author.

Chapter 49: The Power of Purpose

1. Bartlett, *Bartlett's Familiar Quotations,* 560.

Chapter 50: The Law of Prayer

1. James Reimann, ed., *Finding God's Peace and Joy* (Grand Rapids: Zondervan, 1999), n.p.
2. Neale Donald Walsch, *Conversations with God* (Eugene, Ore.: Harvest House Publishers, 1993), 9.
3. Reimann, ed., *Finding God's Peace and Joy,* n.p.

Chapter 52: The Law of Faith

1. Dr. Norman Vincent Peale, *The Power of Positive Thinking* (New York: Prentice Hall, 1956), 96.
2. Ibid., 14.

Chapter 53: The Law of Uniqueness

1. Og Mandino, *The Greatest Miracle in the World* (Frederick Fell Publishers, 1975), 114.
2. James J. Thompson, *Tried As by Fire* (Macon, Ga.: Mercer University Press, 1982).

Chapter 54: The Law of Solitude

1. Charles Swindoll, *Intimacy with the Almighty* (Dallas: Word Publishing, 1996), 30.

Chapter 55: The Law of Wisdom

1. Reimann, ed., *Finding God's Peace and Joy,* n.p.
2. Mandino, *The Greatest Miracle in the World,* 30.

Chapter 56: The Law of Powerful Living

1. Ted Engstrom, *High Performance* (San Bernardino, Calif.: Here's Life Publishers, 1988), 100.
2. Reimann, ed., *Finding God's Peace and Joy,* n.p.

Where Do You Go from Here?

"Achieve True Wealth!"
Todd M. Duncan

You have the Power inside you to accomplish all that you have ever wanted. All of your dreams, your desires, your aspirations, and your goals are moments away from becoming your reality, transforming your life now!

Todd Duncan would like to send you a FREE resource to help you achieve a lifetime of wealth.

Call 1-877-833-TODD (8633) for your FREE training today! Or order online at www.toddduncan.com

The Todd Duncan Group

The Todd Duncan Group, Inc., founded in 1992 by Todd Duncan, is committed to adding value and making a difference in people's lives. Todd Duncan has devoted the last 20 years of his life to researching high-performance, successful people, in all walks of life. He shares his findings and personal experiences with audiences worldwide to help them achieve true wealth. You too can learn his success principles on how to develop the **Power** to be your best!

The Todd Duncan Group, Inc. is committed to these 5 values:

*P*URPOSE: Helping people discover their focus

*O*PTIMISIM: Assisting people in developing their attitude

*W*ILLINGNESS: Empowering people to greater commitment

*E*QUIPPING: Giving people life management resources

*R*ELATIONSHIPS: Encouraging accountability relationships

To contact Todd Duncan or any division of The Todd Duncan Group, call, write, or E-mail us:

The Todd Duncan Group, Inc.
7590 Fay Avenue
Suite 402
La Jolla, Ca 92037
877-833-TODD (8633)
www.toddduncan.com

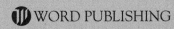

4X Made Easy Program
Simplify & Diversify.
—The Forex Market
—6 Currencies

— End.. Marriott Feb 6th
   North   7th 1&1
3645 River Cross.
   Parkway in td.   8th 9 & 1